Building A Financial Services Marketing Plan:

*Working Plans For
Product and Segment Marketing*

Bank **M**arketing **A**ssociation

FINANCIAL **S**OURCEBOOKS
NAPERVILLE, ILLINOIS

Financial Sourcebooks
A Division of Sourcebooks, Inc.
P.O. Box 313
Naperville, Illinois, 60566

First printing 1989.

Cover design by Creative Mind Services.

This publication is designed to provide accurate and authoritative information in regard to the subject matter covered. It is sold with the understanding that the publisher is not engaged in rendering legal, accounting, or other professional service. If legal advice or other expert assistance is required, the services of a competent professional person should be sought.

From a Declaration of Principles Jointly Adopted by a Committee of the American Bar Association and a Committee of Publishers and Associations

Library of Congress Cataloging-in-Publication Data

Building a financial services marketing plan.

    Includes bibliographical references.
    1. Bank marketing. 2. Market segmentation.
I. Bank Marketing Association (U.S.)
HG1616.M3B85 1989   332.1'068'8   89-23301
ISBN 0-942061-02-0

Printed and bound in the United States of America.

CONTENTS

PREFACE

For over 40 years, Bank Marketing Association has been sponsoring a two-week, two-year school for experienced financial services marketers. As part of the curriculum, students are required to submit either a marketing plan for their bank or a research report based on the student's independent investigation of some area of the financial services market. Those marketing plans and research reports that are well written and considered to be an exceptional contribution to financial marketing receive special recognition and are placed in BMA's Information Center.

The Bank Marketing Association in cooperation with Financial Sourcebooks has developed this publication as a guide for preparing marketing plans. The sample plans contained in this publication are among those plans that have received special recognition from BMA over the last three years. They are excellent examples of overall marketing plans, product plans, and plans for specific market segments or specific marketing techniques.

Each marketing plan is unique to its banking environment. However, each plan contains the essence of planning—careful consideration of the environment, objectives relating to the goals of the organization, and appropriate marketing strategies, tactics and budgets designed to meet the objectives. It is our hope that you will be able to use this publication as a reference source and training tool in creating your own firm's marketing plans.

Bank Marketing Association

Note: The authors listed worked for the banks mentioned at the time they were students at the School of Bank Marketing. In some instances, the authors no longer work at that institution.

INTRODUCTION

The Market Planning Process: A Working Model

Patrick Kennedy
The Northern Trust Bank

Marketing planning is an exercise in organizational dynamics. At its best, it involves the collective efforts of every business unit in the organization. The objective of marketing planning is to invoke a planning discipline that provides a short-range road map for improving communication in the organization and for guiding managerial action.

This chapter discusses marketing planning and some basic principles in the development of a marketing plan. It also presents a "generic" marketing plan for a small bank and outlines its uses and limitations.

Marketing Planning for Financial Institutions

The marketing plan format for a financial institution is similar to that of other industries. The most striking differences occur in developing the marketing strategy and in the marketing mix. Financial institutions, like all service businesses, sell an intangible product, that is, service. Thus, the problem is in making the product tangible and in controlling the quality of the service at its point of delivery (which is also the point of consumption).[1] The point here is that the basic elements of a marketing plan are consistent from one industry to another. The differences are in the composition of those elements and the methods used to develop and implement the plan.

Another important element that distinguishes financial services from consumer and industrial goods is that we are in a people business. Technology may simplify that process, but at its heart, our product involves a high level of human interaction. As a result, managing internal and external communication in a financial services firm is a significant challenge.

The Role of Marketing Planning

A marketing plan is the short-range component of the organization's strategic plan. It flows from the strategic plan and is interdependent with other operating plans, for example, finance, operations, and production. Generally, a marketing plan is developed in conjunction with a financial budget and an operations plan once the long-range strategic plan is in place.

The Corporate Planning Process

The corporate planning process is typically a four-level hierarchy. Each level addresses certain questions related to the future of the organization and the interest of the stockholders, management, employees, customers, and community.

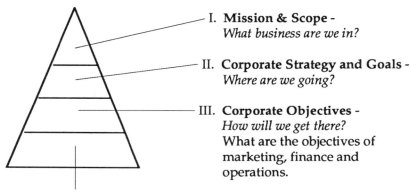

I. **Mission & Scope -**
What business are we in?

II. **Corporate Strategy and Goals -**
Where are we going?

III. **Corporate Objectives -**
How will we get there?
What are the objectives of marketing, finance and operations.

IV. **Marketing Strategy and Goals -**
What will we do? (The Marketing Plan)
- Who will buy our service?
- How will the environment affect us?
- What are the elements of the marketing mix?
- What resources do we need?
- How will we implement the plan?
- Who is responsible for each action step?
- How will we control and revise the plan?

The corporate planning process is an ongoing and integrated information process. The corporate strategic plan takes a long-term perspective in answering questions at levels I and II. Level III is the link that joins the strategic plan to the marketing plan and to the other annual operating plans.[2]

In a competitive environment, the marketing plan should drive the financial and operations plans. It should be used as a request for, and justification of, the annual budget. Only by demonstrating exactly how the money will be spent, who will spend it, and what effect it will have on the attainment of the company's marketing objectives can management have a basis for approving or disapproving a budget request.

Laying the Foundation

Developing the ideal planning process for an institution requires a thorough understanding of the organization and strong communication skills. The planning process is often a revolutionary process, as well as an evolutionary one. There are two important prerequisites in this process:

1. **Management at all levels of the organization must be committed to the marketing concept.**

    Marketing is more than a group of activities; it is a state of mind. All successful organizations, that operate in a dynamic marketplace, understand that long-term growth and profitability depend on a conscious devotion to the satisfaction of market needs. In Peter Drucker's words:

    Marketing is so basic that it cannot be considered as a separate function ... It is the whole business seen from the point of view of its final result, that is, from the customer's point of view.[3]

2. **The marketing plan must be an integral part of the strategic planning process.**

    The strategic plan and marketing plan differ in scope and emphasis. The more dynamic the environment, the more important the marketing plan becomes. Today, the environment seems in a constant state of change. The efficiency and effectiveness of financial institutions depends on their ability to adapt to change. Under these conditions, the role of marketing, and the organizational discipline of market planning, become critical to both the short-term and long-term success of the institution.

The Rules of the Road

Every organization is different. What drives the organization, its values and beliefs, strengths and weaknesses, structure, and many other factors determine the format and areas of emphasis of a firm's marketing plan. The planning format is critical in building an effective marketing plan. If the format does not conform to the accepted principles, behavior and values of the organization, the plan will never be implemented.

There are several common approaches to marketing planning. Some institutions prefer the top-down approach because of its ease in implementation and high degree of control. Others use what I call napkin planning, an informal process reflecting the consensus of a few knowledgeable people regarding the most appropriate strategy. Yet others use a bottom-up approach where each division formulates a plan that is later integrated either via consensus or by management.

What is important is that the planning process be market-oriented and encourage two-way communication, both up and down the organization. In order to be effective, the planning process must adhere to the organization's philosophies and mission, seek the involvement of line management, and focus on meeting the needs of customers.

Some Ground Rules

Of course, there is no magic formula for developing an effective marketing plan, but there are certain rules.[4]

- **Obtain commitment.** Sell the planning process to senior management. If they don't buy in, it doesn't matter who else does.

- **Seek participation.** Even a top-down planning format requires senior management to obtain information from, and the involvement of, staff and line managers. Participation accomplishes two fundamental requirements of planning: the flow of timely information and the commitment of key personnel. Those who are accountable for the marketing plans should participate in their development (notice we don't say they should write the plans).

- **Educate the organization on the costs and benefits of marketing planning.** In real estate, the secret is location, location, location; in marketing it's communication, communication, communication.

- **Keep it simple.** The planning process should be easy for everyone in the organization to understand.

- **Invoke a discipline.** Don't reinvent the wheel every year. The plan and some elements of the process will change as the environment changes and the planning system matures, but the structure should remain constant. Synchronize the marketing plan with the budget, allow sufficient time, and begin implementation as soon after the planning process as possible.

- **Allow for flexibility.** The act of planning implies change. In a dynamic environment, the plan will be in a constant state of revision. Anticipate change and adapt. Be sure to inform everyone that a flexible plan is necessary in a dynamic marketplace; in other words, everyone should expect change.

- **Customize the process.** The blend of operational activities is not alike at any two organizations. Build a flexible planning process around the organization and its key personnel.

- **Get real.** Be realistic, measure performance, and pay attention to detail. Keep accurate records. Don't expect others to assemble the information. Budgets must reflect costs, and goals must be achievable. Dreams have no place in marketing plans.

Stages of a Marketing Plan

As previously mentioned, no two organizations are functionally alike. The marketing planning process should be adapted to the individual requirements of the institution. However, certain stages are essential to the planning process. These stages are outlined as follows:

1. **Marketing Objectives**—The marketing objectives should be established by the institution's strategic plan, and the objectives must be measurable.

2. **Situational Analysis**—An internal and external assessment should be made, with emphasis on marketing strengths, weaknesses, opportunities, and threats (SWOT).

3. **Marketing Strategy**—"What must we do to accomplish our objectives?" This is a creative task that generates alternatives. Quantitative research from stage two can play a major role in choosing among the alternatives.

4. **Programming the Marketing Mix**—"What is the strategy and objective of each major component of the marketing mix, that is, product programs, service quality, distribution programs, and communications programs?" In addition, this step should address the numerous subprograms, for example, marketing research, sales management, advertising, direct marketing, public relations, and promotional activities.

5. **Developing Action Plans**—"Who will do what, when will they do it, what do we expect from it, and how much will it cost?"

6. **Submission and Approval Process**—The senior management review process is usually iterative. Management reviews the plan, raises issues, requests changes, and the cycle starts again.

7. **Implementing the Plan**—The execution of the plan involves a high level of communication, close attention to detail, clear definition of expectations, and the support of line management. It is essential that line management be involved from the beginning of the planning process.

8. **Auditing**—Action plans will change as the plan is implemented, and as market opportunities arise. It is important, therefore, to monitor and control the action plans to ensure that they don't deviate from the marketing strategy. Tracking results and reporting status, at least quarterly, is essential. Senior management may want to adjust the marketing strategy or marketing mix when the environment changes significantly, or if performance fails to meet expectations.

The "Generic" Marketing Plan

Having told you that all marketing plans are different, I will now present a "generic" marketing plan. This may sound somewhat contradictory, but as mentioned previously, the stages of the planning process are very similar. This plan is really an outline that can be tailored to the needs of different kinds of institutions. Since the culture and philosophy of an institution have much to do with the final results of the process, this "plan" is structured as a series of questions or topic areas that must be examined before you can formulate a plan suited to your situation. The planning format and the composition of the plan will obviously vary among institutions. The objective is to build a process that works and that produces the expected results.

This "generic" marketing plan is designed for smaller financial services institutions. It is a simple, pragmatic, and functional format that can be adapted to almost any organization. There are a number of marketing components that are abbreviated, or not included, in order to simplify the process (e.g., communications, advertising, product, and research plans). This does not mean that these elements are not important, only that they may not be as necessary or applicable to smaller institutions.

The elements that drive the organization, such as its values and beliefs, strengths and weaknesses, structure, and many other factors, determine the format and areas of emphasis. For example, in an autocratic structure (strictly top-down) all components of the marketing plan, except the action plans, may originate from senior management. In this case, the budget often drives the marketing plan.

The "generic" plan is designed to facilitate two-way communication. The corporate mission and objectives are communicated down through the organization, and marketing strategies and budget requests are communicated up.

This format assumes that the organization has a corporate strategy in place, and defines its marketing strategy by either product line or market segment. The "generic" marketing plan is divided into three sections:

    A. **Senior Management Summary**—This section contains the corporation's mission statement, marketing goals, marketing objectives (the profit-and-loss effects of the plan), the marketing budget, and business-unit marketing strategies. The senior management summary links the marketing plan to both the strategic plan and the budget approval process. Business unit managers should attach a narrative summary of the marketing strategy for their product line or market segment.

B. **Situational Analysis**—This section reviews the internal and external environment with emphasis on strengths, weaknesses, opportunities and threats (SWOT). A detailed analysis of the competition is usually part of this section.

C. **Marketing Strategy**—This section contains marketing strategies and action plans for each product line and target market. This part of the process includes establishing priorities, determining a rational approach to the market, defining the role of each product, and requests for additional resources.

The "generic" marketing plan is a simple model. Together with the marketing plans presented in this book, the "generic" plan can give you a good foundation for developing a planning process that is right for your institution.

One Last Word
Remember, a marketing plan (or strategic plan) is not a substitute for leadership. A successful plan provides guidance and directs resources to those areas where they will be used most efficiently and effectively in accomplishing the objectives established by management. But it takes leadership to create the vision, to prioritize the opportunities, and to motivate the troops. ◆

---

[1] James Donnelly, Leonard Berry and Thomas Thompson, *Marketing Financial Services: A Strategic Vision*, (Homewood, Illinois: Dow Jones-Irwin 1985).

[2] Mark E. Stern, *Marketing Planning: A Systems Approach*, (NewYork: McGraw Hill 1966).

[3] Philip Kotler, *Marketing Management: Analysis, Planning and Control* (Englewood Cliffs, New Jersey: Prentice-Hall 1976).

[4] James C. Makens, *The Marketing Plan Workbook* (Englewood Cliffs, New Jersey: Prentice-Hall 1985).

GENERIC MARKETING PLAN

BANK: _____

FOR YEAR: _____

===

I.   It is my understanding that the mission statement of our bank is:

II. It is my understanding that my bank's marketing goals are the following: (Qualitative)

III.   ORGANIZATIONAL SUMMARY OF MARKETING OBJECTIVES

The marketing objectives for our bank (reasonable & achievable) over the next three years are as follows:

($ in thousands)	Current Year (Yr.1)	Next Year (Yr.2)	Year 3
Average Assets ($) % Change	_____ _____	_____ _____	_____ _____
Avg Earning Assets ($) % Change	_____ _____	_____ _____	_____ _____
Average Loans ($) % Change	_____ _____	_____ _____	_____ _____
Average Deposits ($) % Change	_____ _____	_____ _____	_____ _____
Net Interest Inc. ($) % Change (After LLP)	_____ _____	_____ _____	_____ _____
Trust New Business ($) % Change	_____ _____	_____ _____	_____ _____
Total Other Income ($) % Change	_____ _____	_____ _____	_____ _____
Net Income ($) % Change	_____ _____	_____ _____	_____ _____

Recommended Marketing Budget (Current Year)

	Current Year	Last Year
Media Advertising	$_____	$_____
Special Sponsored Functions & P.R.	$_____	$_____
Sales Promotion (e.g., brochures, premiums, etc.)	$_____	$_____
Miscellaneous	$_____	$_____
Total	$_____	$_____

Bank President: _____   Date: _____

Marketing
Manager: _____   Date: _____

BANK MARKET PLAN SUMMARY

Bank: _____

($ 000 omitted)

Product Line/Market Segment	Product Strategy	Budget $		Objectives
		Planned	Actual	

A-3

BUSINESS UNIT

SITUATIONAL ANALYSIS

===

I. It is my understanding that the mission statement of our bank is:

II. My unit's marketing goals are the following: (Qualitative)

III. <u>ENVIRONMENT</u>

The key environmental elements affecting my business under each of the topics below are:

A.   Economic: _____

             _____

             _____

             _____

             _____

B.   Technology: _____

             _____

             _____

             _____

C.   Demographic: _____

             _____

             _____

             _____

             _____

D.   Social/
     Cultural   _____

             _____

             _____

             _____

E.   Legal/
     Regulatory   _____

             _____

             _____

             _____

IV. Competitive Factors:

I perceive my competitive situation to be the following?

_____
_____
_____
_____
_____
_____

List Major Competitors:

Competitor	Asset Size	Strategic Thrust
_____	$_____	_____
_____	$_____	_____
_____	$_____	_____
_____	$_____	_____
_____	$_____	_____

V. Customer Analysis:

A. My current three most profitable market segments are:

1. Product Line/Segment _____

   Description _____
                _____
                _____

   Estimated Annual Growth Rate   _____%

   Estimated Local Market Size _____   Market Share _____%
   (# of Households/Businesses)

2. Product Line/Segment _____

   Description _____
              _____
              _____

   Estimated Annual Growth Rate   _____%

   Estimated Local Market Size _____   Market Share _____%
   (Households/Businesses)

3. Product Line/Segment _____

   Description _____
              _____
              _____

   Estimated Annual Growth Rate   _____%

   Estimated Local Market Size _____   Market Share _____%
   (Households/Businesses)

VI. <u>Internal Analysis</u>

   Strengths-Weaknesses-Opportunities-Threats (SWOT) Summary

1. Our bank's major marketing strengths are:

_____

_____

_____

_____

_____

2. Our bank's major weaknesses are:

_____

_____

_____

_____

_____

3. We perceive our major opportunities in the future to be:

_____

_____

_____

_____

_____

4. We perceive the major threats, which could prevent us from reaching our
   objectives, to be:

_____

_____

_____

_____

_____

MARKETING STRATEGY

Business Unit: _____

(Please complete the following three pages for <u>each major target market</u>
you intend to focus on in the next 12 months; include segments addressed
in section V on page B-3 and targeted segments for future growth)

Our marketing strategy will concentrate on the following market segments.

VII. <u>Marketing Plan</u>

Product Line or Segment: _____

A.   The target market description is:

_____

_____

_____

_____

Estimated Annual Growth Rate _____%

Estimated Local Market Size _____   Market Share _____%
(# of Households/Businesses)

B.   The financial needs of this target market are:

_____

_____

_____

_____

C.   The financial products/services necessary to satisfy the needs of
      the target segment are: (If you do not have the product/services
      necessary to meet these needs, please indicate the resources
      required in section VIII.)

_____

_____

_____

C-1

D. Our objectives for this segment are: (Please indicate those that are applicable to your product line/market segment)

	Current Year(Yr.1)	Next Year(Yr.2)	Year 3
Objectives ($ 000 omitted)			
Average Deposits:	$ _____	$ _____	$ _____
Average Loans:	$ _____	$ _____	$ _____
Total Net Interest Income:	$ _____	$ _____	$ _____
Total Fee Income:	$ _____	$ _____	$ _____
Other: _____	_____	_____	_____

E. The marketing strategy is:

1.   Product: _____
     _____
     _____
     _____
     _____

2.   Distribution: _____
     _____
     _____
     _____

3.   Promotion:

   (a)   Advertising: _____
         _____
         _____
         _____

(b)   Sales: _____

_____

_____

_____

(c)   Sales Promotion: _____

_____

_____

_____

4.   Pricing: _____

_____

_____

VIII. Please indicate extraordinary resources required to accomplish the
      objectives outlined in section VII-D.

_____

_____

_____

_____

_____

_____

IX.   Marketing Tactics: (See Attached Marketing Tactics Schedule)

Unit Manager: _____   Date: _____

Marketing
Manager: _____   Date: _____

IX. Marketing Tactics   (First Year Schedule)

Business Unit: _____   Planning Year: _____

The following is a summary of our action plans for this target segment. (You may attached further explanations, pert diagram, or calendar

Product Line or Segment Name/Unit: _____

($ 000 omitted)

* Action Required	Responsibility	Schedule		Goal ($ or accts)		Budget ($)	
		Start	Finish	Plan	Actual	Plan	Actual
(_)							
(_)							
(_)							
(_)							
(_)							
(_)							
(_)							
(_)							
(_)							
(_)							
						==========	==========
	Total Plan Budget					_____	

* Please indicate: (A)..For Media Advertising
                    (E)..For Events
                    (P)..For Public Relations
                    (S)..For Sales Promotion (i.e., brochures, premiums, etc.)
                    (M)..For Miscellaneous

C-4

Marketing Plans for Small and Midsize Banks

CHAPTER 1

Marketing Plan for 1988

Margaret L. Gilpin
Bank of Hanover and Trust Company
$180 million assets

Environment, Trends, and Analysis

Bank of Hanover and Trust Company, the oldest financial institution in Hanover, Pennsylvania, is strategically located in the western section of York County close to the Maryland line between Baltimore, Maryland, and Harrisburg and York, Pennsylvania.

Bank of Hanover's primary market area is the Pennsylvania communities of Hanover, New Oxford, and McSherrystown. Approximately 70 percent of the bank's business comes from these communities. An additional 10 percent comes from Wellsville.

The completion of Maryland Route 795 is bringing an increase in the Hanover area's population. Many people are moving to our market area from the cities of Harrisburg, York, and Baltimore. It is becoming better known that the Hanover area can offer lower housing costs and, in general, a lower cost of living than Harrisburg, York, or Baltimore.

Demographic and Social Factors

The average Hanoverian is white, between thirty-two and thirty-six years of age, owns a home in the $45,000 range, and has a family with two children. The family consists of two wage earners; their occupations are manufacturing related, with an annual income of $25,000 to $39,000.

As is the case nationwide, our customers' knowledge of financial services is increasing. No longer do they opt only for a basic checking account and savings account. They are asking more and more questions to determine the best value of an account for their money. As a result, we are finding less loyalty in our customers. They are price sensitive and want to do their banking in an easy, convenient manner with knowledgeable, customer-oriented tellers.

During the next five to ten years, the migration from larger cities could dramatically alter the characteristics of our market. Our customers, now employed in Hanover, will probably be employed outside our trading area, and most likely will have white collar rather than blue collar jobs.

This migration will bring a new Hanoverian who will be better educated, more knowledgeable, more mobile, and in all likelihood more aggressive in financial affairs. This new Hanoverian will undoubtedly enjoy a higher income. It is possible that our native Hanoverians may not be able to keep pace financially with their new, more affluent neighbors.

Competition

There are six other banks and three savings and loans competing for customers in the Hanover area. Our toughest competitors are Farmers Bank and Trust Company with assets of $376,720,000 and Adams County National Bank with assets of $328,621,000. Farmers Bank is very aggressive in all aspects of management style, business development, pricing, and credit policy. They have a large asset base, a large market area and convenient banking hours—open most nights until 9:00. Within the last three years, Adams County National has commanded a larger share of our market. Once considered a secondary competitor, Adams County National is now aggressively pricing loans and deposits, offering low service charges, and fast turnaround on mortgages.

The strengths and weaknesses of Bank of Hanover and our competitors are listed as follows:

Adams County National Bank

Strengths

1. Locally owned
2. Aggressive price competitor—low loan rates, good deposit rates, low service charges
3. Fast turnaround on mortgages, limited loan documentation, curbside appraisals
4. Participates in regional ATM network; is installing a Cash Stream machine in McSherrystown

Weaknesses

1. Not as convenient—fewer locations, shorter office hours
2. Not as flexible—no fixed rate morgages, primarily a collateral lender

Farmers Bank and Trust Co.

Strengths
1. Local ownership, local decision making
2. Very aggressive in management style, business development, pricing, and credit policy
3. Large asset base, large market area, strong resources
4. Organized for growth—management depth, large DP staff, elaborate training programs
5. Larger local market share
6. Convenient hours and locations; maintains proprietary ATM network

Weaknesses
1. Image problems—"getting too big," "trust department fiasco"
2. Lacks efficiency, more error prone
3. Rumors of poor employee morale, high employee turnover

Hamilton Bank (Corestates)

Strengths
1. Large financial institution, broad market area and customer base, strong financial resources
2. Wide range of products and services, larger loan limit, high-powered investment products, regional ATM network
3. Good local market share
4. Aggressive price competitor, especially on loan rates

Weaknesses
1. Out of town bank, no local decision making
2. Policies not always consistent or flexible
3. Fewer local locations, less convenient to local customers
4. High service charges on deposit accounts

Dauphin Deposit

Strengths
1. Large bank, broad market area, strong resources
2. Aggressive price competitor on both loans and deposits

Weaknesses
1. Out of town bank, no local decision making
2. Poor local locations, not very convenient to deal with, no local ATMs
3. Poor service

Captive Finance Companies and Mortgage Companies

Strengths
1. Very convenient—loans are originated at the point of sale, applications are taken in the customer's home or at the realtor's office
2. Aggressive price competitors, willing to buy market share
3. Operating on a national level, strong financial resources

Weaknesses
1. No personal relationship with the customer, poor cutomer service after the sale
2. Out of town financial institution

Broker's Insurance Agent Financial Planners

Strengths
1. Wide variety of products
2. Strong sales orientation
3. Promise higher rates of return
4. Operating on national level

Weaknesses
1. Poor image, lack credibility
2. Not as visible in the local market
3. Not as convenient to purchase
4. Complicated products
5. Greater risk to the customer

First Federal Savings and Loans

Strengths
1. Aggressive price competitor—free interest checking, higher deposit rates than other institutions
2. Locally owned

Weaknesses
1. Weak management, poor service, very inefficient
2. Problems with savings and loan image
3. Not as convenient to deal with—fewer locations, shorter hours, no ATMs
4. Financially weak

Finance Companies

Strengths
1. Strong financial resources
2. Easy credit, quick approval, willing to make smaller loans
3. Operating on a national level

Weaknesses
1. Narrow product line
2. Weak image
3. High loan rate

Bank of Hanover and Trust Co.

Strengths
1. Locally owned and managed
2. Friendly and efficient staff
3. Good reputation as a strong, safe financial institution, providing good customer service
4. Good locations and convenient hours—proprietary ATM network, with more machines than anyone in Hanover
5. Competitive products and services
6. Strong share in local market
7. Low employee turnover

Weaknesses
1. Small trading area
2. Not aggressive in the areas of business development, credit policy, loan pricing, and deposit pricing
3. Not a bank for the little guy—too aggressive with service charges on deposit accounts
4. Primarily on-the-job training, with bank products and policies not universally known or applied
5. Less effective advertising
6. Lack of management depth—not enough of the right kind of people, no formal management training program

Legal and Regulatory Considerations
As is the case nationwide, mergers and acquisitions are commonplace in our market area. As would be expected, this presents both opportunities and threats. Within the last two years, independent community banks as well as larger regional banks have been acquired. The possibility that Bank of Hanover may be acquired is very real.

While these threats are recognized, there are also a number of opportunities for expansion. Quite possibly, community banks smaller than Bank of Hanover would consider merger offers from us. Smaller banks often need to participate in commercial loans, and a bank the size of Bank of Hanover could be an excellent source of new loans. A loan production office in Maryland is another way that Bank of Hanover could expand its market area.

Financial Performance
The financial performance of Hanover Bankcorp for the first ten months of 1987 may be summarized as follows: On an after-tax basis, return-on-average assets and average equity was 1.18% and 14.54%, respectively. This compares to planned ratios of .99% and 14.67%. Total average assets have increased by 4.6% from $175 million in October of 1986 to $183 million this year. Average assets are slightly below the level planned for 1987. The sale of new stock in 1986 and improved profitability have increased our capital-to-asset ratio from 7.29% in 1986 to 8.57% this year. Loan growth is slightly ahead of plan. At the end of October, our loan-to-asset ratio was 63%. This compares very favorably with our loan-to-asset ratio in 1986 of 53%.

Customer Mix
The majority of our bank customers have lived and worked in Hanover all their lives. Our customers are heavily influenced by family tradition when choosing a bank. Often a customer's loyalty will be with the bank that approved their first loan (mortgage, installment, etc.). Most of our customers are within a ten-minute drive of one of our branch locations, and they usually do their banking as one of many stops they must make.

The average bank customer is between twenty-five and forty-four years of age with an annual family income of $25,000 to $40,000 (dual wage earners). The average customer has a high school education, has a manufacturing-related job, and is married with two children. The average customer is likely to have a noninterest-bearing checking account and a passbook savings account. Both total deposits on hand and installment loan balances are often between $5,000 and $10,000.

As mentioned previously, our market is changing; and within the next three to five years the profile of our customers may change considerably.

Market Share
Bank of Hanover's market share in the Hanover area has stayed relatively stable in the last three years.

Current dollar volume of deposits and loans are as follows:

Demand	$13,180,000
NOW Account	11,990,000
Money Market	43,021,000
Passbook Savings	24,800,000
Time Deposits	73,939,000
Commercial Loans	52,000,000
Installment Loans	21,350,000
Mortgage Loans	42,407,000

Problems and Opportunities

Bank of Hanover's problems and opportunities are best summarized by Patrick Reilly, vice president of operations, in the summary of our September 12, 1987, planning meeting.

On September 12, 1987, the Planning Committee of the Bank of Hanover met to review and update our long-range plan for 1988. The following is a summary of the committee's discussion:

A. Geographic Market—Over the next several years, Hanover Bancorp may need to transform itself from a single company bank holding company to a regional multi-bank or multi-company organization serving south central Pennsylvania and northern Maryland.

B. Distribution Strategy—Our distribution strategy must be tailored to suit our objectives. The right combination of technology, products, and marketing should enable us to enter new markets in a cost-effective manner. The traditional full-service branch office will play an important part in our delivery strategy, as will telemarketing and electronic banking.

C. Product Service—While competition, deregulation, and technology have changed the way we do business, basic banking services are still in demand. We believe the majority of bank earnings will continue to come from the sale of basic community banking services. Other types of financial services will be considered and may be offered if it can be determined that we are capable of offering these services in an effective and profitable manner.

D. Customers—Our target customer group will continue to be middle-income families, builders and developers, small-to-medium-size businesses, and professionals. These segments offer the greatest profit potential to our corporation. We realize, however, that competition for these customers will be keen and that these customers are becoming more sophisticated and will be demanding a higher level of service.

E. Personnel—The corporation's competitive advantage is going to have to come from our personnel. Traditionally, Hanover Bancorp has enjoyed a low turnover level. As a result, we enjoy a reputation for generally fast and efficient service. We must maintain and enhance the professional image of our corporation and build a strong sales, service-oriented organization. To accomplish this, our personnel policies must seek to reward above-average performance in such a way that if the corporation prospers the individual prospers as well.

F. Shareholders—Our goal is to remain an independent banking company. To do this will require above-average financial performance and consistent growth in earnings. We believe the appropriate earnings growth rate for our organization is between 8% and 12% each year.

Status of 1987 Action Items
Expand Our Geographic Market Via Mergers
An investment banking firm was retained during 1987, and a number of opportunities were explored. We plan to continue our efforts in this area but do not see any significant progress in the near future.

Expand Our Geographic Market Via New Facilities
We are opening a loan production office in Westminster, Maryland.

Increase Loan-to-Asset Ratio to 60%
At the end of October, loans outstanding were up 18% over the prior year. To achieve this growth, we increased our staff in the commercial lending area; maintained competitive pricing; introduced Quick Cash Plus, a home equity line of credit; and devoted over 80% of our marketing budget this year to the acquisition of new loan business. At the end of October, our loan-to-asset ratio was 63%. Gross loans totaled $116.5 million, and we are almost $700,000 ahead of our December 31, 1987, goal for loans outstanding.

Expansion of Electronic Banking Services
During 1987, our customer service representatives did an excellent job of cross-selling Nice cards to new deposit customers. A number of programs were implemented to increase ATM usage. As a result, both our cardholder base and the number of transactions per month increased significantly this

year. Our cardholder base increased by 16%, from 4,062 last October to 4,710 this year.   Average monthly transactions, including balance inquiries, increased by 42%, from 7,400 transactions during 1986 to 10,500 this year. The information necessary to evaluate the Mac and Cashstream networks is being assembled and a recommendation concerning Bank of Hanover's participation in one of these networks will be forthcoming before the end of the year.

Develop a Long Range Facilities Plan
The Building Committee of the Board of Directors has selected Bank Building Corporation to assist us with this item. Department space planning questionnaires, employee job summaries, and historical operations data have been supplied to Bank Building, and interviews with various department heads will be scheduled during the next few weeks. After these interviews are completed, and the data we submitted are analyzed, Bank Building will present an analysis of our ten-year facilities requirements and the costs of the various options available to us to meet these requirements. We should receive a report from Bank Building no later than January of next year.

Maximize Earning From Our Investment Portfolio
We have continued to work with an outside investment advisor to improve the performance of our portfolio. Through the end of October, the income from our investments was running at the level we had planned for 1987.

Marketing Budget for 1988
As is evident from our marketing budget, summarized below, in 1988 we plan to spend the bulk of our marketing dollars on public relations, sales promotions and direct marketing.

Newspaper	$21,000
Radio	20,000
Agency	14,500
Research	8,004
Outdoor	9,995
Public Relations and	
Sales Promotions	72,501
Direct Marketing	61,000
Total	$207,000

Marketing Objectives
  I.   Expand our geographic market area
 II.   Develop a stronger sales and service orientation
III.   Improve the quality and professionalism of our staff

IV. Explore a regional ATM network
V. Develop a plan and timetable for the expansion and renovation of existing bank facilities
VI. Maximize earnings from our investment portfolio
VII. Continue to emphasize loan growth
VIII. Establish a formal product development program

Goals, Strategies, and Tactics

I. Expand Our Geographic Market Area
A. Redefine our primary trading area to include northern Maryland, southern Adams and northern York counties.
   1. Identify areas within this region that have the greatest potential for Hanover Bancorp, Inc.
   2. Determine the most effective way possible to enter this market such as new branch office, loan production office, direct marketing, or an officer calling program.
   3. Develop a plan to enter these market areas.

B. Establish Hanover Bancorp as a regional institution by the end of 1990 by continuing efforts to identify and attract merger partners from the south central Pennsylvania or northern Maryland trading area.

C. Increase shareholder earnings by gaining new customers through a call program (two calls per officer per month to new customers in the expanded market area).

Resources required:
• Management commitment
• More employee time devoted to selling bank services
• Additional sales training and qualified staff, and larger budget for marketing and other operating expenses
• Better sales management system

Evaluation: Evaluate results with CEO on a quarterly basis

Completion date: Third quarter 1988 and ongoing

Assigned to: CEO

Support from: The Marketing and Operations departments, and the Loan and Branch Administrator

II. **Develop a stronger sales and service orientation**
  A. Increase profitability via new business
    1. Investigate a commission sales program for both inside and outside sales personnel
    2. Hold monthly meetings to train personnel on product knowledge; include "how-to" sales information
    3. Establish an "automated" sales information system to monitor and report monthly results
    4. Establish a telemarketing department to sell more services to new and existing customers.

  B. Enhance career opportunities for existing staff members
    1. Revise job descriptions and assignments of all customer contact personnel to emphasize sales and customer service
    2. Include individual sales performance in job evaluation

  C. Continue to emphasize service as a priority
    1. Shopper Program
      a) Revise content of the evaluation forms used in 1986
      b) Hold two shopper programs in 1988
    2. Develop a closed account survey

Resources required:
• More employee time devoted to selling bank services
• Additional sales training coordinated by the Marketing Department
• $2,400 for Shopper Program
• $39,000 to establish Telemarketing Department

Evaluation:
• Monitor results of monthly cross-sell report
• Monitor results of monthly telemarketing report
• Monitor results of shopper survey

Completion date: Second quarter 1988 and ongoing

Assigned to: Loan and Branch Administrator and Marketing

Support from: Human Resources and Operations departments

III. **Improve the quality and professionalism of our staff**
  A. Rescue long-term salary and benefit costs via retention of key personnel and lower staff turnover
    1. Identify the skills and talents our staff must have to compete successfully in the changing environment

2. Establish and define career paths within the organization to encourage personal growth and staff retention

B. Increase staff morale and productivity
   1. Review and revise compensation programs as necessary to ensure that we are offering a competitive program
   2. Emphasize pay for performance via sales commissions and bonuses

C. Improve customer service by educating and developing our staff at all levels within the organization
   1. Internal training program
   2. AIB Certificates
   3. Seminars

D. Increase management depth
   1. Review job description, table of organization, and job assignments
   2. Ensure that we are properly organized and staffed to meet the needs of our customers in a changing environment

Resources required:
- Management commitment
- Management time
- Additional staff
- Budget for training programs
- $2,500 for sales commissions and bonuses

Evaluation: Review progress quarterly

Completion date: Third quarter 1988

Assigned to: Human Resources and Marketing Departments

IV. **Explore a regional ATM network**
   A. Consider joining an ATM network to enhance our customers' use of ATMs
   B. Enhance competitive position as a retail financial institution
      1. Continue incentive program for our new Nice cardholders
      2. Offer two incentive programs for our Nice cardholders
         a) Nice Sweepstakes in March
         b) Demonstration Days in September to increase transaction volume
      3. Offer an incentive during February and August to tellers,

CSRs, and bookkeeping personnel to bring in new cardholders the months before the cardholder promotion
4. Use the bank's employee publication *Bank Notes* as a source
of information on ATMs in general and as a place to publish
"high salesperson" of the quarter for selling new cards

Resources required:
- Management time
- Increased expenditures for new hardware, software, and processing
- More marketing
- Incentive programs: $3,000 for Sweepstakes and Demonstration Day

Evaluation:
- Monitor progress with Vice President of Operations quarterly
- Monitor cross-sell report for number of cards sold
- Monitor monthly ATM Report

Completion dates:
- Second quarter 1988 (item A,1)
- Ongoing (item B,1)
- March and September 1988 (item B,2)
- February and August 1988 (item B,3)
- March, June, September, December 1988 (item B,4)

Assigned to: Marketing and Operations Departments

V. **Develop a plan and timetable for the expansion and renovation of existing facilities**
   A. Develop a plan to expand, renovate, or add an administration branch and other facilities to accommodate future growth
   B. Improve customer service and management control
   C. Enhance our bank's image in the community by improving our facilities

Resources required:
- Management time
- Budget for new facilities and/or renovations

Evaluation: Monitor results quarterly with Operations

Completion date: First quarter 1988 and ongoing

Assigned to: Operations Department

VI. **Maximize earnings from our investment portfolio**
  A. Better yield on bank investments—Continue to work with an outside investment advisor to improve the performance of our investment portfolio
  B. Maintain growth in net income of 8% to 12%; ROA of 1% to 1.15%; and ROE of 14% to 15%

Resources required:
- Management time
- Investment Advisor

Evaluation: Monitor monthly financial reports

Completion date: Ongoing

Assigned to: Investments Department

VII. **Continue to emphasize loan growth**
  A. Increase commercial loans to $45,000,000
    1. Aggressively seek commercial loan business via business development officer calling program in our present and expanded market area
      a) Increase required number of calls to six per month— three prospect calls and three professional courtesy calls
      b) Continue using branch manager monthly meetings to conduct sales training via speakers and videotapes
      c) Investigate a commission sales program for officers in the officer call program
      d) Include individual sales efforts as part of job evaluation
    2. Work with advertising agency to develop small-business ads for radio and newspaper
    3. Investigate using a monthly/quarterly newsletter to send to our current and prospective business customers
    4. Investigate the possibility of using "how-to" seminars for small community businesses
    5. Have the branch managers commit to attend the monthly Chamber of Commerce breakfasts at least twice a year

  B. Increase installment loans to $21,600,000
    1. Maintain marketing program to sell Quick Cash accounts, home equity lines of credit and other credit products
      a) Work with Sheshunoff & Company to get a list of customers who would be the best prospects for tele-marketing of credit products

        b) Develop a direct marketing plan to market our loan products—involves telemarketing and direct mail
2. Continue to advertise our loan products via newspaper, radio and billboards
3. Investigate a better tracking system for our cross-sell report
4. Use cash incentive programs to reward sales efforts of our loan products that were successful in 1987
5. Use teller meetings to educate and train our tellers regarding our loan products

C. Increase mortgage loans to $45,000,000
1. Continue to use newspaper, radio, and billboards to market our bi-weekly mortgage product, Accelerated Mortgage Plan
2. Consider holding a reception for builders and contractors to encourage referrals for new home construction mortgages
3. Have advertising agency investigate the effectiveness of a "new home construction" advertisement
4. Develop an "all-in-one" brochure listing all the types of mortgages available (new home construction, convertible ARM with bi-weekly and monthly payments available)
5. Consider retaining outside commission-paid loan originators to improve our marketing efforts

D. Develop new sources of dealer loans such as:
1. Used car dealers
2. Leasing program to be offered in the first quarter of 1988
        a) Educate our employees regarding benefits of leasing
        b) Newspaper and radio ads to market leasing program

Resources required:
- Management commitment and time
- Additional facilities
- Additional marketing

For (A) Commercial Loans:
- Video tapes—$250 (item 1,b)
- Speakers—$1,500 (item 1,b)
- Small businesses ad—$1,250 (item 2)
- Quarterly newsletter—$4,000 per year (item 3)
- Two seminars—$1,800 (item 4)

For (B) Installment Loans:
- Sheshunoff—$1,500 (item 1,a)
- Tracking system—$2,500 (item 3)
- Incentive Programs—$850 (item 4)

For (C) Mortgage Loans:
- Reception for area builders—$900 (item 2)
- "All-in-One" Brochure—$750 (item 4)

Evaluation:
- Monitor monthly officer call report
- Monitor monthly cross-sell report
- Monitor monthly loan report
- Monitor monthly leasing report

Completion dates:
- Ongoing (item A)
- January 1988 and ongoing (item B, 1a)
- March 1988 and ongoing (item B,1b)
- April 1988 and ongoing (item C)

Assigned to: Lending Department

Support from: Marketing Department

VIII. **Establish a formal product development program**
    A. Create more appealing product line by evaluating existing services and products

    B. Increase profitability and market share by changing, adding, or eliminating products as needed to appeal to target markets

    C. Research offering new electronic services
        1. In-home banking
        2. Insurance services
        3. Direct deposit
        4. Non-cash deposit pickup for small businesses

Resources required:
- Management time
- Increased expenditures for computer software and other programs—$5,000 to $10,000
- A better system of cost and product profitability analysis

Evaluation:
- Evaluate existing services by June 1988
- Research on new services by September 1988

Completion date: Ongoing

Assigned to: Marketing and Operations departments and Comptroller

Statement of Summary

The preceding pages have outlined the Hanover area market and Bank of Hanover's position in the marketplace. We are very aware of the weaknesses of our bank in relation to our competitors and the need to capitalize on our strengths.

If we are to remain a strong, independent community bank, we must strive to continue to be proactive, not reactive, to the ever-changing economic environment. We expect our market area to continue to grow and be prosperous, and we plan to be part of that growth.

While we know that the strategic planning process is vital to the future of Bank of Hanover, it will only be through the hard work, cooperation, and dedication of our employees that we will be able to accomplish our goals and objectives in 1988. ◆

CHAPTER 2

Developing a General Marketing Plan for the "New" Valley Bank of Nevada

Daniel C. Gentry
Security Bank of Nevada
$480 million assets

The impending merger of Security Bank of Nevada and Valley Bank of Nevada has created an opportunity to demonstrate the strengths of the marketing function in today's continually changing banking environment. During the merger process, the marketing function must protect the "new" Valley Bank of Nevada from becoming vulnerable.

Indeed, the transition will be a logistical nightmare. We must not, however, allow a preoccupation with converting systems, general ledgers, personnel, and services to cause us to neglect our most precious asset—our customers. They must be protected throughout the process and beyond.

The purpose of this document is to organize not only the thought processes, but also the philosophical changes, necessary to properly market the bank during and after the merger.

Situation Analysis
Nevada Population Data
The 1980 census of population reported that Nevada was the fastest growing state in the Union, with a 63.8% growth rate since 1970. Both Las Vegas and Reno/Sparks were in the ten fastest-growing standard metropolitan statistical areas (SMSAs), with Las Vegas increasing 69.5% and Reno, 60.1%. While the entire state experienced rapid growth, Reno/Sparks and other nonmetropolitan areas did not grow as quickly as the Las Vegas area.

During the 1980s, Nevada has continued to be the fastest growing state, with the Las Vegas area leading the way. Nevada's population is now more than a million. The Las Vegas area has more than 600,000 residents and is among the top 100 of the country's major urban areas. The Reno/Sparks area, with a population of over 230,000, ranks near 150th in size.

The rapid migration to Nevada is expected to continue through the 1980s, with the growth rate anticipated to be 37.8% from 1980 to 1990. A slight leveling off of the growth rate is anticipated through the 1990s, with a 27.9% increase projected between 1990 and 2000.

Demographic Profile
The median age of Nevada residents is 30.3 years. Almost one-third of the population is between twenty-five and forty-four years old, an age group typified by individuals at the peak of their earning power.

The greater portion of adults are young, with 45 percent of the Las Vegas SMSA and 43% of the Reno/Sparks SMSA under the age of forty-five, with a median adult age of only forty-one.

Income
The demographics of income groups in Nevada follow the national patterns: higher income groups have higher educational attainment; the youngest and oldest groups have lower median incomes; and people between the ages of thirty-five and forty-four have the highest median incomes.

Married couples' households have the highest median income, reflecting the national trend toward two-income families. Also consistent with the national income patterns is the low median income of households headed by single females.

Employment and Economic Development
Nevada ranked first in the nation for employment growth in 1986. It is expected to continue growing at rates above those of the nation through the year 2000.

The Nevada labor force totaled 520,000 for first quarter, 1987, with total employment of 490,000. The unemployment rate in Nevada was 6.3%, well below the 7.1% rate recorded for the nation.

Service industries account for 44.2% of total employment in Nevada, followed by trade (19.9%), government (14.1%), transportation/public utilities (6.0%), construction (5.0%), manufacturing (4.8%), finance/insurance/real estate (4.6%), and mining (1.5%).

Nevada's two largest industries, services and trade, are expected to grow steadily, but it is interesting to note that the manufacturing sector is anticipated to grow at a faster pace than the average of all other industries. This is due primarily to the state's diversification efforts. Economic diversification is one of the state's top priorities, and the movement enjoys tremendous state-wide support.

Newcomers
Because Nevada is the fastest growing state, it is important to understand just who is moving to Nevada and why. The primary reason for moving to Nevada is job transfer, with the majority of newcomers being young adults. Due to their age, income levels are lower for this group than the median household income ($22,046 for newcomers, compared to $24,274 in Las Vegas, and $24,890 for Reno).

Most transferring newcomers are locating in the Las Vegas vicinity near Nelis Air Force Force Base, Lake Mead and Hoover Dam. These areas represent high federal government employment.

The second largest group of newcomers is drawn by job opportunities in Nevada's service industries (primarily gaming and tourism). This group is characterized by unskilled and semiskilled workers seeking employment in hotels and casinos. Wages are generally low, with most positions dependent on gratuities.

The development of a new Sun City retirement community in the Las Vegas area should enhance an already favorable retirement image. The quality of life in southern Nevada is highly rated by retirees, particularly in the areas of recreation, shopping, and cultural events.

Newcomers present many interesting challenges for the finance industry. As population growth is spread throughout age groups and professions, the opportunity exists to acquire business from all demographic sectors.

Competitive Environment
Nevada's rapid growth makes it an attractive market for financial services companies. Presently, there are seventeen banks, eight savings and loan associations, three thrift and loan companies, forty-two various credit unions, and numerous brokerage houses and finance companies.

Banks continue to capture the largest total share of market deposit dollars, approximately 60%; however, the share attracted to banks has declined during the past few years. Of the seventeen banks, eight have assets of $100 million or more. Three of those—First Interstate, Valley Bank, and Citibank Nevada—report assets of $1 billion or more. Citibank, however, carries its regional credit card loans as booked assets, which significantly skews its actual in-state existence. Currently, Citibank has only three full-service branches, all located in the Las Vegas area; but it would be wise to monitor their expansion efforts closely.

First Interstate Bank is the dominant Nevada bank with assets of over $3 billion. With 65 branches and 108 automated teller machines (ATMs), First Interstate's proprietary delivery capability is presently unmatched. Additionally, it is a member of the CIRRUS nationwide ATM network. First Interstate has roughly 49% of the commercial bank deposit dollars in Nevada. An interesting observation is that First Interstate's market share has been on a slow, but steady, decline since 1980 when, then known as First National Bank of Nevada, it enjoyed a 55% market share. The bank is now stronger in the urban areas, rather than being equally strong throughout the state, primarily because of gains by credit unions in the rural communities of Nevada.

Valley Bank of Nevada (assets $1.6 billion) is the second largest state-wide bank and the largest state-chartered bank. Valley currently has 38 branches and 106 proprietary ATMs. Valley has been very aggressive with regard to electronic banking and plays host to the In Nevada Network (INN), which links twenty-five banks, savings and loan associations, and credit unions together via ATMs. The network, of which First Interstate is not a participant, has over 200 locations state wide. Valley also participates in the Plus, Star, Instant Teller, Master Teller, VISA and American Express networks. This allows customers access to their funds at over 17,500 ATMs worldwide. Valley Bank has a 26% share of commercial bank deposit dollars in Nevada.

Nevada National Bank (NNB) is the third largest statewide commercial bank with assets of just over $600 million. NNB has 25 branches and 28 proprietary ATMs. They participate in the INN and Plus ATM networks and have a 10% share of commercial bank deposit dollars.

Nevada National has suffered from poor earnings the past few years. Numerous ownership and managerial changes have left them with an identity crisis. However, things are beginning to turn around for NNB. Security Pacific National Bank has agreed to purchase Nevada National effective January 1989, when Nevada's interstate banking laws are nullified. This union will give Nevada National the ability to compete head-to-head with the largest of the state's financial institutions. Already a renewed sense of pride and direction can be observed at NNB.

Security Bank of Nevada, with assets of $480 million, ranks as the fourth largest bank in Nevada. Security Bank has 18 statewide branches and 18 proprietary ATMs. They, too, are participants in the In Nevada Network and Plus nationwide network of ATMs. Security Bank holds an 8% market share of dollars deposited in commercial banks in Nevada.

Security Bank is rebounding from a disastrous 1986 fiscal year in which the bank realized a net operating loss of $682,000 due to significant non-performing loans. An in-depth analysis of Security Bank of Nevada and its impending merger partner, Valley Bank of Nevada, is presented in the comparison section that follows.

Nevada State Bank and **Pioneer Citizens Bank** have a 4% and 2.5% share of the market, respectively. Both banks are under $200 million in assets and are considered community-oriented banks. Although Nevada State Bank has been acquired by Zion's Bank of Utah, it has not yet expanded from the southern region of the state. Pioneer is statewide but has only seven branch offices throughout Nevada. Nevada State has been a steady performer, with return on assets consistently above 1.5%. Pioneer has felt the pain of loan losses and management indecision but has recently appointed a new president who is market driven. His concern for customers and employees has greatly enhanced Pioneer's image as a caring bank, sensitive to customer's needs and expectations.

Savings and loan associations are well received and have made tremendous inroads into the financial services market. They consistently pay higher rates on savings and CDs than their commercial competitors. The two largest savings and loans, **Nevada Savings** and **First Western**, have assets in excess of $1 billion dollars. The savings and loans in Nevada have overcome the consumer skepticism of the early 1980s and now attract roughly 35% of the total deposit dollars in Nevada. Additionally, they are aggressively marketing their adjustable rate mortgages and home equity lines of credit.

Of the numerous **credit unions** in Nevada, **Nevada Federal Credit Union** has the most significant impact on the urban financial services market. It is usually the rate and price leader in the Las Vegas and Reno/Sparks areas. In the rural areas, particularly Elko and Hawthorne, the credit unions have taken a large share of commercial bank business. Again, higher deposit rates and lower leading rates, particularly in installment lending, have been the big drawing cards.

The major **brokerage** firms include Dean Witter Reynolds, Shearson/ American Express, E.F. Hutton, Merrill Lynch, Paine-Webber, Prudential-Bache, and Burr-Wilson. Account executives at these brokerage firm do not hesitate to ask clients to open an asset management account or to transfer their IRA.

Obviously, more could be written on the competition. With the major retailers diversifying into financial services, up-start banks taking advantage of a growing economy and acquisition offers, and major out-of-state financial institutions vying for a piece of the Nevada market, the ability to attract and retain customers demands proactive, innovative strategies that consistently meet the needs of the consumers.

Comparison of Valley Bank of Nevada and Security Bank of Nevada
Overview of Valley Bank and Security Bank
The merger of Valley Bank of Nevada and Security Bank of Nevada is anticipated to be consummated by January 1988. The event will have significant impact on the financial services industry and the banking/consumer public in Nevada.

The "new" Valley Bank of Nevada will be the second largest financial institution in the state with over $2.1 billion in assets. It will employ 2,000 people statewide.

Market coverage will include 56 branch offices and 124 proprietary ATMs. Through the In Nevada Network, customers will have access to over 200 ATM locations throughout Nevada. Deposits will total in excess of $1.8 billion, with total loans exceeding $1.3 billion.

Valley Bank brings to this merger a very successful reputation with business (wholesale) customers. Their Commercial Lending Division and Priority Banking Program offer prompt, professional service for business and large retail clients. Valley's sales force actively solicits new business throughout the marketplace. Valley Bank's management firmly believes in the use of commissions and bonuses to reward performance. At the retail level, Valley is very progressive with regard to the development of expanded product lines and fee-based services. Its electronic banking services are especially advanced compared to competitors in the Nevada financial services market. Valley Bank's highest visibility is in the southern region of the state, where its expertise in commercial business development has allowed it to capitalize on one of the top-five fastest-growing metropolitan areas in the nation.

Security Bank of Nevada has historically been perceived as a retail-oriented bank. Its strengths have been in personal service and concern for the consumer. Hovering at the $500 million asset level, Security has experienced growing pains while trying to decide whether to become more wholesale oriented or to exploit its retail status. The business customers that Security serves express great satisfaction in their banking relationship. The major complaint is that Security is not big enough to service all their financial needs. Security Bank's presence in the Reno/Sparks area and in the northern and eastern rural communities ideally complement Valley Bank's southern region prominence.

Five-Year Performance (1982-1986)
During the past five years, both Valley Bank and Security Bank have endured economic hardships, loan losses, and increased competition. Over the 1982-1986 period, Security Bank's return on assets (ROA) averaged 0.36% compared to Valley Bank's 0.61%. Return on equity (ROE) for the same period averaged 5.32% for Security Bank and 10.50% for Valley Bank.

Security Bank experienced a more favorable capital adequacy ratio of 7.24% compared to Valley Bank's 6.58% for the five-year period. The net charge-offs to average loans was 1.1% for Security Bank and 1.8% for Valley Bank.

Total assets at both banks grew at a compound rate of just over 10%. Valley Bank's loan portfolio grew at a faster rate (11.4%) than Security Bank's loan portfolio (9.5%). Total deposits grew at the compound rate of 10.8% at Security Bank compared to 10.4% at Valley Bank.

Valley Bank experienced a compound growth rate of 8.4% in net income. Since Security Bank had a net loss in 1986, the five-year growth rate could not be applied.

Valley Bank has performed slightly better than Security Bank in terms of ROA and ROE. However, when compared to their competitors, both Valley Bank and Security Bank can be characterized as below average performers.

Deposit Portfolio Growth and Mix
Both banks have enjoyed a strong core deposit base over the last five years. For comparison purposes, core deposits are defined as total deposits excluding time deposits over $100,000 and public funds. The core deposits grew at a rate of 14.1% at Valley Bank and 11.1% at Security Bank. Core deposits represented 88% and 85% of total deposits at Valley Bank and Security Bank, respectively. As percent of total assets, core deposits were 73.4% at Valley Bank and 74.6% at Security Bank.

Major growth areas for both banks were the ATS/NOW and savings deposit categories. Valley Bank experienced growth of 39.6% in ATS/NOW and 16.2% in savings deposits; Security Bank showed 21.6% in ATS/NOW and 1.3% in savings deposits. Security Bank had stronger growth (14.4%) in money markets and CDs than Valley Bank (13.2%).

Loan Portfolio Growth and Mix
Both banks experienced growth in commercial real estate lending over the last five years. Security experienced a 12.2% growth, and Valley grew 11.0%. In residential real estate, Security Bank had modest growth of 0.9%; Valley had not been active in this area and showed a negative growth rate of 17%. In consumer lending, Valley Bank grew 11% compared to 9% at

Security Bank. Valley Bank has been very active in state, county, and municipal lending, showing a growth rate of 5.5% compared to a negative rate of 6% for Security Bank.

The loan portfolio mix reflected the growth patterns given above. Security Bank's total commercial loans (commercial real estate and industrial) represented 59.3% of total loans in December 1986, up slightly from 58.5% in December 1981. Valley Bank increased its percentage of commercial loans from 68.5% of total loans in 1981 to 72.1% in 1986. Conversely, Valley Bank's consumer loans (installment, lines of credit, and residential real estate) decreased from 29.5% to 17.1% of total loans from 1981 to 1986. For the same period, Security Bank increased its loans to consumers from 32.6% to 36.5% of total loans.

Over the last five years, Security Bank's loan mix has remained somewhat constant, whereas Valley Bank has shifted from consumer lending to commercial and governmental lending.

The "New" Valley Bank of Nevada: Strengths, Weaknesses, Opportunities, and Threats

Strengths
- Beginning market share of deposit dollars. The merged bank will hold approximately 34% of the deposit dollars in Nevada.

- The distribution network will include 56 branch offices, 124 proprietary ATMs, and the following ATM network affiliations: In Nevada Network (INN), Plus, Star, Instant Teller, Master Teller, VISA, and American Express.

- The deposit services mix includes a lifeline product (low service charge, no-frills account); noninterest- and interest-bearing checking; an exclusive senior package; and various savings, IRA, and CD products.

- Strong sales orientation with senior management support.

- "High Tech." Innovative, market leader in electronic delivery systems including ATMs, point of sale, and bank by phone.

- "High Touch." The potential is there to integrate Security Bank's existing philosophy of personal service.

- Internal/external communications network.

- Appropriate commitment of budget dollars to advertising.

- Training capabilities.

- Large bank with the ability to meet most needs.

Weaknesses
- No discernable image.

- Customer information file (CIF) limitations. This area had not been enhanced by either institution and lags behind other banks' abilities to use their CIF as a primary resource. Our ability to take advantage of opportunities is in part dependent on expanding our CIF capabilities.

- Difficulty recognizing potential impact of deregulation on our market.

- Large bank that is perceived as not caring about retail customers.

- Lack of marketing culture.

- Lack of marketing organizational structure and authority.

- Lack of commitment to an advertising agency, making long-term positioning and image building difficult.

Opportunities
- Diversify product offerings, particularly fee-based products.

- Gain new account relationships due to the increased convenience of the merged bank and the continuing growth of Nevada.

- Create a market-oriented institution that understands the customer's financial needs and caters to them.

- Offer innovative products and services to the Nevada retail market that are focused, appropriately positioned and priced.

- Develop a customer-oriented image.

Threats
- Loss of customers, particularly during transition due to existing or created ill-will that has not been addressed.

- Inability to deliver quality services because the staff is not "in tune" with management's philosophies.

- Inability to maximize profits owing to a lack of marketing culture.

- Making large capital investment errors owing to a lack of sufficient research.

- Mishandling of customers owing to an incentive-driven sales force pushing unnecessary or unwanted products and services.

- Competition that may serve the market's needs more favorably and may use this merger period to aggressively pursue our customers.

Corporate Objectives

The establishment of objectives for the "merged" banks is the most critical part of this plan since these objectives define the direction we plan to take.

Both long-range (three-year) and short-term (one-year) objectives are reviewed in this section; however, long-range quantitive objectives had not yet been released by senior management at the time of this writing. Therefore, long-range objectives are of a qualitative nature and, although difficult to translate into numbers and to measure, their contribution to the success of the merged banks is unquestionable.

Long-Range Qualitative Objectives

- Differentiate ourselves from the competition.

- Protect our existing customer base.

- Generate profitable new retail relationships.

- Explore earnings opportunities through the expansion and improvement of fee-based product lines.

- Increase the staff's abilities and knowledge through effective sales and product training at all levels of the bank.

- Establish a professional, caring image.

Short-Term Growth Objectives

Bankwide growth goals for 1988 have been set at 11% for deposits and 17% for loans. Based on the estimated 1987 year-end totals, deposits are anticipated to be $1.9 billion at year-end 1988. Loans should total approximately $1.3 billion at year-end 1988. Net income is expected to exceed $25 million.

Again, specific growth rates for individual deposit and loan types have not been determined at this time. However, based on the characteristics of the Nevada market, competitive factors, forecasted economic conditions, and the existing focus of both Valley Bank and Security Bank, the following marketing objectives have been developed.

Short-Term Advertising Objectives—During the Merger

- Create positive awareness and interest in the benefits of the Security/Valley merger.

- Develop a strong positioning statement that properly defines our market presence.

- Establish an image for the bank that complements, and is consistent with, the bank's positioning.

- Maximize customer retention and increase overall market share.

- Measure the effectiveness of the merger campaign and the public's perceptions of the merger.

Short-Term Advertising Objectives—Post-Merger
- Continue positioning and image building campaigns that are natural transitions from the merger campaign.

- Develop new, effective advertising to introduce new products and services for the "merged" banks, and expand awareness of existing products and services.

- Maintain an advertising production-to-media expenditure ratio of 30% production to 70% media.

- Effectively use media dollars to affect the defined target markets.

Advertising Strategies and Tactics
The following target markets have been identified for the "New" Valley Bank of Nevada:
- Valley Bank customers
- Valley Bank employees
- Security Bank customers
- Security Bank employees
- Retail banking marketplace
- Business community

Strategies
- Develop and implement an aggressive communications plan, which consists of both media and public relations, directed towards each of these target markets.

- Develop and implement a comprehensive customer notification program directed toward the existing retail and commercial customers of both banks.

- Develop and implement an educational program for employees of both banks that clearly communicates the following:
  - Customer benefits of the merger
  - Changes affecting current and future customers
  - Information regarding the advertising and public relations campaigns being executed during the merger

- Develop and implement a program to provide customers with quick, informative, and accurate answers to their questions regarding the merger.

Tactics

- Marketec, a Reno-based research firm, will survey approximately 600 Security Bank customers during the last two weeks in November. The research will address two primary areas:

  1. Reasons for banking with Security Bank

  2. Merger awareness and concerns of the customer

  It is felt that the Security Bank customer will be the most sensitive to the merger. Valley's customers are gaining additional convenience, but existing product lines and corresponding service charges will not change. The survey will assist us in preparing direct mail and other tools that directly address the concerns of existing Security Bank customers.

- The public relations campaign will be directed primarily towards the Security Bank customers, using direct mail and personal contacts. The direct mail messages will be determined from the Marketec research. The following pieces are planned:

  1. A personal letter to all Security Bank customers tailored to meet specific concerns.

  2. Statement stuffers with strong, condensed "what's-in-it-for-me" messages. Valley Bank customers will receive a slightly different message. These stuffers will also be the vehicle used to generate participation in a customer sweepstakes.

  Personal contact should be made either in person or via telephone to select customers, as determined by branch and department heads.

- A sweepstakes promotion will be developed for customers of the two banks. It will be introduced in the statement-stuffer mailings and will be designed to encourage visits to the branches. The time frame for the sweepstakes is roughly January 15 through mid-February 1988. Because sweepstakes by law must be open to all persons, branches will have entry forms for noncustomers and may be able to generate new retail customers at that point.

- To generate enthusiasm among both Security and Valley employees, it is suggested that a "learn and earn" campaign be developed that rewards employees for answering a questionnaire based on information provided to the employee about the merger. The following information would be included:

  1. An overview of the new bank

2. A welcome letter signed by senior management officials

3. Copies of advertising campaign materials

4. A question-and-answer sheet based on research findings and pertinent operational procedures

5. Materials that the Human Resources department may want to provide

The employee kits would be given out at breakfast meetings attended by all Valley and Security employees. They will be hosted by senior management and should be held the first two weeks of January.

A sweepstakes/incentive program, similar to the one being done for customers, would be conducted for employees.

- A press kit will be developed and delivered to the media on merger day. It should be completed by December 31, 1987. A public relations budget is presented on the following page.

Two-Phase Merger Campaign
Phase I will create a unifying theme that will directly place the fact of the merger out front and deliver a strong customer benefit statement: "Together for You." Phase I will utilize the names and logos of both banks to reinforce the joining of forces. Customer benefits must always shine through. Ads should be simple in concept and bold in approach. Phase I must be ready for implementation no later than December 31, 1987, and will run for four weeks, starting the day after shareholder ratification.

Phase II takes the campaign one step beyond the merger announcement. It will portray potential questions and answers that customers may ask. These questions will be determined from the research conducted by Marketec and from secondary research gathered on other bank mergers. The "Together for You" theme will now be replaced by ads showing only the Valley Bank logo and the tag line, "Nevada's Bank." Phase II will immediately follow Phase I, and will also run for four weeks.

A media mix of television, radio, newspaper and outdoor advertising will be utilized to fulfill our objectives. The recommended mix and budget is provided on the following page.

Post-Merger Advertising Strategies and Tactics
During the remainder of 1988, the primary thrust of the advertising plan will deal with the continuing push for positioning and image. Individual product support has not yet been determined, as the blending of the two

PUBLIC RELATIONS BUDGET—MERGER CAMPAIGN

Customer research	$ 8,000
Direct mail (35,000)	14,950
Statement stuffer/sweepstakes (190,000)	11,940
Employee/press kit folders (3,000)	3,061
Employee letters (2,000)	1,600
Customer sweepstakes	31,000
Employee sweepstakes	15,500
Buttons for employees	1,365
Banners for lobby (20)	3,155
Posters for lobby (200)	1,813
Brochures for lobby (100,000)	14,845
Counter cards for lobby (200)	2,218
Total	$109,447

banks' products is not complete. Product advertising will be fresh and fit under the image umbrella, giving continuity to the total campaign.

The requested budget for production and media placement is $1.5 million for the year. This is in addition to the merger budget previously outlined.

Department Objectives
Long-Term (Three years)
- Establish a strong, unique existence in the state through a consistent positioning strategy.
- Develop a loyal customer base by maintaining a distinct image.
- Continually monitor and evaluate performance.

Short-Term (1988)
- Create an atmosphere of stability amid the merger transition to alleviate the concerns of the two banks' customers and employees.
- Begin the development of a marketing culture within the bank.
- Blend the products and services of Valley Bank and Security Bank to result in the most advantageous mix for the markets we wish to serve.
- Improve employees' customer service skills.
- Create a newcomers program to take advantage of the rapid statewide population growth.
- Operate under the constraints of the approved budget.

ADVERTISING BUDGET—MERGER CAMPAIGN

Las Vegas
Television
- 2,000 GRP's @ $36 cost per point $72,000

Radio
- 1,800 GRP's @ $21 cost per point $37,800

Newspaper $47,000

Outdoor
- 28 panels for 30 days $10,416

Reno
Television
- 2,600 GRP's @ $32 cost per point $83,200

Radio
- 1,800 GRP's @ $12 cost per point $21,600

Newspaper $35,500

Outdoor
- 16 panels for 30 days $ 5,360

Rural
Newspaper $29,000

Media Budget Recap

Total Las Vegas	$ 167,216
Total Reno	145,660
Total Rural	29,000
Total Campaign	$ 341,876

Total Merger Budget Recap

Public Relations	$ 109,447
Media Placement	341,876
Advertising Production	100,000
Total	$ 551,323

Department Strategies and Tactics

- Develop and implement a new customer information hotline:
  Answerline. This will be a toll-free line to handle customer concerns
  about the merger and other general questions. Answerline should be
  open from 8:00 A.M. to 5:00 P.M., Monday through Friday. Implementation should coincide with the merger announcement (year-end,
  1987). Responsibility for developing the hotline will be spearheaded
  by Marketing.

- Establish an organizational chart for the "merged" bank's Marketing
  Department. Obtain the endorsement and support of senior management. Presently, the marketing functions at the two banks are handled
  quite differently. At Security Bank, the director of marketing oversees
  research and product development, pricing, advertising and promotion, internal and external communications, public relations and
  training. At Valley Bank, although all components are in place, the
  Marketing Department is primarily an advertising and promotions
  function. Product development, research, pricing, sales, and communications are handled outside the jurisdiction of Marketing. It is
  imperative that a functional organizational chart be developed as soon
  as possible. A recommended structure should be submitted for the
  approval of senior management. Realizing that these changes won't
  occur overnight, it is hoped that the marketing director will be in place
  by merger date (the position at Valley is currently vacant), and that the
  various functions will fall under his/her control within the year.

- Create and maintain an image of stability that is consistent with the
  new positioning of the bank. The initial campaign for image building
  and positioning is discussed in the "Advertising Strategies and
  Tactics" section of this report. Unfortunately, the advertising agency
  has been awarded only the merger campaign, and no long-term
  relationship has been contracted. It is recommended that the new
  bank enlist the services of a full-service agency. The agency should
  become involved in the annual marketing and advertising planning to
  help ensure the continuity of positioning and image building and to
  alleviate the sporadic advertising that is the result of contracting
  creative help on a project-by-project basis. The agency proposals
  should be reviewed and the contract awarded as soon as possible—
  no later than January 31, 1988.

- Establish a product review committee to examine the existing
  products/services of both banks, and make recommendations on
  which existing products to keep and which to eliminate. Committee
  membership should include marketing, operations, finance, legal, and
  credit. This committee should also make pricing recommendations

based on costs, competition, and perceived value. All product and service offerings should be integrated and uniformly priced by year-end, 1988.

- Establish an ongoing training program to teach employees about our products and how to match products with customer needs. It is recommended that this program be administered by Marketing. Working hand-in-hand with the product review committee, the Marketing staff can hold product training sessions as needed. Security Bank will bring into the merger several people who are excellent in this capacity.

- Continue to hold the "Success Through Selling" classes that are currently attended by all customer-contact employees at Security Bank. "Success Through Selling" was designed and is marketed by John Pratt and Associates, a subsidiary of Deluxe Cheque Printers. The program focuses on determining customer needs and developing banking relationships. Bank products are also reviewed as part of the training. These classes are for existing and newly hired personnel, and are endorsed and fully supported by senior management.

- Develop a newcomers kit and distribute it to realtors, the Chamber of Commerce, and company personnel directors. The kit should include a welcome letter, maps and community information, and general information on Valley Bank products and services. The development of the kit will be the responsibility of Marketing and should be targeted for a June 1988 implementation date.

- Enlist primary research to monitor and evaluate advertising awareness and effectiveness, customer satisfaction, the competitive environment, and the constantly changing market. The responsibility for marketing research should be brought into the Marketing Department.

- Adopt a budget for the newly formed Marketing Department that includes not only advertising expenditures, but also appropriate funding for research, product development, donations and charitable contributions, staffing, training, and communications. It is not possible to develop long-term marketing planning and effectiveness without a formalized departmental budget.

Conclusion
The convenience the "new" Valley Bank is as good as any financial institution in the state. Our product offerings are competitive. The financials are rebounding and appear stable. So what could possibly keep this bank from realizing its potential? The lack of a sound marketing philosophy.

Management must realize the importance of being a customer-focused organization that understands and effectively serves its markets. In other words, our business is not the delivery of bank services but the creative satisfaction of customers' financial services needs. It is hoped that this observation is construed as the constructive recommendation it is intended to be.

Working in a supporting role to all areas of the bank, marketing can provide guidance towards the attainment of corporate goals and can help maximize the return on invested corporate capital. Most importantly, good marketing can accomplish these goals in ways that satisfy our customers. ◆

PART 2

Market Planning for Specific Product Lines

CHAPTER 3

Developing and Implementing a Home Equity Line of Credit

Sharon Butcher
Bank of A. Levy
$527 million assets

There are many challenges facing bankers today. As product options become more complex, we must consider changes in existing products and consider new products that would best serve our customers' needs, and keep us competitive.

Recent changes in consumer borrowing habits and attitudes have had an impact on banks' ability to develop consumer loans. Consumer loans are generally priced with wider margins than commercial loans, and they provide a stable base of earnings. Consumers are responding to those financial institutions, traditional and nontraditional, that provide convenient access to borrowed funds. Equity lines of credit, a revolving line of credit tied to the equity in the customer's home, can provide a convenient source of credit.

This chapter provides a plan to develop an equity line of credit to accommodate this customer product need. Phases of development include: 1) tracing an equity line from the design stage through product introduction, product/sales training, and promotion; and 2) developing a plan for future marketing of the equity line product by analyzing and evaluating the results of the first direct mail and promotion efforts.

SITUATION ANALYSIS—EXTERNAL
General Consumer Trends
Many of the issues affecting equity lines of credit are the same as those applicable to consumer lending as a whole. The primary factors are changes

in consumer borrowing habits and attitudes. Today, borrowing is most often done at the "point-of-sale," rather than through the more traditional method of obtaining a loan from a lending institution with a fixed amount and term. *Convenience* is the primary reason for this type of borrowing. As lives become busier and more hectic, consumers are increasingly willing to pay a premium in order to buy time.

However, consumers, spurred by the Tax Reform Act of 1986, are becoming aware that equity lines may provide tax benefits. After the phase-in period, finance charges for debt not secured by primary real estate will not be tax deductible. Polls in the *American Banker* have indicated that consumers will decrease outstanding debt that is not tax advantaged. An article in the May 4, 1987, issue of the *Los Angeles Business Journal* indicates that equity lines have become the "belles of the lending ball." Previously unpopular, equity lines now provide flexible credit lines with comparatively low interest rates.

Market Profile
Ventura County, which is Bank of A. Levy's primary market area ranks twenty-sixth in size and twelfth in population[1] among California's fifty-eight counties. Nearly half of the county lies within the Los Padres National Forest. Ventura County ranks seventeenth [2] in the nation in terms of agricultural production and is California's fourth leading oil producer. Because of its proximity to the Los Angeles area, high-technology-related businesses, light manufacturing firms, and corporations in the service industry are relocating to the county.

Some 25% of the work force is employed by some branch of the government. The service and retail industries make up about 40% of the nonfarm-related employment.[3] The county's labor force is well educated. According to the 1980 census, 42% of the working population over the age of twenty-five have attended college. At present Ventura County's population tops 650,000 and is growing rapidly.

This population growth has been accompanied by inflated values in housing and a higher cost of living. These factors have increased the popularity of equity lines of credit in the Ventura County area because the equity line of credit is tied directly to owning a home.

A recent Bank Marketing Association study[4] indicates that more affluent consumers (annual household income of $75,000 or more) are 45% more likely to obtain equity lines of credit. Households with incomes ranging from $50,000 to $75,000 are far less likely to purchase equity lines. Ventura County has approximately 19,183 households with incomes of $75,000 or more, representing 9.26% of the population. The national average is 4.5%. Thus, Ventura County can provide a substantial base for equity line sales.

Competition
Financial industry competition in the state of California is sophisticated and aggressive. Major commercial banks and non-banks provide specialized services to various sectors of the population.

For the purpose of developing this plan, Bank of A. Levy's competition in Ventura County is defined as California Federal, Security Pacific National Bank, Sears, Home Federal, Bank of America, Wells Fargo Bank and First Interstate Bank. Each of these competitors actively solicit financial services in the Ventura County market, particularly, equity lines of credit. Below is a competitive review of the equity-line product.

COMPETITIVE REVIEW

Bank	Initial Fee	Annual Fee	LTV	Incentives
Cal Fed	$400	$ 35	75%	
B of A.	$400	$ 30	80%	50%-100% off
Levy				initial fee
Sec. Pac.	3 points		75%	
Wells Fargo	$450	$ 45	80%	
Sears	1 point		75%	
First Interstate	$300	$ 30	75%	
Home Federal	2 points	$ 35	80%	

SITUATION ANALYSIS—INTERNAL
Assets
In more than 105 years of operation, Bank of A. Levy has made consistent progress, never failing to add to its capital accounts or to pay dividends. Its growth also has been significant. In 1967, the bank's total assets were $51 million. By the end of November 1987, assets had reached $527 million. Bank of A. Levy currently employs 460 people.

Distribution System
Bank of A. Levy has adopted a delivery sytem which is segmented along product lines. Customers obtain products and services through five regional offices and twenty-two retail offices. In addition, there are two convenience centers that are administered operationally through a retail office. These centers offer customers extended hours, walk-up and/or drive-up facilities, and ATMs. Offices and convenience centers are located throughout Ventura County, with one retail office and one convenience center located in Los Angeles. The chart on the following page details the products and services available through this distribution system, which has been in place for approximately three years.

PRODUCTS AND SERVICES BY DISTRIBUTION POINT

Regional Office	Retail Office/ Convenience Center
Commercial loans	Deposit products
Investment products	Consumer credit
Trust products	Real estate loans
Self-directed IRAs	Merchant deposit services
* Financial planning	Drive-up service
* Trade financing	Walk-up service
	ATMs
	* Home equity lines

*Products in development

Deposit/Loan Profile
While local in orientation, Bank of A. Levy is a major financial institution, being the largest independent bank and third largest in deposits in Ventura County.

Overall deposits have shown an average growth of 12.73% from 1984 to 1986, with the largest growth in the savings category. However, there has been a bankwide decline in consumer lending (15% from 1985 to 1986), primarily due to a decline in automobile financing. This is a direct result of "point-of-sale" borrowing; that is, programs offered by car dealers and manufacturers that include rebates and financing at low interest rates. Financial institutions of Bank of A. Levy's size cannot compete profitably against these programs because they cannot generate the volume necessary to offset operating expenses and cost of funding.

The decline in the number of consumer loans has prompted Bank of A. Levy to restructure the administration of consumer lending by centralizing the credit approval and documentation functions. In addition, the bank has reassigned the customer interface function to newly appointed Personal Bankers who are also responsible for the sale of other retail products and services.

Market Size
On the next page are estimates of Bank of A. Levy's market size for equity lines of credit, along with Ventura County homeowners identified from the 1980 census, recent customer demographic data, internal reports, and a list-and-tape service.

MARKET SIZE

I. Ventura County -- (excluding Bank of A. Levy)
   Assumptions: (three cases)
   1. The percentages represent the percent of owner occupied households that might not qualify.
   2. Total number of owner occupied households equals 105,746.
   3. Of remaining market, after adjusting for percentage disqualified, the following is assumed, based on the 1986 survey by Synergistics.
      —13% have line with another institution
      —48% aren't interested
      —39% indicated some interest

Potential Penetration in Ventura County

	Low (-30%)	Average (-20%)	High (-10%)
Total adjusted # of households	74,022	84,597	95,171
# with another institution	9,623	10,998	12,372
# not interested	35,531	40,606	45,682
Net available	28,868	32,992	37,117

II. Bank of A. Levy—(number of owner occupied households=26,000)

	Low (-30%)	Average (-20%)	High (-10%)
Total adjusted # of households	18,207	20,808	23,409
# with another institution	2,367	2,705	3,043
# not interested	8,739	9,988	11,236
Net available	7,100	8,115	9,129

Organization

In 1983, Bank of A. Levy decentralized the marketing function hoping that managers in the retail offices and the regional offices could assume the role of product managers. However, administrative and supervisory duties prevented these officers from becoming effective product managers.

The current marketing department structure consists of only four people: the chief executive officer in the role of marketing director, the advertising/public relations manager, an administrative assistant, and a consultant on contract to the bank whose role varies depending on our needs.

Budget

There are several categories that are included in the Marketing Department's budget; but for the purposes of this plan, only six apply:

- Advertising production $ 85,100
- Business development   16,300
- Other professional services   51,072
- Collateral   22,025
- Media   228,671
- Employee training   4,500

It should be noted that $40,000 is being set aside from these categories to promote the equity line of credit.

Bank of A. Levy Advantages

Bank of A. Levy has certain advantages:

- Our customer attitude surveys tell us that we have an extremely courteous staff and offer friendly service.

- We have convenient hours—open from 7:00 A.M. to 6:00 P.M., Monday through Friday.

- Our staff members live and work here and, thus, have knowledge of the area.

- Our loans are processed locally; customers don't have to call Los Angeles or San Fransisco to get their loans approved.

Given these advantages, we would position Bank of A. Levy's equity line of credit as "convenient," which has wide market appeal.

DISCUSSION OF PLAN
Why an Equity Line of Credit?

The bank prides itself on being responsive to customers' needs. Customers are asking for equity lines because their borrowing habits are changing. Consumers are now willing to test the equity in their homes. The equity (first, second, or third trust deed) secures the line of credit. More important, recent increases in real estate values in Ventura County have made larger amounts of equity available. Among the factors prompting the offering of equity lines are:

- Bank of A. Levy needs to respond to the competition that is already offering equity lines.

- Recent tax changes have made equity lines of credit one of the few remaining ways to borrow money and still realize tax advantages.

- Equity lines will provide the bank with a new source of income.

- The bank needs to increase consumers loans primarily due to run-off over the last two years.

Product Description

The name selected for Bank of A. Levy's equity line of credit is *Homeowner's Credit Line.* The name was selected because it is descriptive of the product and is easy to remember. The chart below indicates the product's features, benefits, pricing, and uses.

HOMEOWNER'S CREDIT LINE

Features
- Revolving line of credit secured by first, second, or third trust deed.
- Line amounts range from a $10,000 minimum to a maximum of $200,000.
- Variable rate of 3.5% over average one-year U.S. Treasury Securities. Rate to be adjusted quarterly; cap to be set by 12/8/87.
- Maximum term of fifteen years with a renewal feature.
- Line may be accessed by check ($200 minimum) or by a special MasterCard.
- Loan to value of 75%.
- Payment amount equal to 2% of balance outstanding or $200, whichever is greater.
- Funds may *not* be used for the purchase of real property with less than five units.

Benefits
- Easy access to equity line in home that is available at any time.
- Greater control over financial position as line may be accessed, paid, and re-accessed within the available limits according to needs.
- Potential tax advantages for using this form of credit to finance large purchases.
- Convenience of readily available funds easily accessed by check or MasterCard.
- Pricing offers the dual advantages of flexibility (adjusted to market conditions quarterly) along with three-month stability. Also, the index used is an indicator of actual market conditions and is not set by the bank (i.e., reference rate).

Pricing—Fees
- Initial fee of $350, plus out-of-pocket.
- Annual fee, beginning the second year, of $50.
- Late fee of 5% of the payment amount or $10, whichever is greater.

Uses
- Investments or taxes
- Temporary cash-flow needs
- Medical expenses
- Retirement financing
- Education
- Home improvement/remodeling
- Vacations
- Major purchases, for example a new car, computer, etc.

A specially designed MasterCard was developed to allow the customer immediate access to the line of credit, since the checks would take at least a week to process. In addition, Bank of A. Levy's *Homeowner's Credit Line* card accesses the Instant Teller and CIRRUS Networks, which are world-wide. At the time of this writing, no other bank in Ventura County has this specific product advantage.

While most banks were featuring an interest-only payment, Bank of A. Levy's conservative lending policies prevented the equity line product from having this feature. Other institutions also provide an automatic payment feature, but Bank of A. Levy's severe systems limitations did not allow for this feature to be included.

The following marketing communication plan was developed to introduce Bank of A. Levy's new *Homeowner's Credit Line*.

- A marketing representative attended all branch and department staff meetings. Written communications were provided on an ongoing basis to update staff on the success of the promotion.

- A customer-incentive program was implemented to increase sales and help the bank's customers recognize that Bank of A. Levy has a valuable product at a reasonable fee.

- Our customers were solicited through direct mail, which included an application and postage-paid envelope for convenient reply.

- An employee incentive program was offered to encourage involvement and cross-selling.

- Branch lobbies were used to display posters carrying the same theme as the direct mail piece and for distribution of brochures.

FINANCIAL CONSIDERATIONS
An analysis was performed to determine at what point Bank of A. Levy's equity line will become profitable. Consideration was given to implement-

ing the program with a discounted fee and not advertising or promoting the product. Two scenarios were analyzed:

- No promotion or advertising with a $175 initial fee (discounted from $350). The breakeven is approximately 18 lines of credit.

- Product promotion and advertising with a $175 initial fee.   The breakeven point is approximately 122 lines.

The following assumptions were used in this analysis:
- Profitability is at the end of Year 2 and is net after taxes.

- The average line outstanding is $20,000.

- Start-up fees of $7,700 are included in Year 1 calculations and includes the following elements:
    - Attorney's fees $2,000
    - Forms/brochures $5,000
    - Card production $ 700

- Advertising and promotion costs are $40,000 in Year 1 and $5,000 in Year 2.

- Statistics used, that is, cost of funds and index, were as of December 12, 1986.

This analysis showed that the potential profitability of *Homeowner's Credit Line* is improved by advertising and promoting the product. It was estimated by the temporary product manager (a member of the bank's marketing department) that fifty equity lines would be sold by the end of Year 2 if the product was not advertised or promoted.

OBJECTIVES OF HOMEOWNER'S CREDIT LINE
The *Homeowner's Credit Line* is intended to complement the existing credit products of Bank of A. Levy. In conjunction with this, other specific objectives of the equity line of credit are:

- To increase consumer loan totals. The October 1987 Directors' Report published by the bank's planning department indicated the ratio of loans to deposits at 63.9%. In December of 1985 and 1986, this same ratio was 70.7% and 69.56%, respectively. Ideally, the bank's ratio should be at the 70% mark. Quality consumer loans are more profitable to the bank and with these loans running off, money is being placed in securities that are not as profitable to the bank.

- To realign the asset mix between real estate and consumer loans. Equity lines, with their shorter terms, are classified as consumer loans and will assist in this realignment of the portfolio. This will improve

Bank of A. Levy's ability to manage against fixed-rate real estate loans that cannot be sold. Also, it allows for credit diversification away from heavy commitments in real estate construction loans.

The current Directors' Report illustrates a loan mix of real estate and consumer loans as follows:

PERCENTAGE OF TOTAL ASSETS

	10/86	10/87	% Change
Real Estate	32.6%	30.4%	- 6.7%
Consumer	6.8%	5.4%	-20.59%
Total Assets ($MM)	526,832	545,301	+ 3.5%

Equity lines of credit will help to increase consumer loan totals and the percentage of total assets.

An equity line of credit is an easy way to answer a customer need in an innovative manner and generate additional fee income for the bank. As consumer's borrowing habits start to change, equity lines offer a convenient source of funds at rates comparable to most second mortgage loans and without the expenses associated with refinancing installment loans.

After watching Bank of A. Levy's major competitors introduce equity lines of credit, it has become apparent that our credit market share is likely to erode unless we act quickly to develop and implement this product. We believe that enough consumers are actively seeking this product, that our failure to introduce one will provide our competitor's with a means of attracting our customers. At this point, the introduction of this product is important to retain our customer base.

In addition, the new *Homeowner's Credit Line* offers the bank the opportunity to experiment in direct marketing, specifically direct mail.

ANALYSIS OF RISKS INVOLVED
As with any new product, the introduction of *Homeowner's Credit Line* has certain inherent risks:

- Insufficient consumer demand—the projections could prove to be overly optimistic.
- Lack of qualified personnel to sell the product. With the transition

of consumer lenders and new account staff into Personal Bankers, we may have Personal Bankers who lack essential lending skills.

- Bank of A. Levy has been an operationally driven bank for many years, and many of the systems are antiquated. For instance, the bank's system prevents us from charging a one-time fee automatically. Manual procedures have to be used. Gathering statistical data is also a manual process.

- Legislation could remove or limit tax benefits, thus making this a more difficult product to sell.

- In the past, Bank of A. Levy's conservative lending policy has prevented us from booking lines of credit on which the bank could have taken a credit loss. Equity lines of credit offer the same risk.

THE MARKETING MIX
Objectives, Strategies and Tactics
The following are planned to introduce the new *Homeowner's Credit Line* :
- Market research is to be used to do two things: 1) identify Bank of A. Levy customer prospects, and 2) identify Ventura County homeowners. As indicated earlier, there are limited internal resources available. Thus, research was limited to the use of the 1980 Census Report and internal reports generated from the bank's main computer, which provided us with name and address information. A list-and-tape service provided the necessary householding information and allowed matching of customers against Ventura County homeowners. The list-and-tape service also allowed for the selection of accounts based on the following mortgage criteria:
  - Owner-occupied single family homes, condos and apartments with less than four units
  - Original purchase date of 1984 or earlier
  - Original purchase price of $100,000 or more

- The advertising campaign was designed to introduce the product, communicate any special offers, increase sales, and enchance the bank's image as being responsive to customers' needs. In addition, the advertising was intended to prompt eligible customers who were homeowners to take action in applying for, or reviewing, the equity line service with the bank's lending staff. For the introduction of the new product, the advertising campaign was coordinated to include these elements: direct mail, radio, point-of-sale counter cards, lobby posters, brochures, and publicity.

The dominant theme of these elements are "convenience" and the "last loan application you'll ever have to make."

The direct mail campaign was selected to target our existing customer base. Of that base, 8,945 households met the criteria mentioned earlier. The purpose of the direct mail piece was to:
- Announce the name of the product
- Explain what it can be used for
- Explain how you can access your line
- Explain repayment method and what the rate is based on
- Explain how much credit you can qualify for
- Urge customers to apply *now*

Other components of the direct mail were:
1. A discount coupon offering a 50% savings on the initial participation fee of $350, with an expiration date on the coupon.
2. A personalized loan application.
3. A return envelope.

Because of the large size of the direct mail campaign, we did not want to overwhelm our lending officers. Thus mailings were cycled throughout the months of May and June. Radio advertising consisted of a 60-second spot (cycled with other loan-oriented spots) on eight dominant stations, seven of which are local stations in the Ventura County area. The other station, KNX-AM, is a Los Angeles station used primarily to support the branches in West Van Nuys, Conejo and Simi Valley. Two of the stations have an all-Spanish format. The spots ran during commuting hours and during the morning news.

Internally, point-of-sale posters carrying the same theme as the direct mail piece 8-1/2" x 11" and 22" x 28" were prominently displayed in branch lobbies. The posters were displayed from the beginning of the program, May 1, through the end of the program, June 30.

Customer brochures highlighting the features and benefits of *Homeowner's Credit Line* were also produced. An application was included as part of the brochure. These are used in the literature holders in all branches and as a handout when answering inquiries.

- Publicity in the form of articles (aside from purchased media) are used to help educate consumers about the product and forestall negative publicity about a somewhat controversial product.

- Sales training was used to provide product knowledge, enhance the image of the Marketing Department, generate enthusiasm, and describe the marketing communication plan. Staff meetings, including all bank staff, were held two weeks before the campaign began. Acting in the capacity of product manager, a member of the Marketing Department visited all office and department staff meetings to share information about the product and upcoming campaign.

- Salesmanship was motivated through an employee-incentive program that consisted of the following elements:
  What: Win a packaged trip to . . .
  >Catalina
  >San Francisco
  >Palm Springs

When: Sweepstakes drawings will be held throughout the campaign, with the first drawing to be held when 200 new *Homeowner's Credit Lines* are booked and for each additional 50 credit lines booked.

Who: All full-time and part-time employees of the bank are eligible.

How: To refer an applicant, simply write their name on the back of your business card and ask the customer to turn it in with their application. The business card then becomes a chance in the sweepstakes drawing. The more referrals made, the better the "chances." The employee must be employed with the bank at the time of drawing. Walk-ins may not be referrals—Be honest about referrals. There is only one prize per employee.

As mentioned earlier, the bank's "Product Knowledge Guide" provides a quick information source on *Homeowner's Credit Line.* In addition, memos were sent to keep our staff members posted on the number of equity lines booked and any new information on the product.

Results of the Introduction
While the *Homeowner's Credit Line* program continues, preliminary results are encouraging. Through mid-September, the bank's ratio of applications to approved equity lines of credit stood at 50%.[5]

It might be noted, that although the number of lines booked (52 as of this writing) may not reach the bank's goal, the employee incentive goals through 1987 have been changed to reflect high average outstandings.

The components of the direct mail program have been reviewed. According to our Centralized Loan Services Department, the application appeared to be cumbersome and confusing. Some of the problems are noted below:

- No address line for employer
- No address line for co-applicant
- Not enough space to list applicant's additional loans
- Application did not easily fall out of the brochure

When the applications are reprinted, the known problems will be corrected. Other elements in the direct mail package appeared to have been received well by both our staff and by the recipients of the mailing.

Details of promotional expenses to date are given below:

PROMOTIONAL SPENDING TO DATE

Expenditures

Direct mail	$15,196
Advertising (radio, lobby posters, brochure)	7,411
Training materials	300
Reserve for employee incentive program	1,800
Total of program	$24,607

Available funds of $15,393

1. Original budget of $40,000.
2. 50% discount on initial fee is not included, but is calculated in profitability model.

FUTURE MARKETING PLANS

As part of the ongoing effort to market *Homeowner's Credit Line* a postcard mailing to non-customers in the bank's service area is being planned for mid-to-late October. This mailing will provide the bank with an additional opportunity to test telemarketing, which was piloted in the summer of 1987 in support of direct marketing, and to test our ability to sell products and services outside our existing customer base.

The estimated number of postcards to be mailed is 100,000. We can obtain phone numbers for about 50% of this group. The bank has a small telemarketing staff and cannot handle calling the entire group; but, it could further screen the homeowner list for the best prospects. Based on our previous experience, the bank can contact 5,000 clients in a 4-week period at an approximate cost of $6,000. An outside service has been contracted to develop the postcard and do the mailing.

Additional plans for the equity line of credit include a promotional event in January of 1988, when the winner of the employee incentive program for

1987 will be announced. In addition, a second direct mail piece will be developed. This mailing will be provided by an outside source, with bids now being taken for design, printing, and mailing. The bank will use the same list of 110,000 Ventura County homeowners generated for the 1987 mailings, and the mailing will coincide with the 1988 tax season.

Telemarketing efforts for the equity line of credit will take place for a selected group approximately two to three weeks after the mailing. Further, simplified "prequalification" procedures will be used and will replace the lengthy application form in the original direct mail package.

CONCLUSION

In conclusion, this plan has traced the equity line program through product implementation, product/sales training, and promotion. In addition, the plan includes future marketing of the equity line product by analyzing and evaluating the results of the first direct mailing.

Corporate management is committed to continuing promotion of Bank of A. Levy's *Homeowner's Credit Line.* If promotional efforts continue to be successful, Bank of A. Levy will meet, if not exceed, its projections—thus confirming that *Homeowner's Credit Line* is successful in meeting the bank's internal needs and in meeting the credit needs of Ventura County homeowners. ◆

---

[1] *Ventura County Living,* County Profile, 1987, p. 8.

[2] *Ventura County Living,* County Profile, 1987, p. 11.

[3] *Ventura County Living,* County Profile, 1987, p. 11.

[4] Bank Marketing Assn., 1987 Research Project, *Consumer Middle Market.*

[5] Percentage of approved lines tracked and provided by the bank's Loan Administration Department.

CHAPTER 4

A Marketing Plan To Improve and Expand First National Bank's Charge Card Program

Robert W. Arnold
First National Bank
$180 million assets

SITUATION ANALYSIS

First National Bank is located in Sioux City, Iowa, at the corner of the three state area of Iowa, Nebraska, and South Dakota.

Population growth rates for the three states have not kept pace with the national rate.[1] The population of the United States increased 11.5% between 1970 and 1980. Current trends indicate we are continuing our slow growth. The population of Iowa increased 3.2%; Nebraska , 5.8%; South Dakota, 3.8%; and the Siouxland Interstate Metropolitan Planning Council area, 0.6%.

The local population has declined as follows:[2]

Location	1960	1970	1980
Sioux City	89,159	85,925	82,003
Woodbury County	107,849	100,680	100,844

A majority (61%) of the Siouxland Interstate Metropolitan Planning Council area population and 84% of the Woodbury County residents are urban dwellers.[3] Our economy is very dependent on agriculture. Consumers are older, often over sixty-five, and live within a 100-mile market radius. Median family income in 1980 was $19,233.00.[4]

We have a relatively stable economy. Booms, bust, and unemployment have not reached the magnitude experienced on the national level.

We are losing people in the twenty-five to fifty-five age group to more favorable economic areas. Our young people leave the community after we have trained and educated them. Thus, we have a steady population decline with a substantial increase in the over sixty-five age group.

Competition in the local financial industry is intense. There are eleven banks ranging in size from $11,000,000 to $368,478,000, three savings and loan associations, ten credit unions, and eight stock and bond brokerage firms. Iowans continue to respect the dependability and honesty of bankers, although 39% say they have less confidence in the banking system now than they did five years ago.[5]

Financial conditions have forced one savings and loan association to merge with another savings and loan, and two banks have been liquidated because of loan and capital problems. Many competitors are more interested in volume than in profit. We are paying approximately .20 to .25 basis points less for our deposits than our local competition, peer banks in our holding company, or financial institutions on a national level.

Savings and loans continue to pay high rates for deposits and to charge low rates for loans. Credit unions offer low consumer loan rates with free credit insurance. As a result, we have been losing market share to these financial institutions for the last few years.

Our bank is a member of Banks of Iowa, Inc., the largest and strongest holding company in Iowa, with fourteen banks and over $2 billion in assets. We are the second-largest bank in Sioux City and have the strongest capital structure of any financial institution in Sioux City. We have three offices within a five-mile radius. The main bank is located downtown, one office is in an affluent area, and another is in a good growth area.

Deposits include:
    Demand
    Individual $5,300,000. Trend—up slightly.
    Business $13,500,000. Trend—up.
    Due to banks $15,300,000. Trend—down, owing to loss of respondent bank accounts and less available funds for deposit. This has been caused by the agricultural economy.

    Savings
    Regular, money market, and NOW accounts $53,000,000.
    Trend—up owing to investors switching from term certificates of deposit to short-term, easy-access accounts in anticipation that rates will go back up, or to investors temporarily depositing funds while looking for higher yielding instruments.

Time
CDs $53,400,000. Trend—down slightly owing to customers switching to savings/money market accounts for easy access. The drop in yields is causing customers to seek other investments even if the risk is greater.

Loans consist of:
Commercial
Demand $41,900,000. Soft, numerous problems; past dues/charge-offs are up; and there is an increase in nonperforming loans.

Consumer
Installments: $10,500,000 demand. Favorable but difficult to hold volume and yield because of low rates from automobile captive finance companies, credit unions, and savings and loans.

Charge Cards: $2,400,000. Our past dues/charge-offs are up substantially because of the "Preapproved" program and because customers have excessive cards and debts.

We are trying to reach the twenty-five to fifty-five age groups as more than 50% of our customers are over age 55. Research has shown individuals twenty-five to fifty-five are more receptive to using charge cards than are older people. A comparison of our consumer loan and charge card data, as shown below, confirmed our decision to offer charge cards as the product/service with the most potential.

National charge card charge-off ratios are in the 3% to 5% range and consumer loan charge-offs are in the .50% range. Our "Preapproved" charge card promotion, a sluggish local economy, and consumer over- indebtedness and bankruptcies have substantially increased our charge-offs as

1986 YIELD COMPARISON

Individual loans	13.50%
Charge card (includes fees and interest)	17.73%
Difference	4.23%

CHARGE-OFFS

Year	Consumer Loans	Charge Cards
1983	.43%	.15%
1984	.27%	.61%
1985	.49%	1.54%
1986	1.12 %	5.19%*

shown in the table on the previous page. Cardholders now hold anywhere from three to six cards and have overextended themselves. In the year ending September 30, 1986, bankruptcies were up 37% compared to a year earlier. The most common reasons for bankruptcy are job loss, divorce, high medical expenses, and compulsive spending.[6]

DELINQUENCY	
Year	30-day Over/Past Dues
1983	2.06%
1984	1.75%
1985	2.69%
1986	3.89%

Delinquencies for 1983 to 1986 are given in the table above.

Our problems are now being resolved and we anticipate substantially fewer charge-offs and delinquencies in 1988, with greater volume.

Information on consumer demand for charge cards is confusing.

- Jerry D. Craft, chairman of the bank card division of the American Bankers Association, estimates that Americans are responding to credit card solicitation at only half the rate they did three years ago.[7]

- SMR Research Corp., Budd Lake, New Jersey, reports that recent response rates to most solicitations have been poor. [8]

- Research by Payment Systems, Inc., shows that contrary to many bankers' assumptions, the credit card market shows little sign of saturation.[9]

- Synergistics Research Corporation's survey of 500 households with household incomes of least $25,000 suggests that the tax revolution impact credit cards. Only 32% of these credit card users will continue using credit cards as they do now. Sixty-nine percent (69%) of itemizers say their credit use will decline significantly.[10]

At this point, we felt that we needed additional information to evaluate a charge card promotion. We examined the factors that research showed are most important when a consumer is deciding on a credit card. The results are shown in the table on the following page. [11]

After looking at the factors that consumers considered to be important in shopping for a credit card, we were confident that the features of our card were compatible with consumer demand.

SHOPPING FOR CREDIT CARDS

Most Important Factor	% Said most important
1. Interest rate (Our 18.6% is lower than most cards.)	38%
2. Prior relationship with bank (Solicit our own customers.)	21%
3. Annual fee (Our $15.00 fee is less than most cards.)	20%
4. Grace period (30% of FNB customers pay within grace period.)	5%
5. Don't know	16%

Given the importance of interest rate to consumers, we compared the rate on our credit card with that of major banks across the country that issue VISA cards.

INTEREST RATE COMPARISON
MAJOR BANK VISA ISSUERS

Bank	Fixed Annual % Rate
Chase Manhattan	17.5++
Citibank	19.8
Bank of America	19.8
Wells Fargo	20.0
First Chicago	19.8
Manufacturers Hanover	17.8++
Chemical	19.5
Marine Midland	19.8
Security Pacific	20.4
Maryland National	17.9++
First National Bank	**18.6**
Sioux City, Iowa	

++Based on data gathered as of December 1986, only three (out of nine) major bank VISA card issuers offer a rate lower than our 18.6%.[12]

Since 38% of consumers said that interest rate is the most important factor in shopping for credit cards, we also compared our rates and other important factors with those of other metro area Iowa banks. The results are shown in the table on the following page.

Our comparison showed that there are only two savings and loan associations (designated with << in the table on the next page) and no banks offering a rate better than FNB's 18.6% credit card rate.

INTEREST RATE COMPARISON

Financial Institution	Interest Rate	Grace Period	Fee
Bankers Trust Co.	19.8	30	$18
	*15.0		*$40
Brenton National Bank	22.0	none	none
East Des Moines	19.8	25	$18
National Bank	*19.8		*$40
First Interstate Bank	21.0	25	$20
of Des Moines, N.A.			
First Interstate Bank	21.0	25	$20
of Urbandale			
Hawkeye-Capital Bank	19.8	30	$18
& Trust	*15.0		*$40
Iowa State Bank	19.8	25	$18
	*19.8		*$40
Norwest Bank	19.8	25	$18
Des Moines, N.A.	*19.8		*$40
Valley National Bank	18.6	25	$15
	*18.6		*$36
First National Bank	19.8	25	$18
of West Des Moines	*19.8	25	*$40
West Des Moines	19.8	25	$18
State Bank	*19.8		*$40
First Financial Savings Bank	19.0	25	$16
Home Plan Savings	17.9<<	25	$15
and Loan Association	**12.9		
Midland Financial	19.8	25	$18
Savings & Loan	*19.8		*$40
United Federal	18.0<<	25	$12
Savings Bank	***15.0		
First National Bank	**18.6**	**25**	**$15**
Sioux City, Iowa			

Source: *Business Record*, June 2-8, 1986.

* Interest rates and annual fees on MasterCard Gold Card.

** Preferred rate.

*** Interest rate is 18% on balances of $500 or less, and 15% on balances greater than $500.[13]

There has been little charge card marketing in the last six or seven years. Charge card marketing has been done primarily on a one-on-one basis.

Our holding company's largest bank, Merchants National Bank, Cedar Rapids, Iowa, is a charge card licensee bank that provides processing and collection services to us as an agent bank for a fee. We do our own marketing, make our own credit decisions, retain all income, absorb all losses and depend on the margin for a profit.

Our analysis indicates that our experience, our ability to control the program and to make our own decisions, the available market, and the features of our charge card will be valuable assets for a campaign. The ability to coordinate the efforts between management, marketing, and consumer lenders should enable us to successfully implement a plan to improve and expand our charge card program.

OBJECTIVES
Trends Affecting Charge Cards
Several trends have made it extremely difficult to compete for volume and profit. These trends include: extremely low rates offered by the captive automobile finance companies, intense competition from bank and non-bank entities, an unfavorable local agricultural economy, and a sharp increase in bankruptcies. After carefully evaluating our alternatives, charge cards were selected as our most potentially profitable product and service. Charge cards were seen to offer the following positive attributes:

- A higher yield than our other products and services.

- A very favorable delinquency and charge off history.

- Limited local competition as local institutions send their charge card business to out-of-town firms.

- We own the accounts and balances, make our own credit decisions, assume all losses, pay our own expenses, and retain all earnings.

- Noncustomer cardholders become an excellent source for other services.

- The added relationship creates a more loyal customer for the bank.

Given the potential of charge cards, an action plan was formulated to implement a strategy to improve and expand our charge card program. The first thing we considered were the goals and objectives of the plan.

Goals
The overall goals of the charge card action plan were to:

- Solidify our current customer relationship with another service.
- Add new customers for continued expansion of products/services.
- Increase interest and non-interest income.
- Improve the net earnings of the bank.

Objectives
Specific objectives for the charge card action plan were to:
1. Increase income by $400,000 (100% increase)
2. Add 2,000 new cardholders (61% increase)
3. Increase outstanding balances by $2,000,000 (85% increase)
4. Add 37 new merchants (15% increase), which includes new deposit account relationship.
5. Increase merchant volume by $100,000 annually (29% increase)
6. Cross-sell 500 new cardholders on other new FNB services

Action Plan
Once the goals and objectives were in place, we were able to formulate our action plan for the charge card program. The specifics are described in the table below and on the following page.

ACTION PLAN

Task	Responsibility	Due	Completed
Analyze current portfolio	Charge Card Operations	07-86	07-86
Research	Marketing		
• Demand for product/service		08-86	08-86
• Niche positioning		08-86	12-86
• Local market		08-86	08-86
• FNB consumer loan portfolio		09-86	10-86
• FNB real estate loan portfolio		02-87	
• FNB affluent customers		11-86	12-86
• Current FNB cardholders		04-87	
• Commercial loan customers		03-87	
• Respondent bank potential		10-86	11-86
• Affinity market		03-87	
• Summary	Marketing	08-86	08-86
Evaluation	Marketing/Consumer Services/Management	08-86	08-86
Recommendation	Marketing	08-86	08-86
Implementation	Marketing/ Consumer Services	09-86	

ACTION PLAN (continued)

Task	Responsibility	Due	Completed
Marketing Plan	Marketing	10-86	
• Direct mail			
• Statement stuffers			
• Merchant program		04-87	
Advertising Plan	Marketing		
• Brochures		10-86	11-86
• "Preapproved" solicitation		12-87	
Training			
• Operations		09-86	09-86
• Family Bankers (lenders)		11-86	12-86
Budget	Operations/Accounting		
• Expenses		09-86	09-86
• Income		09-86	10-86
Conclusion	Marketing	12-87	
• Reports	Operations/Accounting	Monthly	
• Summary	Operations/Accounting	12-87	

STRATEGY AND TACTICS

An analysis of our June 30, 1986, charge card portfolio provided the following information:

• Current outstanding balances	$2,342,951
• Number of active cardholders	3300
• Average balance/active accounts	$620
• Delinquency (30 days or over)	2.7%

The June 30, 1986, information will be used to make comparisons with information gathered at the end of our promotion in December, 1987.

Principal Features of Our Card

We feel that the following features of our card are conducive to a favorable response to our market plan.
- Annual fee: $15.00 (waived first year)
- Interest rate: 18.6%
- No fee for cash advances
- 25-day grace period if the bill is paid in full each month

Marketing Plan

We wanted to target college-educated, 25 to 55 year old consumers with above average incomes. This group would probably carry larger balances and would have the greatest potential for repayment. Direct mail will be our primary solicitation source, plus brochure "stuffers" in our deposit account statements.

Our "Preapproved" solicitation was to be sent to carefully selected current customers with favorable balances and credit records. Other prospects must complete an application and qualify for credit before receiving a card. We decided not to repeat a credit bureau extraction "Preapproved" program. Past dues and charge-offs substantially increased as a result of this 1985 promotion.

The response rate to this earlier promotion was good, from 2% to 3.85%. Name and address labels were purchased from a credit bureau for direct mailing using the following criteria:

- Three or more trades in file
- Six maximum number of inquiries within last six months
- Twenty-four months in file
- Twenty-four maximum number of months since last file activity
- Zero times thirty days late
- No bankruptcies, judgements, suits, wage earners plan, obituaries, or tax liens
- Alphabetic name listing by zip code

There were two major flaws, however, in the selection process:

1. Some consumers had more than one credit file and there was no cross- reference to confirm consumer identity. The same consumer could have one or more files with derogatory information and one or more files with favorable information; yet *any* file with favorable credit information would generate a name and address label. The result was increased past dues and charge-offs.

2. There was no screening for other charge cards. Other charge card solicitors had targeted the same customers with "good" credit and they ended up with several cards. The result: good customers became overloaded with debt and encountered financial problems.

We found that our "Preapproved" problem accounts were with laborers — average age of thirty-nine, income of less than $20,000, and on-the-job for less than 7 months. The promotion taught us a lot about the marketing of credit cards.

Our present promotion included making arrangements with two respondent banks to participate in our direct mail program. We agreed to develop a marketing plan, pay them the normal first-year annual fee of $15.00, pay for a mailing list, and develop credit criteria. We asked the respondent banks to pay the postage for soliciting accounts in their areas. This arrangement gave us the potential of soliciting 37,000 prospects by direct mail.

Details for this part of the marketing plan by direct mail were as follows:

Brochure: We provided our marketing agency with the concept, and specific features of the card from which they were to develop a brochure.

Mailing list criteria: Our objective was to target homeowners. We selected single-family households that had lived at the same address for two or more years, had an annual income of $20,000 plus, and were twenty-five or older.

Timing: Our intent was to mail the application/brochure so the customer would have the credit card before the Thanksgiving/Christmas shopping season. Unfortunately, our agency encountered difficulties so our plan was delayed almost four weeks.

Local market: We had never solicited in our local market so we felt there was good potential.

Our "Preapproved" marketing plan and strategy were as follows:

Current consumer loan customers (September, 1986). The FNB consumer loan portfolio was screened for potential charge-card holders. A mailing list was ordered to include monthly payment loans (student loans, unsecured credit, and home improvement/equity loans), with loans 25% paid, and no thirty day lates. These customers were sent $1,000 "Preapproved" Master-Card lines of credit.

Real estate (February, 1987) and *Commercial loans* (March, 1987). Real estate and commercial loan files will be screened using conservative criteria for "Preapproved" applications.

Current FNB cardholders (April, 1987). Current cardholders were screened for length of time on the books (minimum 18 months), low lines of credit (anything under $1,000), and good payment habits (no lates). Their lines were automatically increased to $1,000.

Affluent customers (November, 1986). Our computer center generated a list of customers with accumulated balances of $25,000 or more. The following information was to be provided by this report:

1. Listing arranged by zip code
2. Alphabetical listing of name, with address and zip code (within zip code ranges)
3. Birth date

4. Social security number
5. FNB cardholder—yes/no
6. Account number listing of individual accounts with current/ average balances

Qualified customers under age seventy were sent "Preapproved" MasterCard Gold Card applications with $5,000 lines of credit.

Affinity groups (March, 1987). Local parochial schools and colleges; dental, chiropractic and medical associations; the Shriners; and two local hospitals will be offered incentives to recommend our card to their groups.

Statement "Stuffers" (December, 1986).   Brochures and applications were enclosed with deposit account statements.

Advertising Plan
Our advertising plan for direct mail was to use simple, attractive, first- class material that is easy to process. The message was to be direct, personal, appealing, and easy to respond to. Specific target groups, with future product/service potential were selected for immediate response.

Merchant Program
The merchant program will be conducted on a one-on-one basis. Merchants will be targeted for larger ticket high volumes. Competitive discounts with immediate credit for deposits and good "local" service will be the features stressed in our merchant program. Checking account relationships will be established with each new merchant.

Training
Operations /Training: The Merchants National Bank charge card center and loan operations were both advised of the promotion so they could anticipate potential increase in work load. Samples of our forms were provided to them for critique.

Sales Training; Prompt service and professional knowledge are key to the success of this program. A chart oulining the product features of our card to be used in training lenders can be found on page 86. Responsibilities and work flow were stressed with lenders to efficiently expedite decisions and processing.

Credit Evaluation; A committee will review and approve turndowns and credit lines. This procedure will help train new staff members. Two experienced lenders will be authorized to approve decisions by using the criteria shown below. A chart showing our credit criteria is provided on the following page.

Budget

There is no limit to the amount of money that can be spent promoting charge cards, or to the number of businesses willing to handle the program. We considered the following alternatives:

Company A: $50,000 for a 100,000 "Preapproved" mailing in our area with a 5% response.

CHARGE CARD CREDIT CRITERIA

Length of Residence
12 months, unless change is because of upward movement or transfer.

Length of Employment
12 months, unless change is because of upward movement or transfer.

Minimum Income
1. One signer = $750.00 net/monthly.
2. Second signer = $1,100.00 combined net/monthly.
3. Plus an additional $100.00 net/monthly for each dependent.
4. Income-to-debt ratio not to exceed 40% including minimum payment required if charge card credit line is used to full extent.

Credit Limit
May not exceed 75% of the combined or individual net monthly income of the applicant(s).

Credit Background
1. Five-year credit history
2. Ratings per 12-month review
3. No applicant will be eligible for credit if they have any of the following: Collections, suits, judgments, adverse information contributing to bankruptcy, tax lien, or wage earners proceedings.
4. Inadequate credit information. Written confirmation from credible references must confirm that the applicant has adequate income, financial responsibility, and capacity and credit worthiness to qualify for a line of credit or dual cards.

Dual Cards
1. FNB will issue dual MasterCard and VISA cards with the written consent of a division head, group head or executive management.
2. A MasterCard or VISA card may be issued with discretion even though the applicant has a card at a competitive card center.

Credit Approval
Two authorized lenders must approve, sign and date the applications to validate and process the credit line.

PRODUCT FEATURES
(essential for sales training)

1. Annual card fee—$15.00. (First year fee waived)

2. Interest rate—18.6%. (Most cards charge more.)

3. 25-day grace period—No finance charges on new purchases when the bill is paid in full each month.

4. No fee for cash advance.

5. Worldwide cash availability at over 137,000 banking offices.

6. Our card is accepted by over 5 million merchants in 162 countries.

7. One-time approval provides years of benefit. The credit line can be reused again and again as balances are repaid.

8. No collateral required. No second mortgage. The customer's established financial reputation secures the credit line.

9. Group Credit Card Insurance Program, including life, health, accident, and involuntary unemployment.

10. Free second card.

11. Choice of payment—pay in full or minimum monthly payment.

12. Convenient MasterChecking: Free personalized MasterCard checks to use like regular checks to draw against the credit line. Confidential—only the customer knows when they are using credit.

Company B: Their $50,000 initial quote was reduced to $35,000 because of our holding company affiliation. The quantity of the mailing and response rate were similar to *Company A*. They apparently work with larger vendors and our project would be quite small for them, hence the lower costs.

Marketing/advertising agency: They would charge us for development, production, etc. They have no previous charge card experience but have direct mail experience.

In-house: We have our own print shop, have had success with previous direct mail promotions and have experience with direct mail expenses.

After considering the alternatives, we decided to do the project ourselves with the aid of our agency to minimize expenses. The cost was estimated at $30,000 or less. On the following page is a breakdown of expenses and income for this project.

ESTIMATED EXPENSES

	Estimate
MasterCard Direct Mail Brochure	
- Copywriting, proofing, corrections	$ 150
- Art direction, layout, design	375
- Keyline	370
- Typesetting	550
- Model	40
- Separations, lithography, chromalin proof	2,100
- Account service, project coordination, meetings	200
- Shipping, photostats, long-distance calls	150
- Printing	5,950
- Postage reimbursement respondent banks	(2,500)
- Credit reports	2,700
- Return postage	324
- Mail house (stuffing and mailing)	800
- First-year annual fee—respondent banks	3,300
- List rental, $48/M Cheshire Labels	1,723
- Postage 36M x .13 each	4,680
- Envelopes 72M x .023 each	1,656
Consumer Loan Portfolio	
- Name/address labels	30
- Postage/Supplies	180
Affluent Customer	
- Computer report	400
- Supplies/Production	480
- Postage	70
Real Estate/Commercial Loan Portfolio	
- Name/address labels	140
- Supplies/production	100
- Postage	95
Affinity Groups	
- Production	400
- Supplies	200
- Postage	3,800
Current Cardholder Line Increase (programming cost, etc.)	600
Miscellaneous	1,500
Total Estimated Expenses	$29,963

ESTIMATED INCOME		
	First Yr.	Second Yr.
Annual fee	$ -0-	$ 30,000
Interest income, interchange income, cash advance fees, misc. (insurance, merchandise, etc.) less-processing fees.	177,300	354,600
Total Estimated Income	$177,300	$384,600

SUMMARY

The response to our charge card solicitation has been approximately half of what we anticipated. This confirms some of the research in our situation analysis.

Our tactic of using direct mail to solicit homeowners and statement "stuffers" in customers' statements was successful. The following summary of some of the highlights of our strategy and tactics contributes to our understanding of the responses.

Principal Features of Our Card

Cardholders have a certain loyalty to the first card they receive. Twenty percent of the consumers shopping for a card say the annual fee is important. Waiving the first year's annual fee was apparently only partly successful even though our charge is less than most competitors. A card issuer in our trade territory issues a no-fee card that is popular. Thirty-eight percent of card-shopping consumers say interest rate is important. Even though most cards charge a higher rate, apparently consumers still feel our rate is more than they are willing to pay.

Preapproved (Regular, Gold)

Regular "Preapproved" $1000 MasterCard lines to our current consumer loan customers resulted in a 8.4% response. We consider this a success and look for a similar response from our other accounts.

Gold "Preapproved" $5,000 MasterCard lines of credit are just going out and will be completed in the next week to ten days. The response from our affluent customers that have received "Preapproved" applications has been gratifying.

Direct Mail

Brochure:
The brochure was attractive, simple, and easy to use. We received favorable comments from customers and consider it a success.

Mailing list criteria:
The mailing list was suspect. Labels were not in alphabetical order by zip code as requested. Labels were addressed to multiple-unit buildings, as well as, to single-family homes as requested. Numerous non-homeowners returned applications.

Mailing:
Advertising agency production delays caused major timing and delivery problems that may have influenced our response rate because applications were received during the busy holiday season.

Local Market:
Our response in the local market was half of what we anticipated. We had never solicited this area before and by waiving the first year's annual fee, we felt a 2% to 2 1/2% response would be possible.

Affinity Groups:
A respondent bank had a 30,000 member group interested. We lost what we considered to be a very favorable bid to a company with a higher annual fee and no local affiliation. Competition for affinity groups may be too intense and requires careful evaluation.

Advertising Plan
We feel the collateral , statement "stuffers," and direct mail have been successful.

Merchant Program
This is a very competitive program with marginal profit *if* we want to compete with national/regional firms. Our thrust will be toward the smaller proprietorships where the profit potential is greater.

Budget
Preliminary billings indicate budgets should be within 10% of estimate.

Applications
The response rate through January 1987 is approximately 1%. Fifty-eight percent have been approved. There have been an excessive number of applications with inadequate financial information. Many of the applicants already have a card(s).

Niche Positioning
Our mailing list request included rural home owners. It has been a pleasant surprise to receive applications from rural consumers with very favorable credit and no debt. This could be an overlooked group with good potential for credit cards.

Non-customers
It appears a large percentage of applicants were first-time customers.

Credit
Forty-two percent of the applications have been turn downs, primarily due to excessive obligations and unfavorable credit. We are experiencing an unusual phenomenon with some of our consumer loans and charge cards. Customers with very favorable credit records, who have never missed a payment, suddenly file for bankruptcy without warning.

CONCLUSION
It is essential that we carefully evaluate the application information and credit history of potential customers. Charge cards are perpetual credit and substantial financial problems can occur without warning.

Our preliminary experience indicates that we will probably achieve 50% to 60% of our objectives and, thereby, achieve our goals. There seems to be a substantial reduction in solicitation response. Controlling solicitation expenses will be critical as response rates diminish. So far we have achieved 20% of our volume and 14% of our cardholder objectives. We consider the promotion a success to date and anticipate continuing to promote charge cards through December 1987. ◆

[1] *Population in Siouxland.*, SIMCO (1983), p. 1

[2] *Sioux City*, Iowa Development Commission (1985), p. 1.

[3] *Population in Siouxland*, p. 7.

[4] Ibid., p. 44

[5] *Perceptions of Banks and Banking In Iowa.*, IMR/Opinion Research (January 24, 1986), p. 95.

[6] Michael Weinstein, "Banks' Credit Card Operations End Up the Big Losers...," *American Banker*, (January 14, 1987).

[7] Bill Sing, "Consumers Turning Wary Over Use of Credit Cards," *Los Angeles Times*, (June 23, 1986).

[8] *Credit Cards: The New Struggle For Market Share*, SMR , (1986), p. 4.

[9] Jeffrey Kutler, "More Consumers Want Cards, Study of Credit Trends Shows", *American Banker*. (October 10, 1986).

[10] Rod Little. "USA Snapshots," *United States Banker*, (Jan., 1987), p. 9.

[11] "Credit Card Survey." *Bank Credit Card Observer*, (Aug. Survey, 1987).

[12] "Chase VISA Lowers Interest Rate," *Chase Manhattan Times*, Jan. 1, 1987.

[13] "Unsecured Loan Makes Credit Cards Risky," *Business Record*, (June 2-8, 1986), p. 11.

Marketing Tactics

CHAPTER 5

Creating an Image Campaign for Connecticut Savings Bank

Cynthia Avery
Connecticut Savings Bank
$1 billion assets

INTRODUCTION

Connecticut Savings Bank wants to enhance its position as a New Haven based financial institution. As we look at our environment, which is characterized by mutual conversions to stock ownership, mergers and consolidations, and an increasingly high rate of bank failure, it is important that we have a clear idea of what we want to be—the dominant commercial thrift in New Haven serving the personal and business needs of our customers. The marketing plan presented here will provide the elements needed to reach that goal.

SITUATION ANALYSIS

Background History

Connecticut Savings Bank, a mutual savings bank, was founded in 1857. We have emerged as a symbol of strength and leadership in the Greater New Haven community. We have nineteen branch offices in thirteen communities in the New Haven market, serving 25% of the households in Greater New Haven. Our assets have grown to over $1 billion. The New Haven market consists of thirty-one towns and cities, covering 675.3 square miles, with an adult population of 500,000. Our consumers rank well above national norms in income, education and employment.

Connecticut is one of the wealthiest states in the nation, with one of the lowest rates of unemployment. Currently the full-time labor force in the New Haven market is 282,000. This represents a higher percentage of the adult population than is found nationally. Yet, New Haven is one of the poorest cities in the nation. It is truly a unique market. In addition:

- 48% of all adults in the New Haven market have annual household incomes of $35,000 or more.

- 48% of all adults in the New Haven market are college educated.

- 51% of adults in the New Haven market live in households headed by white-collar workers.

Past Strategy
In 1982, Connecticut Savings Bank sponsored a comprehensive survey of the Greater New Haven consumer banking market. The survey was conducted by Kramer Associates, a full-service marketing research firm specializing in the banking industry. It was the first major outside, market research venture conducted by Connecticut Savings Bank.

The survey was conducted at a time of turmoil within the financial services industry: Deregulation, new services, new delivery systems, and increasing marketing sophistication were making it difficult for a bank to maintain or expand its market position without fully understanding the marketplace. The goal of this research was to examine the characteristics, behaviors, and motivations of the market. In essence, what were our customers all about? The survey consisted of 1,600 telephone interviews with adults drawn at random from the general population, in towns where Connecticut Savings Bank has offices. The results of this research (which are discussed further on) led to the development of a corporate strategy that has evolved over the years.

In terms of awareness and usage, Connecticut Savings Bank was one of the leaders among New Haven financial institutions. That position was strongest among the older, upscale segments, while the commercial banks were stronger among younger consumers. Since banking relationships are long-lived, CSB's market position could decline over the long term unless some action was taken. At the same time, Connecticut Savings Bank enjoyed the most favorable image of any institution in its service area. There was considerable receptivity to the concept of a one-stop financial center offering brokerage, insurance and other financial products, as well as banking services.

The research indicated banking relationships in the New Haven area enjoyed tremendous longevity.

Most new customers will remain with the bank for a number of years and will eventually be prospects for cross-selling several additional services. Therefore, the effort and expense involved in attracting new customers should not be amortized over a single year or a single service. It is extremely difficult to lure existing customers away from their present institutions. Therefore, a primary source of growth for all institutions is new residents and newly formed households. [1]

The research indicated that the key groups to focus on would be individuals who could offer particularly high potential for new banking relationships. Newlyweds, new residents in the area, and women were prime candidates in the search for developing new business.

The study pointed out the importance of our customer service and indicated that it would be a key factor in our success. While concentrating on gaining new customers, emphasis should also be placed on developing our cross-selling abilities, all the while strengthening our customer relationships. An aggressive cross-selling program should be implemented. All bank employees, but particularly those who come in contact with customers (or potential customers), should be trained in effective cross-selling techniques.

In addition, the research highlighted the role played by various factors in the selection of a financial institution.

Consistent with virtually every other survey of consumer banking behavior, this survey illustrates the importance of convenience as a selection consideration. If an institution is not convenient, it will generally not even be considered. The primary measure of convenience is physical proximity to home, although other aspects (such as extended hours, fast teller lines, drive-in facilities, etc.) also play a role. [2]

The major themes that became apparent from this study—awareness and usage of CSB, new markets to attract, and service to the customer—provided the basis for the strategy that Connecticut Savings Bank would attempt to implement. There was an opportunity for us to make a statement to our targeted markets and to position ourselves favorably in the New Haven community. We were not trying to expand statewide, but rather to concentrate on the communities we were currently serving.

CSB's desired market perceptions included the following points:

- Maintain a policy of controlled growth and community services— avoid pitfalls of overreaction to deregulation
- Provide a broad range of services to consumers, small businesses, and commercial businesses
- Position ourselves as a full-service institution as defined by our market needs

- Our people are courteous, friendly, while also being knowledge-able, informed and professional
- Our locations are geographically convenient to our customers
- Our operational systems and branch hours are convenient

Our target markets were defined as:

- Households with consumers thirty-five or older, and incomes of $25,000 or more
- Businesses with annual sales of $500,000 or more
- Geographic presence in Greater New Haven, with emphasis on improving presence in Guilford, Branford,Wallingford and Milford

Current Market Position

Connecticut Savings Bank has pursued for several years a long-term strat-egy of enhancing its position as a New Haven based financial institution. We have made the transition from a savings institution to a commercial thrift with a dedication to specific targeted markets in the Greater New Haven area.

The last research done for Connecticut Savings Bank was completed by 1986 by Smith and Company, Inc., and consisted of 2,500 telephone interviews of randomly selected consumers in the CSB DataBank trade area. The highlights of this research are:

1. CSB has a strong competitive position in its primary geographic market. It is a leader in the area and enjoys lender name recognition just below Connecticut Bank and Trust (CBT) and New Haven Savings Bank, two competitors.

2. CSB enjoys its strongest name recognition and resultant market share in the towns of North Haven, West Haven, Hamden, North Branford, New Haven, and Cheshire. Our weakest position is in Milford, Guilford, Wallingford and Clinton. CSB has a branch office located in each of these towns, except Guilford.

3. CSB has an older customer base than many commercial bank competitors. We also have a larger share of lower-income, less-educated consumers.

4. New Haven Savings Bank and Connecticut Bank and Trust appear to be acquiring a larger share of new accounts than is CSB. Our percentage of new accounts opened is not keeping pace with existing market share. This enhances the importance of a strong cross-selling program at CSB.

5. CSB is attracting new customers with demographics similar to its existing customers, that is, less affluent and less educated.

6. CSB's advertising recall was a distant second to that of CBT in the marketplace. As one might expect, CSB had strongest recall in areas in which CSB enjoys a strong market position and weakest recall in CSB's weak market areas.

From this same study came the following customer profile:

Age:
- 25.0% of CSB's customer base is between the ages of 26 and 35
- 20.6% is 36 to 45
- 19.3% is over 65

Income:
- 18.9% of CSB's customer base has household incomes of $15,000 to $24,999
- 14.9% have annual household incomes less than $15,000
- 24.0% of customer base earns in excess of $35,000 per year

Education:
- 36.5% of our customer base are high school graduates
- 25.0% are college graduates
- 11.1% have post graduate degrees
- In general, the CSB customer is slightly less educated than the market as a whole.

Occupation:
- 30.4% of the CSB customer base has a white-collar occupation. This is equal to the market. However, 24.7% is retired, which is 6% higher than the market

This information helped us to develop specific action plans. Our future success is focused on serving targeted consumers and small-to-medium-sized businesses throughout the Greater New Haven area. We will offer a broad array of deposit and loan products and fee-based services, while supplementing traditional banking revenues with returns from expanded financial services and equity investments in real estate ventures.

Our primary business interests can be broken down into two areas, the Consumer Division and the Commercial Division. Both areas are dedicated to fulfilling the banking needs of households in our market area and the needs of our commercial customers. Within these two divisions we focus on particular targeted markets.

Consumer Financial Division: On the consumer side, strong emphasis is placed on protecting Connecticut Savings Bank's preferred position in the marketplace by strengthening and expanding our existing customer relationships.

Savings Bank deposit products have been most attractive to customers whose investment abilities exceed their borrowing needs. Typically, these customers are older with a higher income and a higher net worth. Connecticut Savings Bank has achieved a dominant market share of this older, more affluent group in Greater New Haven. However, these customers are highly attractive to other financial institutions. [3]

CSB's strength in target market segments appears to have declined. This is believed to be the result of financial constraints that have forced us to limit our deposit growth and to improve our profitability by paying interest rates that are generally below the market .

We would like to enhance relationships with younger consumers in order to ensure our preferred position in the future. These customers seek both lending and deposit products.

We want to meet the borrowing needs of our targeted customers. Personal banking relationships will help to improve the profitability of Connecticut Savings Bank. We are continuing to develop a place for ourselves in the market and are trying to increase our share of local fee-based products such as employee benefit programs, cash management services and traditional commercial banking services.

The target markets for our Consumer Division are described below:

Consumer Financial Services	
Acquirers:	Income of $35,000 plus Age 35 - 44
Accumulators:	Income of $35,000 plus Age 45 - 64
Retirees:	Income $15,000 plus Age 65 plus
Private banking customers:	Income $100,000 plus with net worth of $250,000

Individuals who can be identified as Acquirers and Accumulators are credit driven with small-to-medium-sized net worths. Their largest investment is their home. Loan products developed for this group will continue to revolve around the equity line of credit, on both a variable- and a fixed-rate basis where appropriate. In addition, investment services, insurance products, and retirement plans are available to our market.

The Private Banking group continues to provide specialized lending services to the higher-income/high-net-worth portion of the Acquirer segment. These individuals are active investors and want to leverage their existing assets to increase their wealth. These people, who are largely professionals, corporate executives, physicians and entrepreneurs, make up a small group in our primary market area, about 4,500 to 5,000 individuals.

In the area of small commercial business development, our branch locations are extremely important. We are focusing on proprietorships, partnerships, and corporations with annual sales of $500,000 to $1,000,000, as well as existing small businesses. Our branch managers have been trained to service the needs of businesses this size. They have territories with specific goals to be met. The sales effort concentrates on increasing our market share in the following areas:

- Commercial DDA
- Business loans and commercial mortgages
- Employee benefit services
- Merchant banking (VISA/Mastercard)

Competition in the Consumer Market: When we take a look at what our competition has been doing over the past year, we find that we are all advertising the same things. The advertisements focus on:

- CD rates
- Commercial services
- Investment services
- Home equity lines
- Home mortgages

Competition is very evident between banks as they go after the consumer's business. Our goal is to position ourselves in the New Haven market as a bank that stands out among the rest with personalized, creative and flexible service. We are a "hometown" bank; financial decisions are made in our main office, located in New Haven. We do not have to contact someone in Hartford, Boston, or New York for approval. The people you will be dealing with on a daily basis are the people who will be the decision makers.

New branch offices of other banks are being built in towns where we have a strong customer base. We will have to watch their activity and plan accordingly in each instance. New banks have opened in New Haven and are starting to build their customer base. While we do not consider them to be a threat, their presence can only add to the confusion already in the marketplace. In addition, our biggest competitors are spending substantial sums to advertise their commercial services.

In 1987, our advertising in all areas was at a minimum. However, we tried to place our ads where we judged it to be to our advantage.

Commercial Financial Division: Our commercial banking business unit is charged with focusing on the specific target market segments listed below:

- Companies in the Greater New Haven market with sales of $1.0 million to $30 million
- Law firms and individual attorneys
- Accountants

Connecticut Savings Bank is making great strides in the Greater New Haven market as a commercial institution. We have a seasoned staff of twelve commercial bankers who are well versed in offering commercial services. Our branch network is strong and is able to handle commercial dealings. There is interaction between our commercial bankers and our branch personnel as evidenced by the loan referrals that are generated.

Our major competition continues to be the larger commercial banks in our market area:

- Connecticut Bank and Trust (CBT)
- Connecticut National Bank (CNB)
- Bank of Boston - Connecticut
- Union Trust Company
- City Trust

Connecticut National Bank is the most aggressive and has the largest market share due to its purchase of the First Bank franchise. This also provides them with the most extensive branch system. The other savings institutions have yet to become a major factor in our marketplace. The larger commercial banks tend to emphasize companies with $5 million to $10 million and over, but they protect their franchises aggressively with customers smaller than that.

Connecticut Savings Bank is a major commercial mortgage lender in the Greater New Haven market in both the construction and permanent financing areas. We are interested in statewide lending opportunities in order to expand our asset allocation and to achieve growth. Our commercial real estate interest rates are relatively low and are expected to remain that way. Above all, the quality of service provided by our staff is a major attraction for loan production.

With these factors in our favor, we should remain a dominant lender in the New Haven Area with the opportunity to do more business statewide. We would like to keep our production level around $80MM.

Future Trends in Banking

For the past few years, Connecticut Savings Bank has worked with a consultant, Edward Furash of Furash & Company located in Washington, D.C. Mr. Furash has examined the current and past position of Connecticut Savings Bank, as well as where it will be going in the years ahead. The banking industry is an environment characterized by constant change and the continued entrance of new competition from companies such as Sears, J.C. Penney and General Motors. Financial instability at this time is greater than it has been since 1927-1933. Below are some key issues highlighted by Mr. Furash that will be influencing banking in the years ahead.

1. Interstate banking structure. There are four models of institutions present in today's environment—they are:
   - Regional Banks, such as Bank of America, Wells Fargo, etc.
   - High spotters that focus on two to three markets within a region
   - Community banks that focus on a single market
   - Boutiques that focus on a single product or service

2. Changes in distribution. Traditionally bank products and services have been both manufactured and retailed by each bank individually. The growing trend is toward dividing the industry into manufacturers, distributors, and retailers.

3. Rise of global economy. The global economy has developed into a high-speed system due to its electronic connections. The "Triangle Trade," between New York, London and Tokyo, dominates the world economy and results in a 24-hour financial services industry.

4. Increased risk. There are two factors adversely affecting the level of risk within the industry: volatility of rates and credit risks. In addition to being affected by the economy, credit risks are also impacted by the competition. The securities market has historically drawn the best risks away from the banking industry. The result is a permanent deterioration of credit quality.

5. New entrants: The entry of new competition in the financial services industry is causing an influx of products and services.
   - Competition is on the increase.
   - There is an overabundance of points of final distribution.
   - There is a proliferation of products.
   - Financial services are commodities.
   - The only method of price protection is differentiation.

6. Technology will continue to be a driving force in financial services.

7. Regulatory insufficiencies. The regulatory insufficiencies today are permanent. Efforts are focused on reversing previous regulation reductions, so there may be a turn toward reregulation.

8. Capital. The current trend regarding bank capital is to drive ratios upward. This position on capital will drive banks to further instability. In order to maintain the required levels of capital, banks will become more dependent on secondary markets to provide them with increased earnings without a corresponding increase in assets.

9. New consumerism. This is best described as consumerism of the middle class. The issues raised include rate disclosure and credit card rates. Banks are becoming political targets.

During the years ahead focus of management will be very important to the success of CSB. There are six critical factors that should be looked at:

1. Expense control
2. Geographic concentration
3. Development of special line of business to supplement earnings
4. Price protection - differentiation
5. Margin control
6. Credit quality

As we prepare for the future, competition within our market will continue to grow, and emphasis will be on capturing niches within our target markets, both in the consumer and commercial divisions. We have an opportunity to make a statement about ourselves to the New Haven market.

Industry trends of continued mergers and acquisitions by out-of-state banks and by large statewide banks allow us to capitalize on our position of being a leading New Haven-based financial institution.

Strengths and Weaknesses of Connecticut Savings Bank
Strengths
Connecticut Savings Bank maintains a strong presence with the New Haven market in a very competitive environment. Research indicates that we have 11.4% of the depositors within our market area.

Our sales force is effective in penetrating our target markets, cross-selling products and developing relationships with new customers.

Our current competitive product line is their selling base. However, we do not know if all these products are profitable or if our customers want all the products we offer. All individuals involved in sales are given specific goals and are compensated with cash incentives for a job well done. We stress the importance of developing a sales culture within the organization.

We are taking the initiative in developing a financial services catalog. This will be the first catalog produced by a bank in the New Haven market. The catalog will be mailed to all our customer households and will be available in our branch offices. This publication will have information about all product line offerings, a credit application, response cards for specific services and a phone number that will be available to call Monday through Thursday from 8:30 A.M. to 9:00 P.M. and Friday from 8:30 A.M. to 5:00 P.M.

Other strengths of CSB include:
- A widely identifiable name in the Greater New Haven market
- A strong presence in the communities it serves
- Effective delivery systems
- Community involvement of bank leaders
- Development of a public relations plan
- Initiating a first for the New Haven market—a financial services catalog

Weaknesses
CSB's main weaknesses include:
- No committed direction for the bank in the New Haven community
- No direction communicated to employees by senior management
- No ongoing research to determine the fit between our customers and our product line
- Employee morale within the organization is low
- Product driven rather than market driven
- Not thought of as a business bank by business people within the community
- No consistent advertising message to the community
- Not very profitable. Ranks second from last among Connecticut financial institutions
- Loss of deposits, particularly for NOW accounts from 1987 re-pricing
- Banking is in a period of little to no growth on the deposit side

OBJECTIVES
CSB plans to meet the following objectives:

1. Become the dominant commercial thrift institution in the Greater New Haven market area by the end of 1989

2. Increase share of target households that define Connecticut Savings Bank as their main financial institution to 13.0% by the end of 1989.
   * Current share: 11.4%

   * Current position: second place

3. Conduct market research throughout 1988. This research should address issues such as: who makes up our customer base, what our customers want from CSB, and whether the products we offer are right for our customers. This research should be completed by the end of the third quarter in 1988.

4. Maintain existing advertising plans to ensure some level of awareness in the Greater New Haven community.

5. During fourth quarter of 1988 begin development of advertising campaign to be kicked-off in 1st quarter of 1989. The campaign should include television, newspaper, and direct mail, and should convey a specific message to the consumers and business people in Greater New Haven.

6. Continue the development and implementation of PR plan in 1988. This plan will benefit consumer and commercial divisions of CSB.
   * Improve awareness and credibility of CSB as "full-service" financial institution serving business and consumer needs

   * Enhance CSB's image as a responsible and caring corporate neighbor in New Haven and in all branch communities

   * Increase employee loyalty, pride, and knowledge in all CSB programs

7. Increase our business loan portfolio, concentrating on companies with sales between $1MM and $10MM, law firms, accounting firms and small real estate developers.
   * 10% by the end of 1988

   * 5% by the end of 1989

8. Increase DDA deposits by $100,000 per officer by end of 1988 and by $300,000 per officer by the end of 1989.

9. Increase our Private Banking customer base by 20% by the end of 1989. We plan to increase our return on assets by actively managing our spread and gathering fee income. Good opportunity to cross-sell services to commercial mortgage and investment services.

10. Continue to increase commercial mortgage portfolio as a percentage of total bank assets from 22% in 1987 to 30% by 1990.

11. Generate sales of insurance products for fee income in 1988.

- Life insurance—sell $38MM, with fee income of $210,000

- Insurance investment products—sell $7MM, with fee income of $210,000

- Credit insurance—sell $16MM, with fee income of $167,000

STRATEGY AND TACTICS
Research
The information derived from our research will be one of the cornerstones for developing a successful image campaign for Connecticut Savings Bank. We need answers to these questions:

1. What is our current market share?
2. Who are our customers?
3. What do our customers and the general market think of us?
4. How effective is our product line?
5. What is our competition doing?
6. Who are our best prospects?

In order to answer these questions and other important issues the following is recommended:

1. Six focus groups to be held during 1988—two per quarter starting in second quarter

2. Telephone survey of 2,500 random calls in the New Haven market
   - Conduct a 20 minute interview
   - Completion by the end of first quarter, 1988

3. Direct mail survey to a percentage of our existing customers during the first quarter of 1988.

In addition, our internal records can provide us with a customer profile for both the consumer and business customer of Connecticut Savings Bank.

Consumer	Business Customer
Age	Type of business
Occupation	Business size
Education level	Number and types of services used
Income	Age of relationship
Ethnic background	Profitability of relationship

Public Relations
The benefits of continuing to develop a public relations plan will be realized over a long term period of time and can only be realized when a plan is established and adhered to on a consistent basis. The program, begun in 1987, should be continued in 1988 and the years ahead.

The objectives of our public relations program are to:
- Improve awareness of and credibility of CSB as a full-service financial institution serving business and consumer needs.
- Enhance CSB's image as a responsible and caring corporate neighbor in New Haven and our branch communities.
- Increase employee pride and knowledge in all CSB programs.

The strategies of the public relations plan are to position CSB as:
- Possessing one of the best management teams in banking.
- A community-based bank.
- An excellent career opportunity—a great place to work.

Communication elements that would be instituted to convey our strategies to the Greater New Haven market include:

1. Press release program
    - Economic trends
    - Product information
    - Speeches
    - Business activities
    - Events
    - Bank-sponsored community activities
    - Award programs
    - Personnel

2. Featured Articles
    - CSB History
    - Community activities
    - Ghost-written articles
    - Employee recognition at each branch

3. Speeches
    - Business organizations
    - Community activities
    - Charity leadership

4. Events
    - Business
    - Community
    - Employee

Advertising
The research will help us focus our advertising efforts. Ideally, several alternative positionings should be developed based on research findings.

At this point, we should begin to test the advertising themes in our market. The testing should be done in the last quarter of 1988. Based on these advertising tests, we will be able to determine which advertising theme is best received, and spend the time and money in developing the campaign that works best for us.

Our media strategy is the following:
1. Achieve a significant reach and frequency among our target markets both on the consumer and the commercial sides
2. Use vehicles geared toward the primary target audiences
3. Select specific geographic areas to achieve maximum efficiency

The advertising media that we will use for this campaign include:
1. Television
2. Newspapers and magazines
3. Outdoor
4. Direct mail

Television. The use of television will provide us with mass audience coverage in the fastest way possible. A 30-second commercial will be produced in the last quarter of 1988, with a kick-off during the first quarter of 1989. This commercial will be the first in a series developed by CSB. The first spot will present a particular image of CSB to our market area. This commercial can be viewed as an "umbrella," and the rest of our advertising will carry through with its theme. This spot will be run at different intervals during the year. We will concentrate on buying television time during the peak hours of prime time and of news broadcasting. We will buy more media initially to build awareness, stay off the air for a period of time, and then go back on to rebuild awareness. During 1989, a second 30-second spot should be produced, that focuses on a particular product or service of the bank, with the underlying image of Connecticut Savings Bank apparent.

Newspaper & Magazine. While the television commercials are running, the image campaign of CSB should be continually reinforced via newspaper advertisements, magazine advertisements and other point-of-purchase material.

Newspaper advertising is flexible and can provide us with extensive coverage of local markets. In the New Haven market, there is one newspaper that dominates the market, the *New Haven Register*. In our market, 52% of adults read this newspaper, 68% read the Sunday edition. In addition, most communities have their own town newspaper.

Along with newspaper advertising, there are select publications which should be looked at as definite possibilities to complement the other

advertising media. Some magazines to be considered are:
- *Connecticut Magazine*
- *New Haven Business Digest*
- *Intercorp - Business Publication*
- *New England Business*

There are also a variety of other trade publications we should consider.

The advertisements we develop for print should be consistent with what we are running on television. Each should work to complement the other. This will insure reinforcement of our message and bring us the most for our advertising dollars.

Newspaper advertisements should begin with full-page two-color spreads and should continue throughout the year, varying in size and alternating color with black and white. A complete one-year advertising plan should be developed. Magazine ads will be run with much more selectivity given their cost. They will be run in color, or in black and white. Print ads will begin in the first quarter and continue during the year.

Outdoor Advertising. Billboard advertising will support the other media. It is flexible; we can choose the specific locations that will give us repeat exposure in high traffic areas. The message will be brief and consistent—always tying in with our main advertising theme.

Direct Mail. The use of direct mail will allow us to send a personalized message to our existing customers, as well as to our prospects. We plan to use it on an ongoing basis. After our advertising campaign has begun, specific products can be highlighted and print materials developed for a specific audience. The direct mail effort can be conducted in a series of waves. Below is an example:

Product:	Equity line of credit
Elements:	Letter, brochure with application
Target:	90,000 existing CSB customers who have been pre-approved by the New Haven Credit Bureau
Mail:	Three consecutive mail drops, 30,000 pieces dropped every three weeks. Telemarketing follow-up.

In addition, employee information about this image campaign must be disseminated to all bank employees. CSB employees should have an understanding of the campaign. This can be accomplished by one or more of the following:

1. A letter from the President about the advertising campaign and expressing management support.

2. An explanation of the advertising campaign to appear in our employee newsletter.

3. A special viewing of new television commercial along with print advertising to be presented to all bank employees.

Our employees can do more for enhancing the image of the bank out in the community than printed media.

Distribution

In March 1988, Connecticut Savings Bank will be mailing our first Financial Services Catalog to approximately 80,000 customer households in the Greater New Haven area. This will be the first catalog issued in our market area as well as in the state of Connecticut. It is our initial step in setting ourselves apart from the rest of our competition.

This catalog will provide a general description of products and services that CSB offers to the consumer and commercial customer. In addition, a credit application will be attached, and four response cards will be included.

Individuals will have the opportunity to request additional information about various products and also the ability to sign up for financial planning seminars. More important, there will be a telephone number listed throughout the catalog, giving people the opportunity to call from their home and "shop" for bank products at their convenience.

We are looking at this catalog venture as a means to better communicate with our customer base and at the same time provide them with the convenience and service they deserve. Our society is accustomed to shopping at home through a catalog for various other items. We are taking it one step further by offering them bank products and services.

The catalog will also be available to the consumer in all of our branch offices. Our Personal Bankers will be using the catalog as a selling tool each time someone sits down at their desk.

It is hoped that the production of this catalog will eliminate many of the product brochures that we currently use, thus saving us in excess of $100,000 annually. Our direct mail packages will be coordinated to reflect the same artwork that was used in the catalog. This will present a consistent appearance in all point of purchase material that we use. The catalog will be reprinted on an annual basis.

We will be promoting the catalog with posters in branch offices, statement stuffers, and in an announcement in our consumer and business newsletter.

In order to use this catalog effectively, telemarketing personnel and all branch personnel involved in selling to customers will go through a training program. Selling techniques will be discussed on how to best use the catalog. Sales tracking methods will be employed to determine response rates to the catalog. Incentive compensation will be awarded to the individuals who reach their quota for sales using the catalog.

In addition to selling through the catalog, bank employees throughout the organization will be responsible for conveying the message to the community about Connecticut Savings Bank. Their word-of-mouth can be just as effective in "selling" CSB as our advertising.

In the commercial services division, the primary distribution system for loans and fee services will continue to be our 12 commercial loan officers. Our commercial loan officers have the expertise and knowledge needed to sell the varied products needed by the commercial customer. Each lender has his or her specific selling goals. In addition, our branch system continues to grow in its expertise in handling commercial customers. We have implemented commercial, customer teller lines and have revamped transaction procedures.

EVALUATION

To determine the success of our financial services catalog, a tracking system should be initiated to determine how many sales referrals and actual sales have occurred as a result of the catalog. The response cards and the credit application located inside the catalog itself can serve as a means of tracking some of those sales. As was mentioned previously, we plan to produce the catalog on an annual basis. A determination should be made at the end of six months as to whether or not the catalog has generated the type of sales we expected.

The tracking of our advertising efforts is important in determining its effectiveness. Three months after the television and print campaign kick-off, follow-up research should be done to find out if the message we are conveying about Connecticut Savings Bank is clear and concise, is reaching our target markets, and is attracting the customers we want. Has our customer base increased both on the consumer side and the commercial side? If we find out that we are not making any progress, the remaining advertising schedule should be reviewed and possibly revised.

In addition, the product managers responsible for a specific part of the business (for example, deposit products, insurance products, commercial loans, commercial mortgages, investment services, private banking services) must be responsible for reviewing their growth on a quarterly basis.

Reports should be generated on a monthly basis for senior management review. If goals are not being met, the original objectives should be reviewed to determine if they are feasible. The review process should not be left until the end of the year—by then it may be to late.

The call reports generated by the commercial lenders and branch personnel involved in sales will supply us with specific information about the markets we are going after. It is important that this information be shared with the individuals in the marketing department, who would use the information to plot the course for future bank activities.

We should be prepared to revise our objectives and the resulting strategies and tactics should the results we receive after monitoring our efforts fail to achieve our original objectives. ◆

---

[1] Kramer Associates, *Connecticut Savings Bank Study*, 1982.

[2] Kramer Associates, *Connecticut Savings Bank Study*, 1982.

[3] Kramer Associates, *Connecticut Savings Bank Study*, 1982.

Chapter 6

Establishment of a Telemarketing Operation

Marie Nordstrom Rittman
Bank Five
$480 million assets

INTRODUCTION

Telemarketing, although a relatively new tool for the banking industry, can be used by banks to add to their profitability in a number of ways.

Telemarketing can be used to build customer relationships by cross-selling accounts to present customers. Research has shown that the more accounts a customer has with a particular financial institution, the higher the probability that the customer will be retained by the institution. Telemarketing can also be used to introduce new products to present customers and prospects.

Market expansion through the establishment of new branches outside the bank's traditional market area can be cost-prohibitive. Telemarketing, however, is a cost-effective method of reaching new markets.

Customer service quality can be improved through telemarketing. It provides for direct contact for answering customers' questions at a convenient location, the customer's home.

Telemarketing can improve the response rate on direct mail programs. Banks following a direct mailing with telephone calls have found that response rates increased up to 35%. [1]

Bank Five can use this additional marketing tool to assist in meeting its objectives for the future. Telemarketing can increase the bank's customers retention level by cross-selling to existing customers, increasing the effectiveness of direct mail programs, and helping us enter new markets more cost effectively .

SITUATION ANALYSIS
Bank Five's History
Bank Five has experienced strong, steady growth throughout its history. This growth is apparent in the chart below.

DEPOSITS AT YEAR END
Year End - October 31

1860	$ 31,429
1870	248,003
1880	628,960
1890	1,101,379
1900	1,773,790
1910	2,148,058
1920	3,860,180
1930	11,649,442
1940	13,614,995
1950	23,114,225
1960	44,433,230
1970	91,362,340
1980	191,812,877
1985	311,713,845
1986	379.317,423
1987	410,125,773

This growth has been due to intelligently managing the bank's assets, maintaining strong links to the community, and providing the financial services needed by the community. This philosophy is demonstrated in the following mission statement:

> Bank Five for Savings is a high performance, independent bank that prospers by concentrating on those things it does best; namely, helping individuals and businesses to achieve their financial goals; rendering high quality, responsive banking services; and intelligently managing risk. It is an organization made up of highly competent business professionals who, through their individual skills and resourcefulness and prudent use of the bank's various resources, are dedicated to helping customers.[2]

Bank Five's Strategy
Past to Present
Bank Five's goal has always been to be an innovative bank that delivers the services needed by its customers while remaining profitable. The bank has achieved this goal through following a sound asset/liability management policy.

In 1969, Bank Five discontinued lending on long-term fixed-rate mortgages. A policy limiting long-term maturity to five years was established at that time and is followed to this day. The bank does not, however, follow the doctrine of matching assets and liabilities 100%. It has developed a portfolio management system using a 25% positive or negative mismatch strategy. In periods of low rates, which the bank feels will rise, we lend shorter than our liability time frame; and in periods of high rates, which the bank feels will drop, we lend longer than our liability time frames for up to 25% of our portfolio. By constantly monitoring the economy and accurately forecasting interest-rate swings, the bank has remained profitable.

Another key to Bank Five's successful asset/liability management policy is the retention of surplus. Surplus, measured as a percentage of deposits, is the retained earnings of the bank. The bank's goal has always been to have a 10% surplus position. It is advantageous for the bank to have this strong surplus position. It contributes to the bank's profitability by creating an excess of earning assets over liability. It also can give the bank a competitive advantage by allowing the bank to affordably offer a higher rate to attract deposits when desired.

In order to retain a high surplus position, Bank Five does not advocate growth for growth's sake but practices a doctrine of controlled growth. Deposit products are priced to attract money only to the point where the bank will be able to match that growth with an increase in surplus. This underlying policy works well in any economic cycle and has made Bank Five a sound and profitable bank.

The following two charts show the net income, surplus position, and deposit growth of the bank over the past four years.

NET INCOME
(Percentage of Assets)

	1984	1985	1986	1987
Gross income	12.1%	11.3%	10.3%	10.1%
Dividend	7.9	6.8	5.8	5.7
Spread (net interest margin)	4.9	4.5	4.5	4.4
Operating expense	2.7	2.7	2.5	2.9
Net income	2.1	1.8	2.0	1.5

SURPLUS AND DEPOSIT GROWTH
(Percentage of Deposits)

	1984	1985	1986	1987
Yearly deposit growth rate	9.0%	18.5%	22.0%	9.0%
Surplus (yearly figure)	9.9%	9.2%	10.0%	10.0%

Future

Future goals and strategies of Bank Five have been developed from the bank's mission statement and essentially follow our past goals and strategies. The major addition to past strategies will be in the area of operating expense control. The Net Income table on the previous page shows that this area has increased as a percentage of assets in the 1987 fiscal year as the gross income percentage has dropped. This is a potential trend that the bank will take immediate action to correct.

Major strategies for Bank Five for 1988 and beyond are:

- Pursue and implement all possible means of both expanding its sources and reducing its relative cost of funds

- Implement a bankwide policy to further control and reduce relative operating costs

- Achieve optimal operating efficiency through the organization and systemization of work, application of improved automation techniques, and the development of an in-house capacity to monitor, evaluate, and effectively apply relevant advances in technology

- Precisely and effectively capitalize on the opportunities presented within its primary consumer market

- Become positioned as a major force within its primary market [3]

Primary Retail Market

The primary consumer market area of Bank Five consists of the towns of Arlington, Bedford, and Burlington and the city of Woburn, Massachusetts. This market area contains a very stable population.

The population in Bank Five's primary market area is composed of high middle-income white professionals, administrators, and blue collar workers. The median income of the market area falls into the high middle-income category with $38,000 being the median income for the combined four communities.

There is a high percentage (over 30%) of the population who are professionals and executives, with only 21.8% in blue-collar jobs.

This combination of a stable population with a median income in the high middle category, employed primarily in professional occupations, creates a lucrative market for Bank Five.

Competition

Arlington. Arlington, home of Bank Five's main office for over 125 years, is the only town in the primary market area in which the bank has the largest market share, although this market share has been declining. The greatest inroads into the Arlington market have been made by Bay Bank Harvard Trust, a member of an extensive bank holding company. Bay Bank has been consistently seeking the young professional market, using their 600-ATM network as a selling point.

The total dollar market in Arlington has grown 53%, while Bank Five's deposit base is approximately the same as in 1982, and its market share has dropped 22.1%. This is a reason for concern in a market whose population is stable.

Bedford. Bank Five holds the third-largest percentage of market share for Bedford. Bedford is another town in which Bank Five is losing market share while Bay Bank is gaining.

The total market, excluding the Hanscom Federal Credit Union, grew 114%. While Bank Five's deposit base increased 71%, its market share dropped by 6.4%. Bedford is another area of concern for Bank Five.

Burlington. Again while Bank Five's deposit base increased 86%, its market share in Burlington dropped from 6.1% to 5.8%. This is another area of increasing dollars but decreasing market share.

Woburn. Woburn is one community in which Bank Five has gained both deposits and market share. With the purchase of Tanners National Bank in 1983, the Tanners/Bank Five deposit base increased substantially and its market share grew 11.4%. The total market grew 147%. Two facts are significant: 1) Strong inroads were also made by Bay Bank which increased its base 456% and its market share 6.7%; and 2) Woburn Five, once the dominant bank of Woburn, increased its base only 22% and lost 27.7% in market share.

Total Primary Market. The deposit base for Bank Five's primary market grew 93% in the time period from 1982 to 1986, taking into account the aforementioned adjustments. Bank Five's deposit base grew 40% while its market share dropped from 33% to 24% during this time. Some of this market share decline is due to bank's philosophy of controlled growth, as well as aggressive market expansion by competing banks.

Strengths and Weaknesses of Bank Five
Background. Bank Five has a strong branch network in its primary market consisting of eight branches, seven of which are located on major roadways and are easily accessible. The eighth, a Woburn branch, is located in a large office/light-industrial park in which Bank Five has exclusivity for a bank branch. Each branch, with the exception of one small branch in Arlington, is managed by a branch officer and staffed with one or more customer service representatives to assist customers with complicated transactions and account openings. Five years ago, the bank changed the title of the teller position to that of financial agent in an attempt to upgrade the image of this often negatively viewed position.

Six of the eight branch locations have an ATM; and by May 1988, all eight will have one. Bank Five recently made a move to expand usage of its card by joining the Yankee 24 ATM Network. This move provided the bank's customers with access to over 2,000 locations at which to use their ATM cards around New England, as well as nationwide through affiliation with the CIRRUS and Cashstream networks.

Four years ago, a cross-sell program was instituted for branch officers and customer service representatives. The program pays commissions for cross-selling accounts and recognizes attaining and exceeding goals with prize awards. The program has successfully generated 4,500 cross-sold accounts and $8 million in balances on average each year.

Deposit Mix. The deposit mix of the bank has remained the same over the past three years, as indicated in the table that follows.

BANK FIVE DEPOSIT MIX

Type	% of Total Deposits		
	1985	**1986**	**1987**
Passbook Savings	28%	24%	24%
NOW Accounts	4%	3%	4%
CD (1yr. or less)	15%	14%	14%
CD (1-3yrs.)	11%	9%	7%
CD (3 yrs. and over)	N/A	1%	2%
IRA	10%	15%	18%
MMA	28%	22%	22%
Super NOW	1%	8%	3%
Demand Deposit	4%	5%	5%
Brokered Deposits	--	--	1%

The only significant shifts have been in the areas of IRAs, money market accounts, and Super NOWs. The bank has been aggressively pursuing deposits over the past three years through the use of high interest rates. In August 1986, the bank introduced the Super NOW in a consolidated statement package with a rate higher than the money market account. A combination of new money and transfers from the money market account resulted from this promotion.

Loan Mix. The loan mix of the bank has shifted slightly over the past three years as indicated in the table below.

BANK FIVE LOAN MIX

Type	% of Total Loans		
	1985	**1986**	**1987**
Real estate loans	74%	68%	70%
Commercial loans	18%	24%	21%
Personal loans	8%	8%	9%
Total loans as a %of total assets	78%	67%	74%

The shift has been toward growth in the commercial loan portfolio. The bank has been working to build in this area since the purchase of Tanners Bank in 1983. The small gain in the personal loan category was caused by the introduction of and marketing of an equity line of credit in 1987.

CIF System. One of the weaknesses of Bank Five is the lack of a central information file (CIF). Bank Five does not have its own data processing center and must rely on an outside service company. The bank has been in the process of switching to a new service over the past two years. Completion of the CIF is not expected for at least one to two years.

Marketing. Bank Five began a strong marketing effort in 1982 with the formation of a marketing department. Previously the marketing effort was handled, along with the personnel and accounting functions, by the vice president of administration. The effort consisted of little more than advertising placement and premium promotions. Today, the Marketing Department is responsible for the bank's research, product development, advertising, direct mail programs, public relations, promotions, customer communications, and publishes the in-house newsletter.

The Marketing Department works with an annual advertising expense budget of approximately 0.1% of the bank's assets. The forecasted breakdown for 1988 is found in the table on the next page.

1988 MARKETING DEPARTMENT BUDGET
(by percentages)

Category	Percent
Public relations	4%
Market research	2%
Agency fees	7%
Printed material	5%
Radio	22%
Promotions	10%
Annual report	4%
Newspapers	16%
Magazines	1%
Direct mail	16%
Production	8%
Employee incentives	1%
Product literature	3%
Presidential group activities	1%

The department's philosophy is to advertise in a campaign using a combination of direct mail, radio, newspapers, statement stuffers and lobby displays. Promotion of any product or service must highlight its advantages to the customer.

Strong emphasis is placed on direct mail. The department finds this marketing tool to be one of the most effective methods of reaching targeted segments of the marketplace.

Product development is research-based to ensure that new products will meet the needs of the consumer and will be priced to be profitable to the bank, while still being competitive.

Bank Five has a good mix of both loan and deposit products. The recent addition of tiered pricing on certificates of deposits and the money market account, of a package of services for the fifty-plus market that is centered on social activities, and of an equity line of credit loan have made this mix more competitive.

ESTABLISHING A TELEMARKETING OPERATION
Objectives

Objective 1
  To increase the customer-retention level by increasing accounts per customer.

Strategy
Increase the number of deposit accounts held by present customers through the use of an outbound telemarketing program to cross-sell additional accounts to existing customers.

Goal
To contact ten customers per day, per telemarketer, and bring the customer account ratio of those contacted to 1.2.

Objective 2
To increase the retention of certificates-of-deposit customers as their certificates mature.

Strategy
Contact customers prior to the maturity date of their certificates to sell them on renewing for the same or another term.

Goal
To increase renewals of maturing certificates by 10%.

Objective 3
To increase the effectiveness of our direct mail programs.

Strategy
Use both inbound and outbound telemarketing in combination with the bank's direct mail programs. The inbound program would consist of placing the phone number of the telecenter in the direct mail package so customers can call and take advantage of the program offer. The outbound portion of this telemarketing effort would consist of telephone follow-up calls to those consumers who did not respond to our direct mail offer.

Goal
To increase the direct mail response rate from the present level of 1%-3% to 10%-15%.

Objective 4
To expand the retail base beyond the bank's primary market, increasing the total deposit base by 1%.

Strategy
Use outbound telemarketing to contact select market groups ouside the primary market area to sell them on bank programs or products geared to that particular market.

Goal
To contact 2,000 prospects and to sell accounts to 20% of those contacted.

Program Development
Advantages of Telemarketing

One-on-one selling. Telemarketing provides the method closest to "face-to-face" selling outside of personal contact. The telephone is an intimate medium that provides the opportunity to speak directly with one individual.

Confidentiality. It provides the opportunity to speak about one's financial information without the chance of being overheard.

Interaction. Telemarketing allows for feedback and provides the caller with the opportunity to adapt to the customer's needs.

Personalization. It allows the caller to address the customer by name, to anwer specific questions, and to eliminate confusion.

Influence over the buying decision. Telemarketing provides the opportunity to complete the sale and to cross-sell additional services.

Target Marketing. It allows for contacting qualified prospects with a product designed specifically for that target segment.

Multiple applications. Telemarketing has many uses. It can be used to generate leads, conduct research, introduce new products, cross-sell to existing customers, renew maturing accounts, support direct mail and advertising programs, and respond to customer inquiries.

Disadvantages
Start-up costs. A new program will incur expenses for furniture, equipment, and telephone lines.

Shortage of trained personnel. Telemarketing is a relatively new area for banking. There is not a readily available supply of trained people to handle this function.

Customer resistance. For the most part, customers are unfamiliar with receiving telephone calls from bank personnel attempting to sell them bank services. This unfamiliarity will create some resistance.

Program failures. Telemarketing is much more than simply reading a sales script over the phone. If a particular program is not designed to reach specific segments with a product geared to their needs, there is a strong chance that it will fail.

Inbound programs
Inbound telemarketing refers to calls that are made by customers to the bank, either to the bank's normal telephone or to a toll-free, 800 number. These programs are used in conjunction with direct mail and advertising for product inquiries, service questions, and customer complaints.

Outbound programs
Outbound telemarketing is telephone sales. It refers to bank personnel directly calling specific bank customers or prospects with a product offering, or calling to follow-up on a direct mail offer. Use of a WATS line is recommended for this purpose.

Location
A relatively small space is required per person for a telemarketing operation. A cubicle, five feet by six feet, is the necessary space required for each telemarketer. Four cubicles placed side-by-side and back-to-back form a "pod" which can be placed in a space ten feet by twelve feet. Minimal additional space would be needed for filing cabinets.

Bank Five is currently not using one-half of the bottom floor at the branch located at 89 Elm Street, Woburn. The space available is eighteen feet by twenty feet. This space would be an ideal location for the telemarketing operation. It is a quiet location and is available at no additional cost to the bank.

Equipment
Equipment needed to establish a three or four person operation includes:
- A four-station pod, complete with chairs, computer workstation tables and soundproof dividers
- Four telephones with headsets
- Four IBM terminals
- Four fifty-megabyte hard drives with networking capability
- Four modems
- One letter-quality printer with switchbox
- Two five-drawer file cabinets
- One 800 telephone line
- Four WATS telephone lines
- Four telemagic software packages

Personnel
The telemarketing operation should be staffed with three or four telemarketers, one of whom will be the supervisor. These positions would be either full-time or full-time equivalent positions, as four-hour shifts are most productive for people in telemarketing positions. The supervisor would be a full-time employee. The telemarketers should be placed at the CSR I (customer service representative) level with the supervisor at the CSR II level. Ideally these candidates should possess the following qualities:
- Understanding of human nature
- Articulate speech
- Pleasant voice
- Good listening skills
- Enthusiasm

- Good sense of humor
- Ability to close a sale
- Courteousness
- Ability to accept rejection well
- Self-motivation

The telemarketing staff would work under the direction of the Marketing Department.

Compensation

The bank's CSRs are currently paid a salary plus commission. The commissions are based on a cross-sell incentive plan. The telemarketers should be paid in a similar fashion. They should receive a salary comparable to CSR level I and II but should have a commission program designed for their particular function. Cash commissions should be established for the following categories:

1. Sales per call, with the dollar amount increasing with each additional sale made to one customer.

Recommended Schedule

		Total
1st Sale	$2.00	$2.00
2nd Sale	$2.50	$4.50
3rd Sale	$3.00	$7.50
4th Sale	$3.50	$11.00

Additional sales would continue at the same rate of increase.

2. Renewals for maturing certificates of deposit based on dollar amount renewed

Recommended Schedule

$1,000 - $10,000	$1.00
$10,000 - $25,000	$1.50
$25,000 - $50,000	$2.00
$50,000 and over	$2.50

3. Special bonus programs should be run from time to time during specified bank promotions.

Training

Training should be conducted in these areas.

Product Knowledge. Bank Five has a comprehensive product information manual which was developed for the cross-sell incentive programs. This manual breaks down all products into the areas of benefits, features and related products. It also provides updated information on competitive products and pricing. This manual is distributed to each trainee and is used as a guide in an in-house training class for those in the cross-sell program. Telemarketing personnel would attend this class.

Sales Skills. Bank Five has an in-house sales skills training class which is also used to train employees in the cross-sell program. Telemarketing personnel would also attend this class.

Telephone Skills. It is recommended that an outside training company be used to provide a telephone skills class. Among the topics to be covered in this class:

- Use of the head phone set
- Proper answering methods such as greeting customers and identifying oneself
- Developing articulate speech through use of pitch, tone, rate, and volume
- Use of a pleasant voice
- Listening for auditory clues
- Accepting rejection cheerfully
- Following scripts
- Placing customers on hold
- Transfering calls

Scripts. Scripts should be used to insure that accurate information is given to customers and prospects. The scripts would be kept short, three to five minutes and should be written in simple, jargon-free language. Questions should be used that involve the customer in a two-way   communication process and allow for feedback. A script should include the following sections:

- Introduction: Customer's/prospect's name should be used, identification of caller and bank given, and customer/prospect told why he or she should listen.

- Qualification: Questions should be asked that will qualify or disqualify the customer/prospect for the product and to uncover other financial needs.

- Body: A sales message should be presented along with pertinent information about the product. Time should be allowed for interaction and for overcoming objections.

- Closing: Ask for the sale and state the action needed to open account. Always thank the customer.

Monitoring Results

Results in a telemarketing operation are easy to measure because of the nature of the activities. Calls made, accounts sold, and dollars gained can be quantified. The Telemagic software package, recommended for this operation, is designed to track all activity, as well as to provide for on-screen scripting and automatic dialing. Reports can be generated that provide information on:

- Calls made
- Customer type—new or existing
- Services sold
- Calls-to-services-sold ratios
- Deposits generated

With this information, it will be relatively simple to determine if the stated objectives have been met.

COST/BENEFIT ANALYSIS

Costs

The expenses that will be incurred in establishing the telemarketing department will be:

Start up costs (one time)

- Space
  Presently available   -0-

- Equipment
  Four person station $1,800
  Four telephones with headsets $1,400
  Four IBM terminals $2,000
  Four 50-megabyte hard drives $2,000
    with network capability
  Four modems $600
  One letter quality printer with switchbox $850
  Two five-drawer file cabinets $750
  Four Telemagic software packages $3,200

- Training
  Emanacom group training (32 hours) $4,000

  Total one time expenses   **$16,600**

Ongoing costs
- Telephone charges
  One 800 line, monthly line charge
  12 months x $39.25 $471

Monthly usage
12 months x 60 hours x $11.25/hour $8,460

- 4 WATS Lines
  Monthly line charge
  12 months x $29.50 x 4 $1,416

  Monthly usage charge
  12 months x 96 hours x $7.90 x 4 $36,403

Compensation
- Salaries
  Three telemarketers at CSR I level Base
  $14,000 x 3 $42,000

  Commissions (estimated)
  $2,500 x 3 $7,500

  One telemarketing supervisor
  at CSR II level $16,500

  Estimated supervisor commissions $2,000
- Employee benefits $20,400

  Total ongoing expenses   **$135,150**

  Total first year expenses   **$151,750**

Benefits

The previously stated objectives will benefit the bank in the following ways.

Objective 1. Increasing the customer account ratio to 1.2 for those customers contacted should result in 20% of those customers having two or more accounts. A Whittle and Hanks' report states that customer retention increases according to the following chart: [4]

Services Used	Retention Probability
Checking account only	1:1
Savings account only	1:1
Checking and savings	10:1
Checking, savings and consumer loan	18:1
Checking account and mortgage loan	50:1
Checking, savings, loan and safe deposit box	200:1

The retention level of the customers who are cross-sold an additional account should increase to a ratio of 10:1 at a minimum.

The second benefit from meeting this objective would be a 3% growth in the deposit base. This should result in an additional $533,456 increase in revenues before expenses. Calculations are based on four telemarketers each contacting ten customers per day for 200 days a year with a sales success rate of 20%.

> 4 callers x 10 calls x 200 days x 20% = 1,600 sales
>
> 1,600 sales/55,000 current account holder base = 3% increase

The return, before expenses on the new money at the October 1987 net interest margin of 4.4% would be $533,456.

Objective 2. Bank Five currently retains 73% of its maturing certificates. Increasing this retention by 10% will result in revenues, before expenses of $486,591.

Objective 3. In 1987, Bank Five conducted three direct mail campaigns, each consisting of about 25,000 pieces at an average cost of $1 per piece mailed. The overall response rate to these programs was 2.5%. This equals about $40.00 per sale.

> 3 programs x 25,000 pieces x 2.5% response = 1,875 sales
>
> 3 programs x 25,000 pieces x $1/piece = $75,000
>
> $75,000/1875 sales = $40.00 per sale

Three similar direct mail programs are planned for 1988. Research has shown that direct mail with a telemarketing follow-up can produce response rates of 20% or more. An increase in the bank's response rate to 10% would result in a cost of $10 per sale, a 75% cost savings per sale.

Objective 4. A 1% growth in the deposit base would result in a $17,817 increase in revenues, before expenses, based on the 4.4% interest margin. Calculations are based on 4 telemarketers, each contacting 4 new prospects per day for 200 days with a sales success rate of 20%.

Analysis
A brief analysis of the costs and benefits for the telemarketing program suggests the following:

First year benefits	$1,197,864
Start-up costs	-18,650
First year ongoing costs	-135,150
Potential revenue	$1,044, 114

CONCLUSION

Bank Five is operating in a stable primary market area. Future growth comes from two important sources: cross-selling additional accounts to present customers and reaching beyond the primary target area.

The Marketing Department recommends that serious consideration be given to the establishment of this telemarketing program. Telemarketing can be a useful tool in helping the bank attain its long-term objective of growth with profitability. ◆

---

[1] Bank Marketing Association, *Marketing Update* (February 1987, Volume 3, Number 4).

[2] Bank Five for Savings, *Corporate Strategic Plan* (November 1987).

[3] Ibid.

[4] *Strategic Planning Update: Telemarketing,* Chicago: Whittle and Hanks, Inc., October 1986, p.3.

CHAPTER 7

Seafirst Crown Women's Cycling Classic: Special Event Marketing Plan

Virginia Stella
Seafirst Bank
$10 billion assets

INTRODUCTION

In 1987, Seafirst Bank experimented with special event marketing, becoming the title sponsor of the first annual Seafirst Crown Women's Cycling Classic.

This chapter will discuss the race's success in 1987, its potential for 1988, and marketing objectives and strategies for the 1988 race. Since sports marketing is relatively new for Seafirst, the same care and planning went into sponsoring the Seafirst Crown as surrounds the marketing of a new product.

As exemplified in this paper, a promotional event can be an ideal marketing vehicle to enhance the bank's image, entertain valued customers and prospects, and strengthen the bank's relations with its employees and the community.

SITUATION ANALYSIS
Background Information
Event Profile

The first annual Seafirst Crown Women's Cycling Classic, sponsored by Seafirst Bank, was a national-caliber women's stage race held May 22-24, 1987, in Redmond, Washington. With more than $10,000 in cash and prize offerings, the Seafirst Crown was the fourth richest race in North America. In addition, the U.S. Cycling Federation selected the Seafirst Crown as one of only seventeen National Prestige Classic (NPC) races in 1987. The

Federation uses results of NPC races to select members of the U.S. National Team for the World Championships and for major European races.

Profile of Riders
The 1987 race attracted one of the most elite fields of any women's race in North America. Eighty of the best women cyclists competed in the Seafirst Crown. The list included Seattle's own Rebecca Twigg Whitehead, an Olympic silver medalist and five-time world champion; Madonna Harris of New Zealand, winner of the 1987 Seafirst Crown and two-time member of the New Zealand World Championship Team; world-champion silver-medalist Janelle Parks, of Kettering, Ohio; 1986 national champion Katrin Tobin, of Ketchum, Idaho; Jane Marshall, of Albuquerque, New Mexico; and Reno's Inga Thompson Benedict, bronze medalist in the 1986 Tour de France and Coors Classic.

Number of Spectators
Over 10,000 spectators came out over the three-day Memorial Day weekend to see the fierce battle between the top women racers.

Courses
The riders covered a total of 130 miles and faced 7,019 feet of total climbing. The race began with a hilly 4.8-mile individual time trial at Chateau Ste. Michelle in Woodinville. On Friday, the riders moved to nearby Redmond for the final three stages on Saturday and Sunday. The routes for the final three stages of the Seafirst Crown had been first used for the 1985 Women's World Team Selection Trials. "These circuits drew unanimous raves back then, " said race director Barclay Kruse. "They provided an ideal mix of tough terrain with plenty of good viewpoints for spectators." The longest and most grueling stage, the 54-mile Meadows Road Race, was held on Saturday, May 23. But the race championship was not decided until the final day, Sunday, May 24, when riders competed in two stages: a 46-mile morning stage on the Classic Road Course and a 25-mile evening criterium at Village Square Shopping Center in downtown Redmond. The New Zealand veteran, Madonna Harris, edged Olympian Ingo Thompson, to take the Seafirst Crown.

Media Coverage
The first year event drew attention from national and local media, which included:

- Four local television stations: KIRO-TV, KOME-TV, KING-TV, KSTW-TV covered pre-event stories and gave live daily coverage of statistics and stories for a total of 25 minutes by all four stations.

- AP wire: Daily stories and statistics were picked up nationwide in cities such as Denver, San Diego, Boston, and Washington, D.C.

- Washington papers: Eighteen Washington-state newspapers, featured daily and prerace stories for a total of over 100 articles.

- One major radio station: KIRO-radio

Historical Position
Sponsorship rationale
The women's cycling event sponsorship was chosen by Seafirst for the following reasons:

- Augment marketing, advertising, public relations efforts. In addition to television image campaigns and public relations efforts, special events enhance a corporation's image in the community. Special events, such as the Seafirst Crown, offered a platform to strengthen the bank's image and to speak directly to target audiences. The targeted audience, cycling enthusiasts and preferred customers/prospects, was selectively reached through Seafirst Crown publicity and a VIP customer reception.

- Title sponsor opportunity. Since it was a first-time event, Seafirst had the chance to become a title sponsor by naming the event the Seafirst Crown Women's Cycling Classic. As pointed out in the article, "How to Win with Sports," in the February 1987 *Public Relations Journal*.:

  > ...if you want credit in the media for the event, you must buy the "title," not a "presenting sponsor" role. The media will generally use the sponsor's name if it is in the title, but tends to drop most other sponsors...[1]

  Seafirst's goal was to be named in all publicity surrounding the race.

- Trendsetting sport. According to the National Sporting Goods Association (NSGA), bicycling last year counted 50.7 million participants. It is America's second most popular participant sport, after swimming, with 73.3 million, and is the fourth-fastest-growing sport in the country. There were 6.4 million new cyclists age seven and older last year. By contrast, the NSGA says that running and jogging, which are thought to be activities that everybody participates in, have only 26.3 million participants, 3.6 million of them new in 1986.[2]

  Seafirst wanted to have a distinctive event. The media is already saturated with triathalons and running events, so Seafirst sought a trend-setting sport which was unique and affordable. As cited by the *Public Relation Journal*, cycling is among the up-and-coming sports, along with walking, snowmobiling, and arm wrestling.[3]

- Opportunity to reach two select target audiences. Cycling enthusiasts and preferred customers/prospects were two key target audiences.

The first target audience the event would reach are cycling enthusiasts. Being the first women's championship race to be held in Seattle since 1985, the three-day event would draw attention from the Northwest cycling community. A *Bicycle Magazine* survey showed 50% of the people who like cycling are 18-34 years old, 73% of them have attended college, and 50% of them have graduated from college. The average household income of cycling enthusiasts is approximately $44,400. Three quarters of the people who like cycling own their own home, and the average value of those homes is over $100,000. Two-thirds of cycling fans are employed in managerial or professional careers. This group closely parallels Seafirst's primary target audience of customers and prospects and is an attractive audience to reach through leisure-time marketing.

The second audience that was to be reached was preferred commercial and consumer customers and prospects. Over 500 select guests were invited to the VIP "Meet the Racers" reception prior to the event. Inviting exclusive customers/prospects to the Seafirst cycling gala was a way to entertain special customers, build upon customer relationships, and identify key prospects. The VIP event offered an opportunity to reach people in a quality, person-to-person setting rather than through a more impersonal mass media approach. Seafirst is carving out a niche as the Northwest's premier financial institution. By staging North America's fourth-largest women's race, Seafirst's position as a leader in the Northwest was strengthened.

Location

Redmond, Washington, was chosen as the site to host the women's cycling event, because of its past experience in hosting major cycling events and because its excellent terrain would challenge the riders. The Redmond course had become known as one of the best in the Northwest since it was first used in the 1985 U.S. Women's World Team trials. In 1987, Redmond hosted five major cycling events with nearly 30,000 total spectators and has achieved the reputation as a hotbed for major, world-caliber bicycle races. Situated only 25 minutes from downtown Seattle, sport reporters find Redmond convenient and accessible.

Time of Year

In 1987, the Seafirst Crown was held over the Memorial Day weekend. With the busy racing schedule, this first-year event found May 22-24 one of the few windows of opportunity to hold the event. The three-day weekend worked well for the racers' schedules. However, it had a negative impact on spectator attendance.

Past Strategy
The main strategies and goals for the 1987 race included:

- Generate publicity. The primary goal of Seafirst Crown in 1987 was to generate publicity. As a newcomer to special-events marketing, Seafirst hoped to link its name with the upscale sport of cycling, as well as to show involvement in the community. The Seafirst Crown was to get us into places where the competition wasn't, namely the editorial section of the sports pages during May. Cycling events were seen as fertile ground for financial institutions and as a way to strengthen image. If marketed successfully on a long-term basis, the Seafirst Crown could eventually become synonymous with elite women's cycling in the Northwest.

- Entertain key customers/prospects. Extending the event to include a special VIP reception was another key element in the selection of the event. The VIP reception provided an entertainment platform for relationship officers to host and mingle with guests, helping to build professional ties with Seafirst. Establishing and building upon relationships is a paramount value in the financial industry and is especially vital with preferred customers. Judging from the positive feedback from both customers and officers, our customers enjoyed the prestige of attending an exclusive Seafirst event.

- Creating a unique identity. Developing a unique identity for the race was an important part of the advertising strategy. The race required a logo to represent the title and image of the inaugural race. The logo was to be included on posters, banners, press kits, and other advertising materials. The materials had to be coordinated, consistent, and professional, thus creating a distinctive identity for the Seafirst Crown.

Past Philosphy
Since the event was a first for Seafirst, it was considered a pilot project. Only after the first year results of media coverage, relationship officers' feedback, and senior management approval had been assessed would consideration be given to staging the event again.

If the event proved successful, Seafirst would build on the event, including getting supporting sponsors and possibly extending the event to include a citizen's challenge. Seafirst hopes that as the event grows it will become an integral part of the Redmond community and of Northwest sports.

MARKET AND EVENT ANALYSIS
Environment
External Environment—U.S. Olympic Road Race
1988 will be a very exciting year for professional cycling in Washington State. The 1988 U.S. Olympic Road Cycling Trials will be staged in Spokane,

Washington, July 22-August 14, attracting top riders from around the county. In the 1984 Olympic Games, seven American cyclists walked away with medals. Among them was silver-medalist and five-time world champion, Rebecca Twigg Whitehead, a local favorite who grew up in Seattle. Besides the excitement of having these lofty Olympians in our state, the Cycling Trials will mean national media attention by network television and in the major daily newspapers across the country. The opportunity to capitalize on the popularity of cycling has never been greater in Washington. The Seafirst Crown precedes the U.S. Cycling Trials and will most likely attract the same strong field as last year's race, competing for valuable points to qualify for the trials. This hot competition at the Seafirst Crown should draw considerable local and national media attention, as well as interest from local racing fans.

2. *Internal Environment - Senior Management*
Selling a promotional event to senior management is a challenge, especially given the large expenditure to sponsor the Seafirst Crown. Although cycling is a cost-effective sponsorship relative to other popular sports, such as golf, tennis, and running events, management has to evaluate the "bottom line." Since the Seafirst Crown is a $50,000 expenditure and is a highly visible event, it is a controversial expenditure. With special event marketing, short-term profitability is difficult to measure and prove in quantifiable terms. The impact on image is also hard to measure, thus the struggle to justify costs. As Clara Lamkin, director of public affairs for Kentucky Fried Chicken, explained after spending $250,000 on two bluegrass festivals in Kentucky:

> You can't judge if the event has actually influenced customers in terms of the bottom line. The bluegrass festivals get lots of press nationally and internationally, and we think it helps our interest. Both are targeted at families, our main customers, and we think it helps our image. We hope it builds brand loyalty, but we don't know. [4]

Even if the event is a good investment, senior management is concerned with profitability. Short-term profits are very important, therefore, management is grappling with the value of a second-year sponsorship.

Competition
Other Banks in Sports Marketing
Competition in the sports marketing area is almost nonexistent. Of the six major competitors in Washington, only one was solidly grounded in a particular sport. Rainier Bank, the second-largest bank in Washington, used to hold the annual Rainier Cup—Professional Skiing Competition each winter. After five years of sponsoring the Cup, Rainier abandoned the event two years ago with no plans to resume sponsorship. Other banks are minor sponsors of sporting events, but have not taken a leading role.

Other Banks in Cycling

Seafirst has two competitors for cycling events:

- Washington Trust Cycling Classic—Spokane
  Washington Trust, a $500 million thrift in Spokane and a minor competitor of Seafirst, was the only bank involved in cycling until last year. Since 1984, Washington Trust has sponsored the Washington Trust Cycling Classic in Spokane, which has seen dramatic growth in size and visibility. The race is now among the nation's top races, and the longest pro-am stage race in the country for men.

- Washington Mutual Grand Prix—Redmond
  Washington Mutual, the largest thrift in Washington, also saw the growth in bicycling and sponsored a major cycling event for the first time last year. The Washington Mutual Grand Prix is a four-day track event scheduled at the Marymoor Velodrome in mid-July; it will be held again in 1988. The four-day session differs from the Seafirst road race because it has paying spectators and a field of both men and women.

With the increasing interest in cycling by our competitors and the U.S. Olympic Trials coming to Spokane in July, there has never been a better time to capitalize on this sport. 1988 is an ideal year to take advantage of the sponsorship and reap the benefits of its full potential. A decision to abandon the Seafirst Crown now could result in negative publicity and community backlash.

Strengths

Established success. The 1987 Seafirst Crown was an important world-class women's stage race that produced dozens of newspaper articles and broadcast features that recognized Seafirst as the major corporate sponsor. Goodwill, community involvement, and a tremendous amount of publicity demonstrated this event to be a success.

Olympic year excitement. With Spokane hosting the Olympic Trials in Washington state, the excitement around the Summer Games and especially around cycling will be heightened. Given that seven world champions competed in the 1987 Seafirst Crown, and that all plan to return, media attention and public interest should be even greater in 1988.

Quality event. Northwest Classics, the company hired to produce the 1987 Seafirst Crown, is a sports promotion company specializing in bicycle racing. Barclay Druse, owner of Northwest Classics, is recognized as one of America's top bicycling promoters and organizers. Since 1983, Northwest Classics has produced over 100 of its own bicycle races. In addition, it has been hired to perform specific media promotion functions at other major events, including the 1984 and 1988 U.S. Olympic Cycling Trials and the

1986 World Cycling Championships. Barclay and his staff managed all the logistics of producing the first Seafirst Crown, including recruiting athletes and obtaining city permits, police coordination, U.S. Cycling Federation permits, site services and a host of other responsibilities. With the capable team at Northwest Classics running the race, the 1988 Seafirst Crown promises to be another quality event.

Second year cost savings. The initial, start-up costs of any project are expensive. After first-year investments, the second-year event will realize certain economies. To plan a similar event for the second year, approximately one-third, or $30,000, can be shaved from the original expenses. The second-year event will benefit from work previously produced, such as logo development, banners, and posters, as well as from areas that can be accomplished more cost-effectively, such as the VIP reception.

Low cost promotion vs. media advertising. A strength of special events is that they are a cost-effective means to advertise image. A special event traditionally cuts through the laboriously slow, costly building factors associated with the traditional promotional mix. Since the Seafirst Crown event is marketed through leisure and lifestyle channels, it is a cost-effective alternative for building a solid reputation.

Promoting goodwill. Sponsoring a community event produces the "Good Samaritan" effect; that is, it shows that a business is concerned about its community and is willing to put something back into it. [5]

Employee participation. The Seafirst Crown provides numerous opportunities for Seafirst employees to get involved and participate. The internal public relations of the event can often build employee morale by making them feel that they are part of the event's success. [6]

Weaknesses
Difficult to measure results. Unlike the measuring of advertising effectiveness through advertising tracking studies, results for special events are difficult to measure. Sports events may help build awareness of the bank and may help in cementing customer relations, but they are more speculative than tangible.

Senior management support. Without tangible results, it is hard to gain support from senior management. Even though they may be well positioned and cost-effective, special events are more difficult to justify. The benefits of the sponsorship are illustrated by the volume of publicity and favorable feedback from customers and officers, but are hard to express in terms of the bottom line.

Time of year. The date of the event is determined by the racers' schedules, not by Seafirst's, and thus is virtually beyond our control. Last year, holding the event over Memorial Day weekend was a deterrent to both spectator attendance and volunteer participation. Also, given the unpredictable weather in May, this outdoor event could be plagued by bad weather—again affecting the spectators and volunteers.

A rival for media attention in May is Seattle's professional basketball team, the Seattle SuperSonics. Last year, the Sonics were in the play-offs, capturing the attention of sportswriters during this period.

Customer entertainment. Aside from the sponsorship cost, the VIP party last year for customers/prospects consumed the major portion of the budget. Over 300 attended the elaborate "Meet the Racers" reception, but it was a costly event, estimated at approximately $80 per person.

OBJECTIVES
Seafirst Crown and Other Current Programs
The Seafirst Crown is one of twenty-one events scheduled in the 1988 Advertising Plan and is the largest single expenditure expected this year. This significant event requires more planning, coordination and involvement than any other sponsorship planned for 1988. To ensure a successful second year, it is essential that the event be coordinated as a collaboration between Seafirst's Advertising, Corporate Communications and Community Relations departments. The sponsorship must have a three-fold effort of advertising, public relations, and event marketing—all under one banner to create a winning event. The "golden triangle" approach of advertising, promotion, and publicity will help position Seafirst as a market leader and make the most of the cycling sponsorship.

The Seafirst Crown in May promises to be one of the most publicized and promoted events staged this year. It is one of only six events requiring indepth planning and coordination between public relations and advertising. Because lifestyle marketing is so new at Seafirst, it is not yet clear under whose marketing domain the event rightly falls. But with the heavy emphasis on advertising and event staging, it is currently under the direction of the Advertising Department.

Profitability Potential
Publicity growth. Although there is little research about the impact of event sponsorships on customer relationships, the impact and potential of the sponsorship in terms of column-inches and on-air time is invaluable. As proven last year with over 100 articles in eighteen Washington papers and 25 minutes of total on-air time on four television stations, the combined

media costs could not have been purchased for what Seafirst paid for the sponsorship. As was pointed out earlier, this is an Olympic year and many hopeful women Olympians will be competing in the Seafirst Crown. The event, therefore, has an even greater potential for media coverage.

Expanded customer/prospect relations. The special event reception for Seafirst's customers/prospects, will give the potential to increase and extend account relationships with new and existing customers. The VIP event in 1987 helped cement customer relationships and reinforced the positive image of the bank. Appreciative letters from customers and positive feedback from account officers acknowledged that the reception was beneficial. The reception not only entertains, but builds upon important, profitable relationships. This type of special event reaches customers that are not easily reached through other channels.

Memorable platform. The "memorable platform" concept is again profitable in the long term but is difficult to measure. The premise of this concept is that through leisure-time and lifestyle marketing, consumers can be reached on what can be called a "memorable platform." That is, if the event is pleasant or a helpful experience, consumers will tend to remember it and associate their good feelings about the event with the sponsor.[7] Given that the 1987 race was positively received by the press and the public, the Seafirst Crown would fall into this category.

Related Risks
Risks at the race. The major risk at the race is a cyclist or a spectator being injured due to the Seafirst Crown. Seafirst Bank and Northwest Classics, the race promotion company, are insured through the U.S. Cycling Federation for up to $1 million. In addition, Seafirst Risk Management Division has insurance policies covering such events in the advent of an accident. All policies are reviewed by both Seafirst Risk Management and inhouse legal council before any contracts are signed.

Naturally, as precautionary measures, local police, race course marshalls, and course officials are all positioned around the course for traffic and spectator control. Hay bales, barricades, traffic cones, diversion signs, and crowd-control fencing is positioned around the course. There were no accidents at or surrounding the 1987 Seafirst Crown.

Objectives for Marketing Mix
The six areas of the marketing mix are: publicity, promotions, advertising and media relations, customer relations, merchandising, community and employee relations. The following are Seafirst Crown's objectives for each element of the marketing mix:

1. Publicity

   - Maximize media coverage by major television networks, radio stations, and statewide newspapers.

   - Continue to support Seafirst's good corporate image statewide.

2. Promotions

   - Attract a minimum of five supporting sponsors to participate in the Seafirst Crown.

   - Enhance the awareness and appeal of Seafirst Crown with Seafirst customers and the general public.

   - Enhance the involvement of the Redmond community with the Seafirst Crown.

3. Advertising and Media Relations

   - Improve and enhance Seafirst's image across multiple markets(personal, business and commercial) by 2% in conjunction with the overall 1988 Marketing Plan.

   - Maintain strong awareness and appeal of the Seafirst Crown with Seafirst customers and adults aged twenty-five to forty-nine with $35,000 annual household income.

4. Customer Relations

   - Increase the number and extent of relationships with new and existing customers following the "Meet the Racers" reception.

   - Create goodwill with prospective and existing customers.

5. Merchandising

   - Increase the visibility of the Seafirst Crown by 100%.

6. Community and Employee Relations

   - Enhance the involvement of the Redmond community with the Seafirst Crown.

   - Increase the number of Seafirst employee volunteers participating from 20 to 100.

   - Increase participation by senior management from two to five senior officers at the VIP customer reception.

STRATEGIES AND TACTICS

The elements of the marketing mix will be successful only if the departments and the people administering the programs are committed to the success of the project and work effectively together. With the most difficult first year behind them, the team working on this project has a proven track record and a historical perspective to assist with 1988 plans.

Publicity Program

1. *Strategy*

   Implement a proactive public relations/publicity effort designed to demonstrate Seafirst's commitment to the Northwest, to sports, and specifically to women's cycling.

2. *Tactics*

   - Create news by announcing Seafirst's second year sponsorship to the media with a kick-off press conference.

   - Continue to enhance already established rapport with local TV, radio and newspaper sportswriters.

   - Develop a news bureau and generate a flow of press kits and news releases aimed at not only sports pages, but business, arts and leisure, and general news pages. All materials will carry Seafirst Crown logo for consistency.

   - Schedule a two-day, prerace media tour for 1987 Seafirst Crown defending champion Madonna Harris, and five-time world champion and native Seattleite Rebecca Twigg Whitehead. Schedule radio and TV talk shows and newscast interviews throughout the two days, allowing time for story and photo opportunities with the press.

   - Stage a sports headquarters at the event and send press passes to all media. Establish a communications channel to send event and postevent results.

3. *Measurement for Evaluation*

   - Compile prerace and postrace media clippings from TV video clips, radio transcripts and newspaper clippings.

   - Compose a post-event evaluation of the event from a public relations perspective, including all press generated before, during and after the event.

4. *Budget*

   - Premedia tour $1,500
     Racers fees and accommodations
   - Photography documentation/video clips   500

        Total $2,000

Promotions Programs

1. *Strategy*
   - Initiate a supporting sponsorship program to help finance the race and increase the level of awareness.
   - Stage a community festival in Redmond during race days.

2. *Tactics*
   - Develop a Seafirst Crown sponsorship package to solicit other supporting sponsors. First, target companies who showed initial interest in 1987 (i.e., cycling related companies). Second, target companies who have established relationships with Seafirst. Third, target Redmond and surrounding area businesses.
   - Encourage supporting sponsors to advertise within Seafirst Crown Highlights Show broadcast following event.
   - Create a community festival at the race course to encourage community involvement and spectator attendance.
   - Pursue interest by the city to host live entertainment, on-site food booths, cycling related clinics, bike repair workshops and other on-site displays.
   - Reinforce Seafirst's sponsorship and the supporting sponsors' participation with the race by staging a Seafirst booth and other sponsors' booths at the event.
   - Develop a promotional tie-in with the cycling, such as a sweepstakes, couponing, contests, or cash saving (i.e.," Use our cash machine to enter" or "Pick up an entry at the Redmond branch and have a chance to win a racing bike or cycling equipment.")

3. *Measurement for Evaluation*
   Estimate the number of spectators on race days versus 1987 event attendance. Determine how many spectators attended the Seafirst Crown versus other Washington cycling events.

4. *Budget*
   Community Festival: There will be no cost to participating businesses. Each company pays for set-up of their own booth in exchange for exposure of their product or service.

• Band	$500
• Promotional tie in	$5,000
—Point-of-sale materials	
Total:	$5,500
• Income from supporting sponsors:	$20,000

Advertising/Media Relations Program

1. *Strategy*
   - Initiate a postrace highlights show with a local TV station to further extend Seafirst's visibility with the world-class cycling.
   - Continue to develop awareness using specially designed logo on advertising, merchandising and public relations material.

2. *Tactics*
   - Query local TV stations for interest in producing a highlights show of the Seafirst Crown.
   - Package a media deal and negotiate with stations interested.
   - Purchase advertising time within the highlights show and encourage supporting sponsors to advertise in the program.
   - Work closely with station to develop a half-hour to one-hour program highlighting scenes from the race.
   - Use logo on all material: ads, posters, premiums, T-shirts, banners, customer gifts, and press kits.
   - Advertise event via 4-color poster previously developed. Display posters in 160 branches statewide, 50 cycling shops and clubs, and 200 locations in Bellevue, Redmond and Woodinville.
   - Advertise event in local newspaper supplements, the event program, and on-site fact sheets.
   - Line streets, bleachers, podium, and awards area with banners.

3. *Measurement for Evaluation*
   - Monitor viewer response to the highlights show.
   - Send a survey to a sampling of Redmond citizens to gauge awareness and interest in the event and to solicit feedback.

4. *Budget*
   - Negotiated cost for highlights show production $5,000
   - 1000 posters - production, printing $4,000
   - Redmond newspaper insert $1,500
   - Survey $1,000
     Total: $10,500

Customer Relations Program
1. *Strategy*
   Host an exclusive evening reception prior to race where preferred Seafirst customers and prospects can meet the racers and help cement relationships with Seafirst officers.

2. *Tactics*
   - Host a party for 200 to 300 Eastside guests at the Chateau Ste. Michelle Winery. The winery was a favorable location in 1987 and can accommodate customers comfortably in a scenic setting.

   - Develop a unique theme appropriate for the event and setting.

   - Produce invitations, wine glasses, name tags, decorations, tying into the same theme and Seafirst Crown.

   - Hire a professional catering company to supply the party with appetizing and festive hors d'oeuvres.

   - Establish an internal communication channel to disseminate information about the VIP reception. Ensure Seafirst officers are aware which customers/prospects were invited, which are attending, and are informed about all details surrounding event.

   - Stage a brief ceremony with welcoming remarks, background of the race and an introduction of the world-class athletes.

   - Involve featured athletes with customers at the reception with autograph sighing and photo opportunities.

3. *Measurement for Evaluation*
   Evaluate response rate to reception versus 1987. Survey relationship officers following event and gauge their response to the party.

4. *Budget*
• Invitations/name tags	$5,000
• Etched wine glasses	$2,500
• Wine - Provided by winery	NC
• Music	$500
• Decorations/flowers	$500
Total:	$8,500

Merchandising Program

1. *Strategy*
   Organize a Seafirst booth at the event to sell Seafirst Crown merchandise and to distribute Seafirst Bank promotional material.

2. *Tactics*
   - Determine viable merchandise and price all souvenirs as self-liquidating (i.e., T-shirts, water bottles, racing caps, posters).

   - Set-up booth on-site during race days to help promote Seafirst's sponsorship and get spectators involved with the race.

3. *Measurement for Evaluation*
   Attempt to track any customer leads as a result of the Seafirst booth

at the event. Monitor how many souvenirs were sold—these people will be walking billboards for Seafirst.

4. *Budget*
   • Booth - transportation and set-up $800

No merchandising costs. All handled though Northwest Classics.

Community Relations Program
1. *Strategy*
   Implement a proactive communications strategy targeted at the local community of Redmond.

2. *Tactics*
   • Develop a basic plan illustrating the impact of cycling in the community, (i.e., economic impact on business, visibility for community).

   • Contact local business and civic organizations to promote the race, discussing the impact of the Seafirst Crown on the community.

   • Involve the local government and police force with plans.

   • Contact local neighborhoods where the race is staged, notifying them in advance of the race and to create goodwill.

   • Provide civic organizations, schools and local businesses with information and poster for the race.

   • Schedule Madonna Harris, Rebecca Twigg Whitehead and a Seafirst Representative for guest appearances at major civic organization meetings (i.e., Redmond Rotary Club) to thank the community on behalf of Seafirst Bank and the cyclists.

   • Present Redmond's mayor with commemorative poster, autographed by the cyclists and a Seafirst momento.

3. *Measurement For Evaluation*
   Send a survey to a sampling of Redmond citizens to gauge awareness and interest in the event and to solicit positive and negative feedback. (Same survey used to measure Advertising Program.)

4. *Budget*
   Previously expensed in advertising program.

Employee Relations Program
1. *Strategy*
   Use Seafirst's communication network and the Seafirst employee newspaper to promote and motivate employee participation.

2. *Tactics*
    - Contact Seafirst volunteers in January 1988, alerting Board of the need for volunteers for the race. Request the event be included on Seafirst's calendar of volunteering events.

    - Provide Seafirst volunteers with information on what would be expected of them, if they choose to participate. Distribute fliers to all potential volunteers with sign-up information.

    - Request a member of Seafirst's volunteers be assigned to Seafirst Bike Race Committee to stay current with event plans.

    - Contact Seafirst News (inhouse employee newspaper) regarding Seafirst Crown information and volunteer sign-up. Request a featured story before, during and after the race.

3. *Measurement for Evaluation*
    Evaluate number of volunteers in 1988 versus the number in 1987.

4. *Budget*
    Only internal "soft" cost, no hard dollars to expense.

SUMMARY
In conclusion, the sponsorship of the Seafirst Crown in 1988 promises to be a quality, well-publicized event. With the Olympic Cycling Trials in Washington, seven Olympic hopefuls competing in the Seafirst race and excitement building toward the Summer Olympics, potential for cycling publicity has never been greater. Attention by local and national press will position the Seafirst Crown as an event on the move in 1988. The value of the publicity alone will outweigh the cost of sponsorship.

Enhanced by the added dimensions of the marketing mix, the Seafirst Crown is a cost-effective means of boosting image, community service and market share for Seafirst. ◆

---

[1] Claire Walter, "Selling America's No. 2 Sport: Bicycling," *Stores*, (December, 1986), p.36

[2] Ibid.,p.36

[3] Jackie Lapin, "Worshop: How To Win with Sports," *Public Relations Journal* (February, 1987), p.31

[4] Jeffrey A. Tractenbers "Beyond the 30-Second Spot," *Forbes*, (December 17, 1984), p.176.

[5] Kathleen Jarvis, "Name Recognition: It Doesn't Have to be Costly," *Credit* (November/December, 1986), p.30.

[6] Ibid, p.31

[7] Lesa Ukman, "Corporate Games-Advertisers Discover the Benefits of Special Events," *Madison Avenue*, (December, 1984) p.32.

CHAPTER 8

Establishing an Effective Calling Program for the Retail Banker

Charles E. Wuertz
Hamilton Bank
$2.7 billion assets

MARKET ANALYSIS
Hamilton Bank's Marketplace

Hamilton Bank country is situated in Pennsylvania's heartland. Shaped by seven counties that stretch from Cumberland in the west to Chester in the east, Lebanon and Berks in the north, and York in the south, the Bank's marketplace is well balanced and diverse. Lancaster, Chester, and Berks counties rank first, second and third in cash farm income in Pennsylvania; York is fifth, Lebanon, ninth; and Dauphin, nineteenth. Twenty-three percent of the state's farms are located in these counties. Agriculture is a mainstay, stabilizing the market from the vagaries of a fluctuating national economy and providing a foundation for the manufacturing and service industries that are concentrated in Berks and Chester counties.

Hamilton Bank [1] is an autonomous, wholly owned banking subsidiary of CoreStates Financial Corp., charged with marketing financial services for CoreStates. These financial services are delivered through operating plans that are developed, implemented and managed by Hamilton Bank on a basis consistent with the philosophies, policies, and strategies established by CoreStates for its banking subsidiaries.

Financial services are provided to consumers, businesses, institutions and other organizations along consumer, trust, and wholesale business lines. Hamilton is the market leader in each business line in its overall trade area but not in all geographical submarkets. This strong presence has been achieved through high-quality personnel with excellent market knowledge, a respected reputation in the marketplace, and an extensive regional branch network.

As a result of Hamilton Bank's past product development and a recent affiliation with CoreStates, it is able to draw on a broader product line, as well as on greater and more specialized resources and expertise, than its primary banking competitors. These products and resources, coupled with Hamilton's high caliber of people, product awareness, knowledge of markets, and professional operating style are a significant competitive advantage in the marketplace.

Market Overview
Combined total deposits , including both Individual Partnership Corporations (IPC) and public, for the six-county market area (data were not available for Cumberland County at the time of the survey) increased 12% over 1984. This is higher than last year's increase of 8.5%, but slightly lower than 1983's increase of 14.1%.

The county shares of total IPC deposits shows Berks with the highest share of 21.29% and Lebanon County with the lowest share of 5.78%. This compares to last year with Berks at 21.26% and Lebanon with 5.99%.

Total IPC deposits increased by 11.01%, which is slightly lower than the increase of 12.0% for total deposits (IPC and public).

The 11.01% increase in total IPC deposits is even higher than the 9.0% increase in 1984. This was true for most of our six county market area except Lebanon County, which decreased to 7.17% growth compared to last year's 9.64%, and Chester County, which decreased to 10.36% growth compared to last year's 11.31%.

The total growth rate of demand IPC deposits was 5.0% in 1985, which is lower than the 6.9% increase in 1984. Chester County had the highest percentage increase of 9.18%, and Lebanon County had the lowest increase of 1. 01%. This compares to Chester having the highest percentage increase of 14.64%, and Lancaster County the lowest (2.28%), in 1984.

Total time (savings and time IPC) deposits grew by 11.67% in 1985, which is higher than the 1984 total time growth rate of 9.2%. Dauphin County had the highest percentage increase, 15.6%, and Lebanon had the lowest increase, 7.75%.

Institutional Type Market Share
Market share for total IPC deposits by institutional type are shown on the chart on the following page.

MARKET SHARE FOR TOTAL IPC DEPOSITS

	1983 Market Share	1984 Market Share	1985 Market Share
Commercial Banks	72.34%	72.08%	71.18%
Savings & Loans	20.02%	19.82%	20.14%
Mutual Savings	2.47%	2.36%	2.07%
Credit Unions	5.17%	5.74%	6.61%

In 1985, credit unions increased their market share by .87%. This compares to credit unions increasing their market share by .57% from the other institutions in 1984.

Total deposits for commercial banks reached $12.1 billion compared with $11.2 billion in 1984. Lancaster County had the largest portion of those deposits, at $2.8 billion. This is consistent with last year's ranking.

Total deposits for savings and loans were $3.3 billion compared with $2.9 billion in 1984. Dauphin County had the largest portion of these deposits, at $874 million. This is consistent with the 1984 ranking.

Hamilton Bank Recap
Hamilton Bank's share of total deposits (IPC and public) decreased from 12.4% to 11.8%. Our total IPC market share also decreased, from 12.3% to 11.9%. Demand and total time deposits also had a decrease of 1.01% and .32% respectively.

Assuming that total deposits in the marketplace increase an average of 12% (total deposits in the marketplace grew 12% between 1984-85) and that Hamilton wants to maintain its current market share of 11.8% through June 1986, Hamilton would need to increase total deposits by $237.8 million. As of March 31, 1986, our FDIC reporting indicated that we have $2.1 billion in total deposits or an increase of $134.5 million since June 1985. This would mean that we need to increase total deposit dollars by $103.2 million during the second quarter of 1986.

Competitive Analysis
American Bank competes with Hamilton Bank in Berks, Chester, Lancaster, and Lebanon counties. When comparing market share for total IPC deposits within the above counties, American Bank has a 15.1% market share. This reflects a slight loss since 1984. American Bank also lost market share in demand and savings IPC deposits. Hamilton Bank also saw a decline in

market share for total, demand, and savings IPC deposits with a current market share of 11.7% for total IPC deposits. When comparing the interest rates offered during the time frame of July 1984 to June 1985, American Bank offered very competitive rates and maintained a slight edge over Hamilton Bank.

Bank of PA competes with Hamilton Bank in Berks County. Market share for total IPC deposits are comparable, with each bank having approximately 14.5%. Bank of PA captures a higher percentage of the market for demand deposits than does Hamilton Bank. Both banks lost market share from 1984 in total, demand and savings IPC deposits. Bank of PA's pricing structure for interest rates was similar to Hamilton Bank. The majority of Bank of PA's interest rates were within thirty basis points of Hamilton Bank's.

Commonwealth National Bank competes with Hamilton Bank in Dauphin, Lancaster, and York counties. Hamilton Bank continues to dominate this market area with 12.9% market share for total IPC deposits and an 8.4% market share. Commonwealth has seen a decline in market share in total and savings IPC deposits since 1984. Commonwealth National Bank and Hamilton Bank had very competitive interest rates.

Dauphin Deposit competes with Hamilton Bank in Dauphin, Lancaster, Lebanon, and York counties. Hamilton has 12.8% market share compared to Dauphin's 10.2% market share for total IPC deposits. Dauphin had little fluctuation in deposits over the past year, except for a decrease in demand deposits. Hamilton and Dauphin offered similar interest rates from July, 1984 to the end of the year. During the first half of 1985, Dauphin Deposit appears to have offered slightly higher interest rates.

Fulton Bank competes with Hamilton Bank in Lancaster county. Hamilton Bank has a 16.5% market share of total IPC deposits and Fulton Bank increased 0.6% to 14.8% market share. Fulton Bank has also increased its market share in demand IPC deposits. Interest rates offered by Fulton Bank were very competitive with Hamilton Bank's rates until the beginning of 1985, when Fulton Bank's interest rates were usually a few basis points above Hamilton Bank's.

York Bank & Trust competes with Hamilton Bank in York County. York maintains a strong lead over Hamilton with a total IPC deposit market share of 21.6% compared to Hamilton Bank's market share of 13.5% (a .7% decrease from 1984). York Bank increased market share in demand IPC deposits but decreased in total and savings IPC deposits. York Bank's pricing structure for interest rates was similar to Hamilton's. When differences did occur, Hamilton Bank was usually slightly higher.

Branch Delivery System
Hamilton Bank has sixty-seven branches located in its seven-county trade area. They are supported by a "MAC" ATM network of forty machines. Hamilton employs 1,600 people of which 369 are officers.

Our network of conveniently located branch and ATM facilities constitutes the primary distribution channel for our products. These facilities, which contribute to Hamilton's overall strength in the marketplace, serve as distribution points for other groups as well. Through their sales efforts, branch personnel generate referrals to the Trust, Metropolitan and Wholesale groups, as well as to Private Banking, Investments and CoreStates Capital Markets.

Product Lines
We offer a broad range of asset and liability products, including group sales to a business customer's employees. Known as Direct Benefit Banking, this service is marketed through employers having a direct deposit payroll relationship with Hamilton Bank. Asset as well as liability products are offered to individual employees who elect to participate in this program.

Our asset products consist of consumer and small business loans, lines of credit, residential mortgages, and credit cards. We offer traditional fixed-rate and floating-rate products. Additionally, we provide wholesale floor plan, third-party financing, and fleet leasing to automobile dealers within our marketplace. Our primary sources of asset-based fee income are line of credit fees, business loan origination fees, residential mortgage origination fees, and installment loan insurance commissions.

Our array of liability products, available to both consumers and small businesses, includes checking and transaction-based accounts, traditional savings products, certificates of deposit, money market accounts and retirement products. Our Individual Retirement Accounts offer the option of diversifying into mutual fund investments. Specialized employee retirement products are available to small businesses, including SEP, ESI, defined contribution pension plans and profit sharing plans.

Our ATMs are affiliated with a worldwide network providing over 10,000 points from which our customers can access their accounts. Liability-oriented, fee-income producers are deposit account service charges, mutual fund fees, and safe deposit box rentals.

Loans and Deposits
A summary of Hamilton's loans and deposits[2] for the past three years is shown on the following page.

HAMILTON BANK LOANS SUMMARY
(in thousands)

	1983	1984	1985
Commercial	451,050	465,268	451,850
Installment	180,983	165,189	188,037
Real Estate	454,474	412,955	435,891
Other	50,469	236,668	616,944
Total:	1,136,976	1,280,080	1,692,722

HAMILTON BANK DEPOSITS IPC SUMMARY
(in thousands)

	1983	1984	1985
Demand	240,463	255,790	254,897
Savings	574,497	129,800	45,095
Time	854,895	1,422,464	1,542,158
Other	120,827	73,131	165,345
Total:	1,790,682	1,881,185	2,007,495

Customer Base

In 1984, Hamilton conducted a Lifestyle Segmentation Study of its market and customer base. The relative size of each lifestyle segment in Hamilton's market was determined by analyzing various demographic characteristics and attitudinal factors of area consumers. The main demographic categories analyzed included age, income, occupation and education. Responses to ten attitudinal statements were used to segment the market. Based on responses to these statements, Hamilton customers felt slightly more secure in their ability to meet near-term financial goals, were somewhat knowledgeable about savings and investment matters and therefore, were less likely to be confused when comparison shopping for financial products. They were also more likely to feel that all credit cards are the same. Fewer of them indicated that they liked to use ATMs.

The market was divided into five types of customers: Indifferents; Older Traditionalists; Mature Cconfidents; Young Professionals; and Need-Driven.

Hamilton Customers versus the Hamilton Market

The relative segment size of Hamilton's customer base versus that of the total market reveals several differences, the most notable being that Hamilton Bank has a similar share of the three main segments (Young Professionals, Older Traditionalists and Mature Confidents), although these segments represent vastly different portions of the total market.

MARKET SHARE OF LIFESTYLE SEGMENTS

% of Total Resp.	% of Indiff.	%of Older Tradition.	% of Young Profession.	% of Mature	% of Need-Driven
Hamilton (13.5)	**15.9**	**14.1**	**13.2**	**13.2**	**9.4**
American (11.1)	10.6	13.6	10.1	10.7	9.4
Dauphin (8.1)	5.3	9.2	9.4	5.4	18.8
Common. (6.9)	8.0	6.5	9.4	6.1	3.1
York B&T (5.9)	5.3	6.0	6.3	5.7	6.3
Fulton (4.5)	4.4	6.0	2.5	4.6	4.7
% Rep. in Hamilton Marketplace (100%)	14%	23%	20%	35%	8%

Mature Confidents, representing 35% of the total market, are the largest segment, and Hamilton Bank has a 13.2% share of this group. Hamilton's largest segment is the Indifferent group, with a 15.9% share, although this segment ranks fourth in size out of the five segments identified.

Market Share

Respondents were also asked to identify the bank that they consider to be their regular or main bank. The data showed Hamilton to have an overall market share of 13% in the seven counties where they compete. The following table shows Hamilton's share of market for each county:

HAMILTON BANK MARKET SHARE
(% Main Bank Households)

Berks	15%
Chester	5
Cumberland/Dauphin	11
Lancaster	34
Lebanon	9
York	10
Total Share	15%

Other Financial Services

In addition to the segmentation questions, respondents were also asked their opinion about two new banking services—debit cards and financial counseling.

Consumer awareness of debit cards is about 33% of the market which is similar to both the Philadelphia area and the rest of the nation. Interest in obtaining this service, if available through their main bank, is approximately 40% of all consumers, with 44% of Hamilton's customers expressing an interest.

The most likely spot for using the debit card (among the four locations specified) is a department store, with 36% mentioning this location. Respondents were not asked to choose a preferred site among the four given but rather to rate the degree of interest in using each of the predetermined sites. Among the lifestyle segments, Young Professionals were the most interested in this service and expressed the highest degree of interest in each of the specified locations.

Consumer interest in obtaining financial counseling and advice was based on four subject areas, including retirement planning, financing children's education, investment and savings strategy, and life insurance planning. The data showed that investment and savings strategy was by far the most popular area in which financial counseling would be sought, with the least interest evidenced in life insurance planning.

Young Professionals appear to be the target market for each of the counseling options since they expressed the most interest of any of the segments. Young Professionals were also the most receptive to obtaining financial counseling from their main bank.

The method of receiving financial advice most preferred by consumers (from the four options presented) is to complete a questionnaire and meet with a planner in person. 43% indicated this was the best method, while only 25% preferred to have a plan sent to them (after filling out a questionnaire) and a similar number preferred to attend a seminar and subsequently prepare their own plan. Virtually no one expressed interest in the home computer option, which would be linked to a bank with all planning completed via electronic mail.

Conclusions/Implications

1. Although Young Professionals are less prevalent in Hamilton's total market, they still represent a sizeable segment.

2. Rather than placing less emphasis on Young Professionals, a two-

pronged marketing approach with greater emphasis on Older Traditionalists seems most appropriate.

3. The substantial number of Older Traditionalists in the Hamilton market suggests that a "package" program could be a successful marketing strategy.

4. Since Young Professionals represent a smaller segment of Hamilton's market, it should be recognized that the adoption of automated delivery systems/services will most likely occur at a somewhat slower pace.

5. As determined in previous research and once again substantiated, there is considerable consumer interest in financial counseling services. Plans for offering of these services should be given priority.

Marketing Philosophy

Hamilton Bank has specifically targeted the Young Professionals, Mature Confident, Older Traditionalist and small business segments of our market. Consistent with our objectives, all potentially profitable relationships will be encouraged.

Young Professionals are between the ages of twenty-five and forty-four, with average annual incomes of $25,000 or greater. While they are organized in their approach to financial matters, they would like to be more knowledgeable about financial products and services, and overall investment strategy. These consumers are the primary users of credit-related products. Convenience is important to them; they are very receptive to self-service products such as ATM's.

Mature Confidents are aged thirty-five to fifty and earn in excess of $40,000 annually, on average. They have achieved economic security and believe that they are in a position to meet both their short- and long-term financial goals. Traditional in their approach to banking, they have a need for a broad range of investment vehicles and information-based services to assist them in their investment strategies.

The Older Traditionalist segment, aged forty-five and over, is conservative by nature and uses financial services accordingly. They are economically established and positive in their financial outlook.

The targeted small business segment is composed of companies with annual revenues of $2,500,000 or less and borrowing needs of under $250,000. This group requires more than a credit relationship and has expressed a need for deposit and noncredit services.

The most recent statistical data available suggests that our target segments comprise 78% of the consumer households in our seven county market area. It is estimated that 18,000 small businesses exist within this market as well.

Of our targeted segments, the Young Professionals and Mature Confidents are growing faster than the population as a whole. Between 1981 and 1990, the fastest growing age group will be thirty-five to fifty-four, expected to grow by 30%, followed by the sixty-five and over age group, seen as growing by 20%.

Demographics and other factors will continue to influence customer behavior, thus altering our market environment:

1. Consumers are devoting an increasing share of their personal savings to financial assets rather than to tangible assets.

2. Consumers are demonstrating increasingly active involvement in savings and investment decision-making.

3. The country is changing demographically. Consumers and small business owners are better educated and informed. There will continue to exist a growing segment of the overall market that is technologically aware, competent, and receptive.

Currently, the most meaningful measure of penetration in our primary market is deposit market share. As of June 30, 1985, Hamilton's share of total IPC dollars on deposit was 11.9%. Our primary bank competitors are Meridian Bank, Commonwealth National Bank, Dauphin Deposit Bank, Fulton Bank, and York Bank and Trust. In order to more fully measure competition from the consumers' perspective, this standard must be expanded to include non-bank competition and loan volume. As we emphasize the principles of relationship banking and management, other measurements, such as financial performance ratios, relationship measurements, and measurements of strategic activities, are becoming increasingly significant.

Traditionally, price and convenience have formed the primary basis for all competition. While our pricing has been competitive overall, our positioning has also been based on our marketing expertise, our knowledgeable staff, our product offerings, and our convenient facilities.

Targeting specific market segments provides us with an opportunity to better channel our marketing approach and prioritize the expenditure of our marketing dollars. Market segments pose potential problems as well— overfocusing on these segments can result in overlooking the remainder of the market and other potentially profitable relationships.

The final deregulation of savings account interest rates provides the opportunity to offer a range of investment products that are tailored to customers' individual investment strategies. This will enable product differentiation to take on increasing importance among competitors in the marketplace.

Key Strengths
Our major strength is the expertise of our employees and their ability to generate and retain loans and deposits, even during periods of unfavorable rates. Other strengths include the diversity of our overall product line, the positive, professional perception of Hamilton carried by our customers, the financial strength of CoreStates and our presence in one of the fastest growing areas in the Northeastern United States.

HAMILTON BANK'S CALLING PROGRAM
Objectives
Our objective is to be the leading provider of financial products and services in our marketplace. The key elements in achieving this objective are pricing, our professional staff, product offerings, promotion and our distribution channels.

We can increase our profit and our share of target market segments but this does not necessarily indicate an overall increase in market share. Progress toward our objective should be measured in the forms of outstandings volume, financial performance and banking relationships within our key market segments.

Purpose
Our purpose is to increase profitability and penetration of our target market segments through an active, well-organized, and systematic calling program. Our market includes Young Professionals, Mature Confidents, Older Traditionalists and the small business segment.

Goals
1. Increase noninterest income 10% over 1986 levels.
2. Increase average loans 11% over 1986 levels.
3. Increase average deposits 7.5% over 1986 levels.

Strategies
We will use the following strategies to accomplish our goals:

1. Gather a maximum level of deposits at a relatively attractive cost compared to other sources of lendable/investable funds available to the corporation.

2. Generate quality consumer and small business loans at a net yield

that will allow attractive spread at all times in the economic cycle, while increasing market penetration.

3. Generate growth in fee income at a percentage rate at least equal to the growth in group non-interest direct expense.

4. Build and expand stable, profitable relationships with an increasing number of consumers, households, small business and our dealer base by providing a broad range of financial services as efficiently as possible.

Background

Hamilton has always had an active calling program. Perhaps in the past the key distinction was the "form of administration," with the emphasis on the importance of making sales calls. The Bank was organized along traditional lines. Each county had its own administrator who was assigned responsibility for loan and deposit growth as well as supervision of the branch network in his particular county. This resulted in various degrees of emphasis on selling and on achievement of goals.

The sales force was also identified in a traditional manner, that is, branch manager, new accounts clerk, installment loan officer. In 1980, the bank began to recognize the need for change. Many of the branch managers were sent to sales training seminars and workshops such as Bankers Business Development Institute, Xerox Sales Training Course, and others to develop and enhance selling skills. A calling program was established. Goals were set and a reporting system was implemented to monitor and measure results. In addition, an incentive program was established to reward and recognize achievement. After three years of experience, we began to focus on changing the culture of the organization from that of a traditional bank to a sales bank, and steps were taken to implement the changes.

Today, the bank has accomplished the majority of its cultural and organizational objectives. It is currently refining and streamlining the sales organization in order to achieve efficiency and flexibility for the future. The bank is organized into two divisions. Each division is organized by clusters composed of sales units supported by operations personnel and sales team members. Each "sales team" consists of an area marketing manager, who acts as the sales team's manager, and an appropriate number of marketing managers, consumer banking officers or specialists, and customer service specialists.

Market Segmentation

The effect of identifying our market via segmentation has presented us with opportunities as well as challenges. For example, it has enabled us to clearly identify customers and prospects who present us with the best opportunity for profit. It has permitted us to "zero in" on those opportunities and to focus our energy on capturing a greater share of these customers.

It also presents us with new challenges, such as:

1. Measuring the effectiveness of the sales team's efforts in developing the markets identified.

2. Establishing operational plans for the sales team which create integration of sales efforts while maintaining unified goals, and providing flexibility for change.

3. Addressing compensation of sales team members to insure consistent performance and fair recognition of achievement.

These issues can be addressed by implementing during 1986 and 1987 the following initiatives:

1. Automation of sales reporting.

2. Establishment of marketing plans for each of the sales units.

3. Establishment of data bank for a future "commission salary" plan.

Marketing Plan
This recommendation will outline the use of the marketing plan as a tool to establish commitments from our sales force to achieve our corporate goals. The first two initiatives from the list above are being addressed by sales management in cooperation with the computer services staff.

Description of Plan
The marketing plan is a tool that will allow each sales unit to organize market information in a concise manner in order to develop the specific action steps needed to achieve their goals. The plan takes into consideration the tendency of the marketing manager to be "action oriented." The plan format allows freedom for the unit manager to plan action steps based on the strengths of the unit without sacrificing the bank's financial objectives.

How It Will Be Used
Each sales unit will be required to complete a marketing plan by January 31, 1987. The unit plans will "roll up" from the branch marketing manager level to the clusters, then through the divisional level and finally the bank. It is essential that the plans be coordinated to reflect the overall goals and objectives of the bank and at the same time provide strategies that are appropriate to the "local" marketplace.

Introduction of Plan
The plan will be introduced to the divisional staff, sales management and

Consumer Banking Group at the November 1986 meeting. Final approval of the plan will be requested at that time. The following steps will be required in order to effect implementation in January.

1. Marketing Department will collect and assemble market data for each branch and division by December 1.

2. Market data and plans will be distributed to sales units during the last week of December.

3. A meeting will be held in January 1987 to formally introduce the use of the plan. This meeting will be coordinated by sales management. The agenda will include the following:
    *   Opening remarks by the consumer banking group head
    *   Comments on 1986 performance and value statement on planning process by the bank president
    *   Concepts, logic and plan development by the sales manager
    *   Peer group exchanges
    *   Wrap-up by the sales manager

Completion
The unit and bank plans should be completed no later than January 31.

Monitoring
The marketing plans will be reviewed each quarter as part of the progress review within each unit of the Bank. The review will enable us to identify action steps planned and completed, as well as results achieved. A divisional and bank summary will be compiled at the end of second quarter to evaluate the effectiveness of the marketing plan as a tool.

SALES MANAGEMENT
Program Administration
Sales Training
We have started a basic sales skills program that addresses every team member. During 1986 and 1987, our goal is to have each member of the sales team complete their unit of training. This training program was developed with the assistance of Mohr Development, Inc. Each training unit was specifically designed to meet the needs of Hamilton's sales people.

The basic sales skills training includes an explanation of core skills, as well as an opportunity to practice those skills in the field. Core skills include needs assessment, probing, conducting a sales interview, prospecting, benefit-oriented statements, reading cues, handling objections, and closing techniques. Each of the courses includes skill practices, role playing, and video behavior models.

Training will be conducted on an ongoing basis until every team member has received the basic course. The training will be conducted centrally through the auspices of the branch training center.

In addition to basic sales skills training, sales management will develop a telephone sales training program which will provide each salesperson with a method of acquiring and developing skills in using the telephone to accomplish their goals.

Emphasis on sales management is critical to achieving our financial goals. "Effective sales management is key to the success of any calling program."[3]

Recognition of this principle has caused us to add the Sales Leadership Seminar to our training program. This program will be presented to the area marketing managers and the marketing managers during the last quarter of 1986 and first quarter of 1987. The training program, developed by the Mohr organization, includes issues such as conducting progress reviews, making joint calls, supervising a sales person, correcting poor performance, and measuring performance.

Product Knowledge
Training will be delivered on a monthly basis. Each group will receive training in products that are appropriate to their area of activity. Product knowledge training will be done by our product managers, sales management staff, and our branch trainers.

Reporting/Monitoring Systems
1. Officer call report. The changeover from a vendor reporting system to our own in-house system began in January. New interview and sales report forms were introduced in January. The form, properly completed, allows us to clearly identify and report activity as well as results on a timely basis. An interview and sales report must be completed for all meaningful sales contacts with existing or pro-spective customers, as well as when a sale is secured. It is the key document for the reporting system.

2. Monthly reports are produced that summarize each officer's activi-ties and sales results. The results are compared with goals defined in the marketing plan for the calling officer. The reports are issued by individuals, cluster divisions and the bank. Sales management will continue to monitor and refine our reporting system through-out 1987.

3. Minimum standards have been established for each sales team member. These will not change in 1987. These standards address thresholds which encourage desired behavior and results.

INCENTIVE PROGRAM
Objectives of Plan

1. Encourage and reward proactive selling.

2. Encourage and reward planned selling activities.

3. Establish a minimum level of selling activity as a threshold before incentive payments are earned.

Eligible Participants
Marketing managers, area marketing managers, consumer banking officers, and consumer banking specialists.

Payment Terms
Payments under the plan will be made when $25 or more has been earned. Eligible employees participating in the plan who are promoted, are transferred, retire, are disabled, or die will receive incentives earned, but not yet paid. Employees terminated either voluntarily or involuntarily will not be eligible to receive incentives beyond their date of termination.

Administration of Plan
The plan will be administered by a committee with representatives from Human Resources, Financial Planning, Sales Management, Sales Training, and Consumer Banking.

This committee, or a member of the committee, will have responsibility for approving all awards made under this plan. All awards may be subject to an independent review by the Audit Department. The committee can make administrative changes, clarifications or changes in minimum standards or incentive payouts when appropriate to meet the corporation's objectives.

The plan will be reviewed on a quarterly basis to ensure that the program enhances the achievement of the business objectives of Hamilton Bank.

Minimum Standards
To receive credit and subsequent payments, the following minimum standards must be met each month that an eligible sale is submitted.

1. Marketing managers
   a. Prospect or customer must be prequalified by submission of the name, no less than five days prior to an account being opened.

   b. Thirty in-person sales contacts per month.

   c. Two fact-finding presentations per month.

   d. Three fact-finding sheets completed per month.

2. Area marketing managers
   a. Prospect or customer must be pre-qualified by submission of the name, no less than five days prior to an account being opened.

   b. Twelve in person sales contacts per month.

   c. One fact-finding presentation per month.

   d. Four joint sales calls with marketing managers per month.

   e. Two fact-finding sheets completed per month.

3. Consumer banking officers/specialists (CBO/CBA)
   a. Process 25 loan applications per month.

   b. Meet the individual minimum standard for Life and A & H Insurance. This will be agreed to by employee and supervisor.

   c. Make 75 sales contacts per month.

It is not necessary for CBO/CBS to pre-qualify prospects/customers.

Eligible Accounts
The accounts eligible to earn incentives are shown in the sales incentive schedule. The incentive is earned for new money to the bank. Internal transfers from any account to new account will not be eligible.

Incentives are not paid for "walk-in" business. Only business generated by the participant's planned, direct solicitation or by referrals from the participant's network of referral sources, qualify. Accounts opened through the customer's own initiative or volition are not eligible for incentive payment. Incentive payments for loans are based on new net loan proceeds.

Incentives
A chart of the incentives that will be paid when the minimum standards have been met follows:

SALES INCENTIVES

Account Type Balance	Commission Rate	Minimum Average Monthly Balance
Individual demand	1%	500.00
Business demand	1%	1,500.00
Statement savings accounts	.75%	1,000.00
Interest checking accounts	.75%	1,000.00
Money market/liquid reserve	.25%	5,000.00
CDs ($25,000 and below)	.10%	10,000.00
CDs ($25,001 and above)	.15%	25,000.01
Cash management services	10%	Estimated annual fee

Method of Calculation

The average monthly balances from the date the account is opened and the two succeeding calendar months will be used for the calculation. Compensating balances are not eligible. To qualify, the account must be open at the time the monthly average balance is determined.

Guidelines and Definitions

1. Sales contact is defined as a discussion verbally with a prospect or customer to uncover additional needs or specifically discuss the sale of a product or service. Seminars or meetings with a group of individuals will count as one sales contact.

2. The interview reports and monthly summary forms are the basis for determining the meeting of minimum monthly standards. The interview reports should be submitted after each call, and all interview reports and monthly summaries must be received by the last working day of the month. Reports should be sent to the Sales Department.

3. To qualify, the prospect must be submitted five days prior to making a sales call. Prospects name should be submitted on a standard form to the Sales Department.

4. Relationship is defined as the sale of one or more products and/or services to members of the same family unit at a common address or to a group of employees working for the same holding company, subsidiary, or business entity. Individual financial planning or fact-finding interviews resulting from Corporate Relationships or Group Banking Sales will be treated the same as any other individual sale.

5. Payment for joint calls will be handled as follows:
   a. Two or more marketing managers, banking officers, financial services officers or retirement sales officers assisting in the sale will share the incentive equally. An equal share will be paid to those meeting their minimum monthly standard.

   b. When an area marketing manager assists a subordinate in making a sale, the subordinate will receive 100% of the incentive earned, as long as all other qualifications have been met.

   c. If an eligible participant in the plan requires the assistance of a noneligible participant of the plan to close the sale, the eligible participant will receive 100% of the incentive. Examples would be calling officers of Trust, Commercial Loan or staff support persons.

6. The services eligible for payment under the Cash Management provision are ZBA, Lock Box ARP, Compulink, and DTC.

7. The minimum standards will be reduced on a pro rata basis if an eligible employee is absent from work as a result of vacation, sickness, special assignment or training for a period of more than five working days in the calendar month. Any rounding will be rounded up. The exact number of working days will be used for the purposes of determining pro rata standards.

8. New accounts opened by existing customers of the bank coming from another institution will qualify, if the account has been pre-qualified and is the result of direct solicitation. Additional accounts opened by customers under their own volition will not qualify.

CONCLUSION

An active, well-organized, and systematic calling program can increase our profitability and penetration of target market segments. Training in sales, sales management, marketing, product knowledge, and operations need to be ongoing, with the thrust leaning toward professional, consultative selling and portfolio servicing. We have already begun to change the culture of the organization from a traditional bank to a sales bank. A structured, proactive calling program, supported by management and ongoing training, is critical to achieving our financial goals. ◆

---

[1] Hamilton Bank, *Mission/Strategic Plan* (January 1986) p. 2.

[2] Hamilton Bank Balance Sheet, 12/31/82, 12/31/83 and 12/31/84.

[3] Arthur R. Miller,*Organizing a Calling Program for Results: A Step by Step Guide*, Sales Development Assoc. Inc.

PART 4

Developing a Sales Culture

CHAPTER 9

Developing a Sales Culture
At SouthTrust Bank of Huntsville

Lonnie A. Hayes
SouthTrust Bank of Huntsville
$150 million assets

INTRODUCTION

Banking as we have known it since WW II is dead. In its place, the financial services industry has arrived. Gone is the protected regulated industry that has been banking since the Great Depression. Gone are the protected product lines that for decades have only been available through banks. Gone is the predictable management of interest margins that existed when banks' raw materials were priced in Washington, D.C. Gone is the protection from geographic expansion. In place of these components from yesterday's banking industry is a deregulated environment characterized by intense competition, shrinking profit margins and a myriad of new products. The rules have changed, or perhaps more correctly stated, are disappearing. Competition is no longer just the bank down the street or the savings and loan next door. New players have entered the game—players used to competing without the protection of the McFadden and Douglas Act, Glass-Steagall, and Regulation Q. Players like Sears, Krogers, J.C. Penney's, and General Motors have entered the game in search of the "$1.3 trillion pot of gold in household deposits" that exists in the United States.[1] Those industries that in the past bordered banking, such as insurance and brokerage services, now are virtually indistinguishable from banks in the products they can offer.

The key word in all these developments is *change*. Banking is an industry in the midst of dramatic change. Those that succeed, and possibly even those who survive this period, will be the banks who do the best job of adjusting to and managing the opportunities created by the changes.

Though change is a certainty in the banking industry, it does not have to be lethal. Once it is understood, it should be the foundation of a bank's planning and positioning.

Thomas Thompson writing in the *ABA Journal of Financial Services,* made this statement: "Taken as a whole, the consequences of deregulation, especially the intensification of competition, form the external dimensions of banking's new selling environment. They also underscore the industry's need to develop, implement, and manage a responsive selling culture."[2]

The purpose of this planning document is to organize not only the thought processes and philosophical changes necessary to become a customer-driven sales organization, but also the specific strategies and tactics that will be used to orchestrate this evolution from order taking to problem solving at SouthTrust.

SITUATION ANALYSIS
An Overview of Huntsville
Founded in 1805, Huntsville was Alabama's first state capital. By 1890 Hunstville was one of Alabama's thriving textile centers. In 1950, the late Dr. Wernher von Braun and his "German space team" came to town.

By 1960, NASA had established the Marshall Space Flight Center. The location of the space industry in Huntsville brought with it the many high-tech suppliers of that industry. Huntsville continues to be a hotbed of high-tech development with companies such as Boeing, Intergraph, Chrysler, and IBM significantly contributing to the city's industrial base.

As technology's importance to our nation has grown, so has Huntsville's population: from 16,400 in 1950 to 142,500 in 1980.[3] Recent statistics released by the Commerce Department's Bureau of Economic Analysis project that Huntsville's population will reach 230,000 by the year 2000. For the same period, per capita income is projected to increase by 43.4% from $11,359 to $16,293. National income growth is projected at 34.7% for the same fifteen-year period.[4] These positive projections make Huntsville a desirable location for growth businesses, including financial services companies looking for healthy local economies.

Huntsville's commercial/industrial future appears bright . The Chamber of Commerce has embarked on a major fund-raising campaign entitled "Huntsville 2000." The campaign's goal of $2.5 million will be used for industrial development and recruitment. The campaign is designed to help Huntsville compete with high-tech cities like Austin, Texas, and Boston, Massachusetts, for relocating growth companies.

Competition

Huntsville's healthy economy makes it an attractive market for financial services companies. There are eight banks, six savings and loan associations, fourteen finance companies, eight brokerage houses, nine credit unions, as well as Sears, Krogers, and J.C. Penney all competing for the same customers.

Of the eight banks in Huntsville, five (including SouthTrust) are part of multibank holding companies, with home offices in the state of Alabama. One bank is a limited production office established by First American National Bank of Nashville, Tennessee. The other two banks are small independent banks. Both are less than one year old and have yet to have a significant impact on the market place. Because several of the banks that are holding company affiliates have begun to blend their assets back into the holding company, an accurate analysis of market share is difficult. Statewide, Amsouth is the largest holding company with total assets of $4.1 billion dollars. SouthTrust is second in total asset size with holding company assets of $3.7 billion; followed by First Alabama, with assets of $3.5 billion; Central Bank, with assets of $3.1 billion; and Colonial Bank, with holding company assets of $681 million.[5]

Amsouth's position as the largest bank holding company in the state was further solidified in 1985 when it purchased First Gulf Corporation, a $1 billion multi-bank holding company. SouthTrust Corporation was an active bidder for First Gulf at the time of its sale. Amsouth won the bidding war because a larger portion of their offer was cash, while SouthTrust's offer hinged on exchanges of stock.

Locally, the market leader (based on total deposits reported by each bank's CEO, June 1985) is First Alabama with total deposits of $280 million. With the acquisition of First Gulf, Amsouth is second with $200 million. Central Bank reported total deposits of $160 million. SouthTrust was at $120 million; followed by Colonial Bank, with $86 million; and Citizens Independent Bank, with $12 million. Of the savings and loans only First American Federal's deposit total was disclosed. It is the largest savings and loan in the city, with total deposits of $225 million. Of the credit unions, Redstone Federal is the strongest with deposits over $250 million. Assets and/or deposits of the other financial services firms are almost impossible to determine from existing information.

As mentioned previously, **First Alabama** is the market leader in Huntsville. Its main office in Huntsville was the first bank in the state of Alabama. First Alabama has traditionally served what some might call " the blue-blood" market. This market would include the businesses of affluent families that have been in Huntsville for a number of years.

It has the oldest and largest trust department in the city. This fact, along with its location directly across from the county courthouse in large part explains the large share of the legal market it controls. First Alabama is part of a statewide holding company and has a good board of directors and senior management staff. Together with Central Bank they are probably our major adversary when competing for major commercial loan projects. First Alabama is a sound institution, with a well-managed bottom line. However, it is not aggressive in its business development efforts, probably as a result of being the market leader for so long.

Amsouth Bank of Huntsville is now operated as a branch of Amsouth Bank of Birmingham. Financials regarding their performance are difficult to assess from their corporate information. Amsouth Corporation, as a whole, has been extremely well positioned by its chairman and CEO, John Woods. As recently as eighteen months ago, Mr. Woods had Amsouth aligned to merge with Trust Company of Georgia (Sun Bank of Florida's new partner in SunTrust) had reciprocal banking become a reality between Alabama and Georgia. Fortunately (for Amsouth's competition) that arrangement dissipated when SunTrust was formed.

Locally the bank has a solid image, although it has been somewhat of a revolving door for city presidents in recent years. Amsouth has long been the market leader in serving Madison County's medical professionals. Its main office location in the center of Huntsville's medical district has contributed to success in that market. Amsouth was the first major Alabama bank to make a concentrated effort to garner the affluent market by providing a private banking area and a composite account— a Personal Financial Account. Along with other enhancements, the account offers a premium rate on a Super NOW, with unlimited checking, a line of credit priced at 1% over Amsouth's prime rate, a MasterCard Gold Card and discount Brokerage, all for a $75.00 annual fee. They have been quite successful in marketing this product to local professionals.

Colonial Bank, which was formerly The Bank of Huntsville has suffered from poor earnings the past several years. Because it was the last bank in Huntsville to be affiliated with a statewide multibank holding company, it is still suffering an identity crisis caused by their acquisition by Colonial.

Citizens Independent Bank is a year old, and while making good progress in the consumer market by stressing its independent bank status, it has been less effective in the commercial area. Its size inhibits large lending projects without the assistance of a correspondent bank.

Central Bank was the first statewide holding company in Alabama. Harry Brock, the corporation's CEO, marketed this to his advantage statewide by proclaiming that Central was "the largest bank in the state." Other bank holding companies were actually larger when the assets of their independent affiliates were totaled. Central has been the most   aggressive holding company in setting up limited production offices outside the state, primarily in Tennessee and is currently the only bank impacting the market in a significant way. Locally the bank has suffered from a vacillating style of management, one year pursuing the retail market and the next year the corporate market. They aggressively pursue new commercial business and are innovative in their statewide product development and advertising. Central recently changed presidents at the local office. Harry Brock, Jr., the CEO's son, has assumed that position. It is still too early to assess the effects of this change.

The savings and loans in town have been slow to use the drastically expanded powers that they have thanks to deregulation. As a group, they are tough competitors for consumers' time deposits. The reserve requirement differentials between banks and S & Ls allow S & Ls to price aggressively. The three largest institutions, **Alabama Federal**, **First American Federal**, and **First Southern Federal**, consistently pay higher rates on CDs than their commercial competitors. Local consumer behavior seems to indicate that people are hesitant to move their money to S & Ls because of the recent problems they have experienced.

The major brokerage firms include **Merrill Lynch**, **Robinson Humphrey**, **Shearson American Express**, **Dean Witter**, and **Thomson McKinnon Security Corporation**. No specific information was available regarding these firms' market share or penetration; however, customer comments lead us to believe that they are beginning to have a major impact locally. The "bullish" environment that the stock market has provided for the past several months has increased the traffic at the brokerage firms. Account executives, who make a living by selling products, have no inhibitions when it comes to asking clients who are buying stock to open an asset management account or to transfer their IRA. Banks have been trying to get their salaried employees to do this for years. We call it cross-selling.

Of the brokerage firms mentioned, Robinson Humphrey seems to be the strongest in stock trades and investment advice. While Merrill Lynch does not enjoy Robinson Humphrey's share of stock trades, its cash management account is still "top dog" when it comes to asset management products.

Dean Witter has two offices locally. One is housed in a Sears Financial Network office in Madison Square Mall. The mall's location west of the city was chosen in anticipation of Huntsville's future expansion in that direction. As the city continues to grow to the west, Sears will certainly be a company to contend with.

Only one credit union has a significant impact on Huntsville's financial services market. **Redstone Federal Credit Union** (R.F.C.U.) services the Redstone Arsenal's employees and their families. R.F.C.U. had assets of $268.5 million as of June 30, 1985. Because of the legislative differences that exist between operating procedures for banks and credit unions, R.F.C.U. is usually the price leader in the city. Each year we loose a number of IRAs to R.F.C.U. because of interest rates. Fortunately, these same customers often return to SouthTrust as loyal clients because they didn't like the way they were treated at the credit union.

More could be said about the competition. Suffice it to say, that South-Trust's competition is no longer restricted to other locally owned banks and savings and loans. As the battle for customers intensifies, proactive, innovative strategies must replace reactive, imitative crisis management that has plagued banking in the past.

An Overview of SouthTrust Bank of Huntsville
SouthTrust Bank of Huntsville is an affiliate of SouthTrust Corporation. The corporation is the second-largest, multi-bank holding company in the state with $3.7 billion in assets. There are twenty-two banks in the system operating 129 banking offices in 62 cities across the state of Alabama. SouthTrust Corporation employs more than 3,200 people throughout the state.[6] SouthTrust Corporation's financial strength has been obvious over the past several years. In 1984, net income reached a record high of $34.5 million, an increase of 24% over 1983. Total deposits were over $2.5 billion. Our return on average assets was a very respectable 1.12%; and return on average stockholders equity, a healthy 18.5%. SouthTrust Corporation's aggressive posture in Alabama is best epitomized by its new corporate headquarters—the SouthTrust Tower. When completed in late 1986, the building will be the tallest in the state and a testimony to SouthTrust's commitment to the state of Alabama.[7]

SouthTrust Bank (STB) of Huntsville has been an integral part of the corporation's financial success. For the past five years, STB has been ranked first or second in the holding company based on return on equity. As of June 30, 1985, STB had total assets of $141,428,000. For the past three years the bank has averaged a 1.72% return on assets and a 23.9% return on equity. In Sheshunoff's compilation of top-performing banks in the state of Alabama, based on five year average returns on average equity, SouthTrust Bank of Huntsville ranked first in its peer group ($100 million-$499 million) with an average return of 23.28%. This outstanding performance is in part attributable to Huntsville's "booming" economy. This is only part of the answer, since our competitors have enjoyed the same economy and not produced equal results. Shrewd management, tight control of noninterest expense, and an aggressive lending posture towards real estate development have been at the heart of our performance. While some might look at the words *aggressive lending posture* and assume a loss of loan quality, such has not been the case. Net credit losses in 1984 were held to .02%. Total loans past due were at 1.25% and nonperforming assets were at .44%. These figures testify to our prudent pursuit of quality credits.

The current loan mix shows that 46% ($44,669,000) of our total loan portfolio is commercial real estate, with loans to individuals a distant second at 28% ($27,208,000). Total loans on June 30, 1985, equaled $97,785,000. Thanks to the healthy economy, loan demand has been good. Intense competition for deposits from nonbanks such as Merrill Lynch has caused deposit growth to occur at a rate slower than total loan growth. Our loan-to-deposit ratio as of June 30, 1985 was an unbelievable 81%.

The deposit mix as of June 30, 1985 showed total deposits of $120,011,000 — $91,620,000 in time and savings deposits, and $28,391,000 in demand accounts. The net interest margin has remained around 6.25% through the first six months of 1985. As is the case with all banks, interest margins are continuing to shrink, making service charge income and non-interest expense priorities for senior managment.

SouthTrust Bank of Huntsville currently has five full-service branches, with two more slated to open by mid-1986. Three ATMs are strategically placed throughout the city. SouthTrust is participating in a statewide ATM network slated to begin operation in March of 1986. The network will be called ALERT and will make the number of ATMs that each bank has less important from a customer convenience standpoint. Our full service Trust department with assets of $35 million also includes an active discount brokerage department.

SouthTrust's product line is competitive. Locally, we offer six types of consumer checking accounts. Our package account, Banker's Dozen, is our best seller to consumers looking for a household account. For a $6.00 flat monthly fee, the account offers unlimited check writing privileges with no minimum balance requirement. Thirteen enhancements are packaged into the account, including free checks, discounts, and free notary service. A similar product, Silver Service, is offered to customers age fifty-five or over at no cost. We offer an array of investment options including Personal Investment Certificates (CDs) and Money Multiplier Investment Accounts (MMDAs).

As mentioned earlier, SouthTrust's financial performance can in part be tied back to our assertive loan behavior. Our commercial department has a reputation for being responsive and flexible. Our CEO is willing to involve himself as necessary to see that major projects get appropriate attention.

The price of our commercial checking account is based on account analysis. We've been very successful in obtaining small- to medium-sized business accounts due to the simplicity of the formula used to price our commercial accounts. While most banks are using a formula based on treasury bill rates, SouthTrust credits commercial accounts a flat $.30 for every hundred dollars of collected balance. Through the corporate office in Birmingham, we are able to offer cash management services to those businesses requesting them. We currently have an agreement with Control Data to provide payroll services.

Our nonbank competitors have many more innovative products than do the other commercial banks and S & Ls in the market. Products such as Merrill Lynch's Cash Management Account and sophisticated financial planning services provided by New England Life are more disturbing at this point than what the other banks are offering. To compete in the financial services industry, banks are going to have to be more creative in product development than we have been in the past.

The Marketing Department
Marketing is no longer a part-time responsibility at SouthTrust, nor is it being accomplished by someone who is pulled in several different directions, nor is it being done by two people and a part-time secretary. Marketing bank services is now viewed as a key component of SouthTrust's future success. Senior management has committed the necessary staff and funding to make marketing a key contributor to the bank's strategic direction.

While in the past, SouthTrust's marketing efforts focused on promoting and advertising the same products that all banks sold, current efforts are being directed toward the areas of product development, market research, sales training and market planning. Having the right people, selling the right products, to the right customers, at the right time, at the right price more aptly describes marketing's current goal at SouthTrust.

The budget provided to accomplish our marketing strategy has increased as marketing's role in the bank has increased. The total budget for 1985 was $129,000. In 1986, Marketing has been allocated $201,600, a 72% increase over 1985. In addition to this figure, $60,000 has been set aside for the lobby sales program and the incentive costs associated with it. Approximately $40,000 of the total budget will be invested in a statewide image campaign that will begin in January. The campaign is a follow-up to 1985's theme of "SouthTrust Bank—Working Harder for You." The message this year is "Hard Work Pays Off." Grand openings at two new branches will also be an added expense in 1986. Advertising for the year will be more closely focused on certain target markets. More direct mail and less newspaper advertising will be used.

OBJECTIVES

Simply stated "objectives define the bank's goals."[8] Since the general objective of this plan is to "map out" an action-oriented set of goals that, when followed, will change our "order-taking" culture into a sales culture, a definition of culture is in order.

In *Marketing Financial Services* the authors define culture as that which is important in an organization: "It is the chemistry of organizational history right up to yesterday: management deeds not just management words; behavior that is rewarded; projects that win approval and funding."[9] One McKinsey and Company partner, describes culture as "the way we do things around here."[10] What counts? What does management reward? Culture is in the hearts and mind of each individual; therefore, cultural change is as much destructive as it is creative. Building a new culture requires rooting out old images, not just suggesting new ones.[11] Clearly, from these comments, an organization's culture can be broken down into attitudes and actions that reflect the values of the organization. Changing anything can be difficult, but changing the attitudes and values of an organization (or industry) that have existed for decades seems almost impossible.

> Redirecting an organization's culture represents major change. It requires a determined, unwavering, systematic, yet evolutionary, process. Internal newness best comes in bite-size pieces rather than all at once. Too much change at one time can be overwhelming and breed fear. The object of a sales culture is to pave the way for a sustainable sales program, one that keeps getting better.[12]

In *Bankers Who Sell*, the authors describe a set of six characteristics, that research has shown must be present to have a true sales culture.[13]

1. Customer orientation—Sales is viewed as a way to help people; a way to serve. (Tom Peters in *Passion for Excellence* devotes a whole chapter to having "The Smell of the Customer").

2. Pervasive selling attitude—People throughout the organization should believe that sales is important to the future of the company.

3. Sense of team—A feeling of family, with group sales goals as well as individual goals.

4. Institutional pride—The attitude of "I work for the best bank, We're winners."

5. Visible top management commitment—Employees can see from senior management's actions, not just words, what is important.

6. Faith in employees—The belief by management that, given the proper tools and training, employees can sell.

SouthTrust's metamorphosis to a sales-oriented bank is to a large degree dependent on our ability to make the six aforementioned characteristics come to life on a recurring basis.

Both long-range goals and short-term goals will be addressed in this section. Each category of goals has been further subdivided into quantitative objectives and qualitative objectives. Long-range objectives outlined in this plan are to be achieved by the end of 1987. The short term goals have varying time tables.

Long-Range Quantitative Objectives
The following long-range financial objectives are easily quantifiable and thus useful. While certain intangible accomplishments are equally important, a concrete means of measurement is necessary in any organization.

Senior management expects total assets to be in excess of $200 million by the end of 1987. Considering the fact that total assets have grown from $80 million in 1982 to $150 million in 1985, the goal appears ambitious, but reachable. Through this same period, loans are expected to increase to $135 million and total deposits to $173 million. Income is projected to reach $3.1 million by the end of 1987. As assets increase, it becomes more difficult to maintain the high ratios on assets and equity that we have become accustomed to during the past few years. Our 1987 goals of a 1.7% return on assets and 21% return on equity are truly ambitious and will require a tremendous team effort in order to become a reality.

Long Range Qualitative Objectives
While many qualitative objectives can be measured, others are observable but hard to translate into numbers. These goals often deal with changing the customer's perception of the bank—the way the customer feels. As difficult as these achievements may be to measure, their contribution will be obvious. The bottom line itself will testify to their importance to the organization. SouthTrust's long range objectives include the following:

1. Differentiate ourselves from the competition through superior customer service. This is no easy task in an industry that offers a commodity product. Many will argue that it isn't possible to differentiate a product such as money in the eyes of the consumer. That may well be a true statement. The argument may be approached by asking: Is money really what banks are selling?

   Charles Revson of Revlon Inc. is famous for his statement regarding the products his company sells. Revlon stated that his factories may produce cosmetics; but in the stores, Revlon sells *hope*. For banks, good customer service can be that hope. People are hungry for good service. IBM has not been a leader in innovative new products for years, yet it remains number one. Why? Because technologically IBM is never far behind its competition and when it comes to service *no one* is ever ahead of them.[14] In order to be a leader in the market, SouthTrust must be synonymous with good service when it comes to banking in Huntsville. Good customer service is more than smiling and saying nice things. Good service is going the extra mile, "righting all wrongs," meeting the customer's need competently and courteously. Customer service is an important factor in a person's choice of a bank. The key is to get good service to work for you, rather than having bad service working against you and for your competition.

2. Permeate the organization with the concept that selling is a must, not an option. In order to survive deregulation, banks have to think of sales in the same way they think about balancing, loan losses and interest rates. It must become the norm for the entire organization. The commitment must begin with senior management and filter through the organization. The idea of selling will not succeed with management's verbal commitment and the continued reinforcement of antisales attitudes.

3. Increase the number of services sold to each customer. Cross-selling has been a buzz word of the industry for years. The logic is simple. The more services a customer obtains from a bank the less likely he or she is to sever his or her relationship with the bank.

   If selling additional services actually enhances a bank's chances of retaining a customer in a dramatic fashion, why isn't cross-selling as important to a bank as technical efficiency in tasks such as cash balancing? Ask CEOs worth their salt and they'll tell you cross-selling is crucial to the bank's success in the consumer market. Ask them how they reward those who excel at cross-selling and the answer could be silence. We plan to elevate excellent cross-selling ability to its proper place on the employee evaluation scale—near the top.

4. Design and implement a successful Newcomers program. South-Trust has been passively pursuing this market for years. The Huntsville Utilities Company reports that an average of 100 new out-of-state residents apply for utility services each month. Considering the demographics of the typical Huntsville resident alluded to in the situation analysis with regard to income, the Newcomer strategy deserves significant attention.

5. Protect our existing commercial customer base. It must be remembered that our best customers are someone else's best prospects. In

the competitive financial services industry that we are now part of, rival salespeople are continually bombarding our best customers with tempting proposals to change banks. Our goal must be to protect this profitable market segment from eroding away to our competition.

6. Generate profitable new commercial relationships. Huntsville's strong economy is an obvious attraction for businesses interested in relocating. SouthTrust's commitment to the corporate lending market makes the pursuit of new business essential. Since the commercial real estate market is a key market for our bank we expect to obtain a disproportionate share of this market.

7. Improve our professional image in our primary market area. Consumers earning $60,000 or more annually were asked in a survey to rank, in order of importance, six qualities used in selecting financial institutions. Image ranked number two on the consumer's list right behind "prior relationships." When a group of bankers were asked the same question, they ranked image last.[15] With the increased sophistication of the industry because of new products and competitors, bankers can no longer afford to be viewed as simple-minded "caretakers" of other people's money. They must project an image of being professional problem solvers, well versed on a broad cross-section of financial matters.

Short-Term Quantitative Objectives
The following short-term objectives have been established for year-end 1985. Total assets should reach $150 million. This would be a 13.8% increase over year-end assets for 1984, which were $131,700,000. Total loans are projected to reach $102 million. This figure represents a 19.8% increase over total loans at year-end 1984. Total deposits are expected to reach $131,000,000 in 1985, compared to $114,700,000 in 1984. Annual earnings are expected to exceed $2.3 million for the year. A 1.7% return on assets is anticipated in 1985, with a return on equity to exceed 22%.

Short-Term Qualitative Objectives
The short-term qualitative objectives have been subdivided into internal sales goals (within the bank) and external sales goals (outside the bank). These objectives should be achieved by the end 1985.

Internal
1. Increase the cross-sell ratio of our account representatives from 1.1 to 1.5 services per customer. The 1.1 starting point is our best estimate of our current cross-sell ratio and is in line with the national average. This ratio is obtained by dividing the number of

services sold by the number of customers served. The purpose of this objective is to increase customer retention.

2. Improve employees' customer relation skills. In a recent article in *American Banker*, it was reported the Citibank was involved in a two-and-a-half-year overhaul of the bank's customer service efforts at a cost of more than $40 million dollars. In the article, an executive from Citibank stated that their research found that people wanted "a friendly, competent, well-trained staff."[16] Like Citibank, we are convinced that good customer service equals positive customer relations.

3. Assess employees' product knowledge and improve it as needed. In an article in the *ABA Banking Journal*, Carol North states that, "building sales skills through training, without product knowledge, is like erecting an igloo on the equator - the end result will be watered down."[17] It is difficult to make people comfortable with the idea of selling if they are not provided with the knowledge needed to explain product benefits to their customers.

4. Remove "speed bumps" that inhibit sales success, such as poorly written brochures, and excessive paperwork. We cannot continue to ask customers to fill out repetitive information and sign their names six times on the same signature card and expect them to enjoy coming to the bank. If the account-opening process is painful for either the employee or the customer, the chances of the contact being a positive one is greatly diminished. Telephone interruptions in the middle of sales presentations, and product brochures that simply list features make it hard for the employee to sell and unlikely that the customer will buy. These seemingly small problems don't prevent a sale, they simply make it more difficult.

5. Begin measuring employees' sales performance. Kent Stickler coined a phrase a few years ago that has been widely adopted and used by bank marketers throughout the country. Kent says, "People do what's inspected, not what's expected." It is virtually impossible to manage people without objective data regarding their performance. We have become a nation of people who thrive on competing and winning. That requires keeping score. Measurement is not just useful for program management but also provides useful feedback to employees that can be a key to motivation.

6. Reward top sales performers with incentive compensation. For decades banks have carried the reputation of paying their employees poorly. In many cases salary increases were distributed without

any regard for employees' contributions to the bank's performance. Consequently, an average employee received basically the same wage as a top performer. What then is the motivation for top performers to continue to produce? The insurance industry realized long ago if you allowed top performers to share in the fruits of their labor, they remain motivated to produce results. Consequently if employees contribute to the company's success, they should be rewarded financially. Because of the ways that banking has changed, selling was not part of most job descriptions when many people were hired. Therfore, it is management's responsibility to impress upon employees the importance of selling, that it will be rewarded and how, and the availability of training, or the opportunity to transfer to a nonsales area where people are compensated according to different criteria.

7. Improve employee loyalty and morale through increased institutional pride. Every affiliate of SouthTrust Corporation participated in a statewide image campaign in 1985. The theme of the campaign was "SouthTrust Bank—Working Harder For You." Before this theme was adopted, a marketing committee composed of several marketing directors from around the state, affiliate CEOs, and top management from SouthTrust Corporation worked to find a characteristic of SouthTrust that set it apart from the competition. Their conclusion was that employees' pride in SouthTrust prompted them to work harder, thus the theme. In 1985, we want to continue to develop our employees' pride in SouthTrust.

8. Convert branch managers into sales managers who "coach" their staff to superior sales performance. Len Berry cites a study that was done by a life insurance company that classified its branch managers (immediate supervisors of salespeople) into two categories: half who were most effective and half who were less effective. The company then watched to see what happened to salespeople who rated "A" (most effective) on their screening tests and were sent to work under one of these managers. The results were significant. Forty-eight percent were successful salespeople under the best managers while only twenty-seven percent succeeded under the less successful managers. Recruits who graded "B" were successful twenty-seven percent under the best managers but only six percent under less effective management. Berry concludes: "The study seems to indicate that persons of indifferent abilities are as likely to succeed under a good manager as are persons of outstanding abilities under a mediocre manager. Or, to put it another way, the quality of first-line supervision has as much to do with the sales staff's success as the drive and ability they bring to the job."[18]

9. Improve employees' task clarity with regard to sales. In a project detailed in a 1980 issue of *Harvard Business Review* task clarity is described as the most critical factor in motivating sales people.

   Task clarity is the degree to which there is a clear and positive relationship between exerting effort and attaining results. If a sales task is unclear, selling can be frustrating. In such a situation, the salesperson will not be able to pinpoint the results of his or her own efforts. Good performance seems to be a random occurrence in no way related to effort. This lack of connection is discouraging and dampens the pride that might otherwise come from accomplishment. [19]

   It is essential that we improve employees' understanding of what is expected of them and give them immediate feedback when it is achieved.

External
1. Establish senior management's commitment to our outside sales effort. Nothing can be successful for long without strong commitment from people at the top. Getting loan officers and branch managers to leave busy desks to pursue additional business is virtually impossible if management's commitment is not clearly communicated throughout the organization. "Commitment is demonstrated to others through participation, goal setting and rewards. To show real commitment senior management must lead by example." [20]

2. Protect our existing customer base through improved account management. Account management is at the core of corporate relationship banking. The relationship must be one that is mutually beneficial and profitably managed to the satisfaction of both parties. Account officers will have to become more adept at selling long-term relationships, rather than individual products.

3. Make officers accountable for enhancing their portfolio of clients. Accountability must be established to get officers to accept responsibility. In a way this ties back to task clarity. Loan officers know that they are responsible for the quality of their loan portfolio. Consequently, good officers will go to great lengths to insure that the credits they put on the books are top quality. Given the same sense of accountability, expanding and enhancing their client's present relationship with the bank should elicit the same response.

4. Track outside sales results. In order to provide employees with the appropriate feedback, quantitative information is critical to manage-

ment as they make cost/benefit assessments of the outside business development efforts. A good tracking system should measure efforts expended and results obtained. The information provided by the tracking system can also be used by management to allocate the rewards to top performers. The very act of measuring some-one's performance shows management's commitment to what is being measured and therefore should be a motivator to those performing the task.

5. Establish a sales manager for the retail side of the bank (branch managers) and the corporate side (commercial lenders) to encourage calling officers, help set call objectives and make joint calls. Dick Kendall makes this observation in *Bank Marketing*:

   In the past, officer call programs have been turned over to the marketing department or to someone else in the organization who has staff rather than line responsibility. The president may be strongly behind that program, but the line managers, such as the executive vice president for lending, the senior vice president for commercial loans, etc., give only lip service to the program. Consequently the marketing officer becomes frustrated because the president is looking to him to do a job without the authority to do it. [21]

   This is exactly what has occurred at SouthTrust in past calling efforts. To be successful, the person asking the calling officer to leave his busy desk and face possible rejection must be in a position to reward that officer's effort or chastise the lack of it.

6. Reorganize the Newcomers Department to increase its effectiveness in our growing market. Because of the large number of new residents moving to Huntsville monthly and since no financial services firm has aggressively targeted this market yet, we should restructure our Newcomers strategy for greater effectiveness. Although our results have been good for the efforts expended to date, we have been unwilling to commit the necessary staffing and funding to do a thorough job. In the next year we want to become the bank that gets the referrals, or reaches the newcomers, prior to their arrival in Huntsville.

7. Improve the task clarity of our outside calling force with regard to sales. Task clarity has already been discussed in detail as it pertains to inside sales. The same principles hold true for outside sales. People have to know what is expected of them and get timely feedback when they accomplish the tasks that are expected of them.

STRATEGIES AND TACTICS
The strategy section has been divided into two broad categories: Internal Sales Strategies and External Sales Strategies. The internal strategies deal with what can be accomplished inside the bank and are primarily directed at the retail/consumer market. The external strategies address outside business development and are primarily applicable to the wholesale/ commercial market. A section is also included on our Newcomers strategy, which is focused on the consumer market.

Each strategy is first stated and explained. Immediately following each strategy are the results to date of implementing the strategy. If the strategy is yet to be implemented, a target date will be given, along with a brief description of anticipated results. Cost figures are given in the results section when applicable. Since this is a three-year plan that actually began January 1985, several short-term objectives have already been achieved.

Internal Sales Strategies
Strategy: **Implement the Financial Selling System** (F.S.S.), a lobby sales program designed to help customer-contact employees become more effective in their jobs by increasing their levels of competency, courtesy and concern when dealing with customers and/or prospects. F.S.S. was designed by the Madison Financial Consulting Group. The system is designed to make each customer contact as effective as possible. The program emphasizes that customer-contact employees can make a substantial contribution to the growth of the organization by professionally administering three specific dimensions of their jobs.

- Customer servicing. Operations—way people are serviced
- Customer relations. Courtesy—the way people are treated
- Customer development. Sales—the way people are helped to solve their financial problems

The program was purchased after a lengthy search for a total system that would allow SouthTrust to differentiate itself from its competition. The common sense theme of the program is simply treating people the way they want to be treated.

Results: The system became operational April 1, 1985. At that point, it was thoroughly explained that the principles involved in the Selling System were not part of another 90-day sales program, but rather a permanent alteration in the way SouthTrust does business. Our consulting contract with Madison is for two years. Though selling was received somewhat reluctantly at first, employees are starting to realize that it is a part of the industry in which they work. Many have accepted the idea of selling enthusiastically and have distinguished themselves with their results. The consulting fee for two years is $28,100.

Strategy: **Hold a "kick-off" rally** for all personnel at the inception of the Financial Selling System to explain its purpose and management's commitment to its success, as well as to create some excitement and enthusiasm about the new opportunities that this philosophy will create for everyone involved.

Result: A kickoff rally was held March 18, 1985. The whole evening revolved around the central theme "The World Series of Sales." Baseball bloopers were shown on a VCR as people arrived (we rented the Civic Center). The area was decorated with baseball paraphernalia. The menu included hot dogs, beer, peanuts, popcorn, and ice cream. All employees received "tickets" to the game which were later used to determine door prize winners. Team jerseys were distributed. A locker room pep talk (management commitment) was given by our general manager (CEO). The consulting group was on hand to explain the nuts and bolts of the system. The evening was a smashing success, as evidenced by the first month's sales going through the roof.

Strategy: **Implement an ongoing sales training program** that teaches employees how to match bank products with customer needs. The initial training classes last three days for new account representatives and two days for tellers. The sessions are led by the executive vice president of administration and the market director. Both attended "Train the Trainer" sessions taught by Madison Financial. The training focuses on the perfect customer interview. Asking probing questions and listening are stressed. Cross-selling and closing the sale are discussed. A SouthTrust definition of selling is given: Caring plus helping equals selling. The teller sessions are for two days and cover much of the same material in less detail. Referring or directing the customer is discussed at length. Tellers also receive a nice "diploma" and copy of "The Winning Play" for their teller windows (which they all display proudly).

Results: The training results have been positive. Vacation season, however, kept us from getting everyone trained as quickly as we would have liked. The training helped take the mystery out of what management expected. By November of 1985 we were able to get all new account representatives and tellers through the initial training. Customer comments indicate that they can see a real difference in employees' attitudes. One customer mentioned an atmosphere of helpfulness. Ongoing training is being conducted in the form of weekly meetings. This initial training revealed that our employees did not know our products, but that most were anxious to learn.

Strategy: **Train branch managers to be sales coaches**: hold sales meetings, encourage sales behavior, and improve employees' product knowledge.

Result: A four day Sales Leadership and Coaching Conference was conducted by a representative from Madison Financial for each branch manager at STB in Huntsville. The training was held prior to implementing the F.S.S. so managers would be ready to assume their new responsibilities as sales managers from the outset of the program. Our first workshop was held February 12 -15. The first two days of the workshop the managers learn many of the same things that their employees learn in their training. The last two days focus on how to conduct effective sales meeting, how to counsel employees individually, leading by example, etc. In November, we conducted our second workshop for new managers and trainees, as well as a one-day refresher for those who went through the first workshop. The managers have reacted positively to their new role as sales managers. They meet with the Program Administrator (Marketing Director) monthly to discuss problems, new formats for sales meetings, success stories etc. The cost of leadership workshops was included in our two-year contract fee.

Strategy: **Implement the F.S.S. computerized sales measurement system** to track cross-selling, sales, referrals, top performers, and products sold, by individuals, branches, regions, and the organization as a whole.

Result: The measurement system was up and running April 1, 1985. It gave us what had been missing in our prior sales programs, a way to keep score. Although we encountered difficulty in getting the tracking program set up properly, for the last several months, the reports have been available without any problem. The input document is called a Customer Introduction Card (CIC). It lists every product we intend to track. The CIC is a four-part NCR form so it will duplicate without carbon paper. The same form is used for referring or selling. The account number is recorded on the form by the employees to provide an audit trail. CICs are sent to the Marketing Department where they are entered into an IBM PC/XT. The software generates the following four reports each month for every employee in the bank.

1. Employee performance report that shows total points earned (the incentive program is discussed later), the cross-sell ratio, points year-to-date, referrals sent, and services sold.

2. Referral journal that shows every referral that was made for the month and if an account was opened.

3. Sales journal that every account an employee opened, along with opening balances and incentive values.

4. Product summary that shows every product an employee sold by product category.

The same reports are generated for each branch, region, and the organization as a whole. Management also receives a top performer report that shows how new account representatives ranked by cross-sell ratio, and number of services sold, and how tellers ranked by referrals made and referrals sold. The measurement system was included in the consulting fees. In addition, a $3,500 licensing fee is paid annually.

Strategy: **Implement an ongoing commission incentive program.**

Result: An ongoing incentive program was created and made available to every employee in the bank. After much debate about whether cash or merchandise should be used, merchandise was chosen as the incentive compensation to be used. An agreement was reached with S & H Motivation to provide a catalog from which employees could order based on points earned. Product values were established based on profitability and converted to a point total. For example, we felt an ATM card could be valued at one dollar. Our conversion ratio to change dollars (cost to the bank) to incentive points for employees is one cent equals one point. The ATM card then is worth one hundred points. Our feeling is that employees were receiving a salary for their level of production prior to the incentive program. We didn't feel they should be "paid twice" by receiving incentive compensation for salaried work.

A base was established for each branch by reviewing account openings for the past three years. Branch activity reports were used to determine how many checking accounts, CDs and installment loans, could be expected if the trend continued. Based on the value we established for each product, a base was established for each branch by multiplying the number of accounts anticipated in each category by their assigned value. The cumulative total became the branch's monthly base and represents the work they are already receiving a salary for. Accounts opened after this base has been met go into an incentive pool, to be distributed to employees at the end of the month based on their contribution to the branch's total point performance for the month.

Branch managers are paid an override based on the total sales performance of their branch. Each manager receives incentive points equal to 40% of the branch's net points over base. The program administrator receives an override of 10% of the total points over base, for the organization as a whole. Incentive costs to date (through November) are $32,000. This is in line with the $35,000 budgeted at the beginning of the year.

Strategy: **Design and produce a new product/services manual** which stresses the benefits of the bank's products.

Results: A format for the manual has been adopted and tested on the new account representatives. The manual uses the terminology used in the F.S.S.

training. Product-in-a-Nutshell (P.I.N.) statements explain the product in twenty-five words or less. One-liners convert features to benefits. The manual should be finished and distributed by January 31, 1986. By placing a manual with each employee, and by reviewing products regularly, lack of product knowledge could be eliminated as a sales barrier.

Strategy: **Rewrite the job descriptions** of all customer contact employees.

Result: This is targeted to be completed by the end of 1985. The result should be improved task clarity, which in turn will improve each employee's motivational level.

Strategy: **Rewrite product brochures** in a more customer-friendly format, stressing the benefits that the product offers the consumer.

Result: This is to be completed by the end 1986. By consolidating several brochures into two we saved money. Because the brochures' format is much simpler, employees have been more enthusiastic about using them.

Strategy: **Adopt a new signature card** that allows more than one account to be opened on a single card.

Result: Two new signature cards are now in place. The cards were designed by our parent company. Theoretically, a customer is supposed to be able to open checking and savings accounts, and apply for an ATM card with the signature cards. The card also acts as the W-9 disclosure. Because of programming problems, the signature cards still can't be used to open multiple accounts. When this "snag" is removed, the cards should make it easier to do business with SouthTrust.

Strategy: **Introduce an in-house sales bulletin** that recognizes top performers and performances.

Result: The first issue of our *Sales Update* was issued in September. The recognition provided by this newsletter turned out to be one of the best motivational devices we have. Each month we recognize the "Branch of the Month" and top performers who have special success stories to tell. We try to get the *Sales Update* out by the fifth of each month. If we're late, we start getting phone calls. Seeing your name in print is a powerful motivator.

Strategy: **Implement a quarterly "shopping" program** to assess employees' product knowledge and sales skills.

Result: We "shopped" our employees immediately following the initial training to see if they were using the skills taught in the workshops. The results were positive. The marketing assistant is in charge of kicking off the ongoing shopping program by the second quarter 1986.

External Sales Strategies—Commercial Strategies

Strategy: **Adopt the Relationship Management Program** (RMP), created by the Omega Corporation, as our formal officer call program. The RMP is designed to give officers the accountability for an assigned group of clients, on a continuing basis. In the past, officer call programs have been based on the number of calls made. A different officer may call on the same business every month. With the RMP philosophy, an account is given to an officer, who sets objectives to be reached with that client, and a time frame in which to accomplish them. Success is measured by the officer's ability to meet these objectives. Account objectives are set with the help of the officer's sales manager.

Annual salary reviews will include a look at the officer's success in meeting his objectives for each client. Has the customer increased the amount of business he does with the bank? The program places the burden of management where it belongs, with line managers rather than with a staff function such as marketing.

Result: The program has been chosen by the holding company for the lead bank, and we have followed suit. The officers who will be participating and managing the program have been trained. The calling effort is slated to kick off in the first quarter of 1985.

Strategy: **Establish the marketing director as program administrator** (P.A.).

Result: This has been accomplished. The responsibilities of this position are strictly administrative. The management function rests with line management. The P.A. and his staff receive the call reports, send out tickler reports, produce management reports, and supply prospect information.

Strategy: **Establish the CEO's commitment to the RMP philosophy** and to its success at SouthTrust, and announce his availability for joint calls.

Result: A meeting of all involved parties is planned for January 1986. This meeting will confirm that this is not another 90-day call program, that will disappear, but a component of future performance evaluations.

Strategy: **Target our top layer of commercial customers** and see that each one is assigned to a "relationship manager."

Result: This process began in May 1985 and was concluded after a tremendous amount of research in July. Approximately 250 of our best commercial clients were assigned to a "relationship manager" by August of 1985. This list of commercial clients will be modified, as needed, to reflect changes in a client's relationship with SouthTrust.

Strategy: **Position the president as the sales manager of the retail officers** and the executive vice president of lending as sales manager of the commercial officers. This positions senior line managers in a role where they are involved in evaluating the objectives set by the officers for the clients they manage and evaluating the officers' success in achieving those objectives.

Result: Both senior officers accepted their roles as sales managers in the RMP in August 1985 and voiced their commitment to help the officers that report to them set realistic, yet challenging, goals, and to assist them in achieving those goals. The intensity and longevity of these senior officers' commitment will be a key component in the program's success or failure.

Strategy: **Have relationship managers set milestone objectives** (long-range), target objectives (short-range), and cultivation levels (call frequency), for each assigned client.

Result: This process began in September and is reaching its conclusion. It is extremely time consuming since each officer must meet with his sales manager on each account. It is vital that the objectives be set thoughtfully, since the officers are in fact creating their own measurement system.

Strategy: **Adopt the computer tickler system** designed by SouthTrust Bank in Birmingham. The system acts as a database for all activity on RMP.

Result: When fully operational in April 1986, the tickler system will be the key to the RMPs administration. Call histories, and cultivation levels will be stored in the system and used to produce monthly ticklers for each officer of the calls that should be made that month. A list of calls that were not made as scheduled is also produced monthly for the officer and his sales manager.

Strategy: **Rewrite calling officers' job descriptions** to reflect their new responsibilities as relationship managers.

Results: The purpose of this strategy is to improve task clarity. It is to be accomplished by the end of 1985 so that the new job duties can be discussed in each officer's year-end review.

Strategy: **Incorporate the officer's RMP performance** into yearly review.

Result: This will first be done at the end of 1986. This information will be reviewed as part of the relationship manager's management-by- objectives interview with the sales manager.

External Sales Strategies—Consumer Strategies
Strategy: **Increase the size of the Newcomer staff** by adding one full-time employee and one part-time employee.

Result: This should be completed by January 1, 1986. Both people are already hired and are being trained. The part-time employee is a former branch manager who retired and wants to work twenty hours per week. Her background will be very helpful.

Strategy: **Call on the personnel directors of the major employers** in the area.

Result: Personnel directors are often involved in recruiting employees from outside the area. By apprising them of our commitment to new arrivals in Huntsville and by explaining the services offered through our Newcomer staff, a mutually beneficial partnership can be created. We can aid them with their recruitment, and they can supply us with leads. Our calling effort is slated to begin in March 1986.

CONCLUSION
Robert Klockars, writing in the *Mid-Continent Banker,* made this observation about the current state of affairs in the financial services industry:

> Today, banking is on the threshold of its most exciting era. Because of changes in banking regulations, and the industry's structure, the business is more competitive than ever. Only the strongest and most innovative organizations will survive, and sales are providing the momentum for today's banks to be profitable.[22]

Without question the opportunities that currently exist in our industry are cleverly disguised as insoluble problems. The key to achieving the success available is the persistent destruction of our archaic remembrances of the way it used to be. Cultural change is a tedious process, but as Admiral Hyman Rickover put it, "Good ideas and innovation must be driven into existence by courageous patience." [23] SouthTrust's transition to a sales-oriented bank may be likened to a statement Amy Gross made in her essay on courage, "One person sees a mountain as a mountain. Another takes it personally, as a thing to be climbed, or else. Awful as the climbing might be, the or-else is worse."[24] ◆

---

[1] James H. Donnelly, Jr., Leonard L. Berry and Thomas W. Thompson, *Marketing Financial Services —A Strategic Vision* (Homewood, Illinois: Dow-Jones-Irwin 1985), p. 3.

2 Thomas W. Thompson, "A Selling Bank in a Selling Culture," *ABA Journal of Personal Financial Services*, Vol. I (Spring 1985), p. 3.

3 Information and statistics provided by the Madison County Chamber of Commerce.

4 *The Huntsville Times*, December 3, 1985, Sec. A, p. 1.

5 Asset totals are rounded off and were taken from each holding company's June 30, 1985 quarterly statement.

6 Roy Gilbert, "Comments from Roy Gilbert," *SouthTrust Bank Paper*, September 1985, Vol. 5, No. 9, p. 3.

7 Taken from *SouthTrust Corporation's 1984 Annual Report*; pp. 2-3.

8 Bank Administration Institute, *A Guide to Marketing Analysis and Planning for Community Banks*, (Rolling Meadows, Illinois: 1984), p. 30.

9 Donnelly, Berry and Thompson, *Marketing Financial Services*, p. 186.

10 Raoul D. Edwards, "The Changing Culture of Marketing," *United States Banker*, November 1985, p. 13.

11 Leonard L. Berry, Charles M. Futrell, and Michael R. Bowers, *Bankers Who Sell: Improving Selling Effectiveness In Banking*, (Homewood, Illinois: Dow Jones-Irwin 1985), p. 41.

12 Ibid., p. 42.

13 Ibid., p. 35-41.

14 Thomas J. Peters and Robert H. Waterman, Jr., *In Search of Excellence: Lessons from America's Best-Run Companies*, (New York: Harper & Row, Publishers 1982), p. 157.

15 Barbara Mantel, "Banks Seek the Needs of the Hands that Feed," *The American Banker* (November 8 ,1985), pp. 16,17.

16 Laura Gross, "Banks are Making a Vigorous Play To Satisfy Customers," *The American Banker* (November 8, 1985), p. 39.

17 Carol Fleming North, "Don't Spend a Dime on Sales Training Unless...," *ABA Banking Journal* (Vol. 76, No.9), September 1984, p. 50.

18 Berry, Futrell and Bowers, *Bankers Who Sell*, pp. 131,132.

19 Stephen X. Doyle and Benson P. Shapiro, "What Counts Most in Motivating Your Sales Force?"*Harvard Business Review* (Vol. 58, No.3), May-June 1980, pp. 135, 136.

20 Laird Landon, "Four Keys to Successful Commercial Business Development," *Bank Marketing* (December 1985), p. 12.

[21] Dick Kendall, "Turning Line Managers into Sales Managers", *Bank Marketing* (December 1984), p. 10.

[22] Robert W. Klockars, "Don't ask me...I wasn't hired to sell!," *Mid-Continent Banker*, Southern Ed. (April 1985), p. 7.

[23] Tom Peters and Nancy Austin, *A Passion for Excellence* (New York: Random House, 1985) p. 415.

[24] Ibid.

CHAPTER 10

Cultivating a Sales Culture

Lynn M. Banks
Household Bank
$330 million assets

INTRODUCTION

How can a company ensure its continued growth? By changing existing attitudes and taking advantage of growth opportunities. To do this, "bankers must recognize that they must sell—that they must go after the business, not just wait for it. Deregulation, intense competition, profit pressures, and a changing product line, among other influences, demand no less. Recognizing the need to sell is not enough but must be translated into action."[1] It is essential to the industry's future that banks cultivate a "sales culture" by becoming customer/market oriented, as opposed to product/operations oriented.

This marketing plan is based on the development and implementation of an action plan that will shift Household Bank from a product-driven institution to a true marketing- and sales-driven facility. While we have begun to shift toward this "sales culture," the few programs we have only begin to scratch the surface. "Public relations and effective advertising programs are no longer sufficient in bringing new customers to the bank. Marketing and sales, often disparaged by the industry, are necessary." The preceding quote from Kent D. Stickler sets the stage for a step-by-step implementation of a bank-wide sales orientation program.

Although Household Bank is currently riding a wave of growth enthusiasm, it nevertheless faces the possibilities of decline. We have reached a level of maturity in the bank's lifecycle that gives us a feeling of euphoria. The maturity stage does not last forever. It ultimately moves into a declining mode that leads to termination if nothing is done to reverse the process. Implementing a sales culture at Household Bank is the best method of combating decline. Becoming a sales bank is a way of lifting Household Bank out of the maturity stage and reintroducing employees and customers to a growth-oriented institution.

SITUATION ANALYSIS
Environment and Trends
In the material that follows, market information is presented for the three counties we currently service. All information was obtained from research completed by the Employment Data and Research Division of the Development Department of Monterey, Santa Cruz, and Santa Clara counties.

Monterey County
Industry—Occupation Overview
Monterey County experienced moderate job growth between December, 1984 and December, 1986. The unemployment rate dropped sharply in 1984 and 1985, and stabilized except for seasonal fluctuations in 1986. More than 40 percent of all new jobs should occur in retail trade and services. These two industry groups account for 40 percent of all the jobs in the county and are very important to the local economy.

Area Profile
Monterey County is situated on the California coast, 106 miles south of San Fransisco, and 241 miles north of Los Angeles. The county covers 3,324 square miles. Salinas, the county's government center and largest city, serves as the industrial, commercial, and residential hub of the Valley. It has also become a regional trade center for the central coast counties.

The Monterey Peninsula and other coastal areas of the county have long been a recreational site for vacationers and tourists. County growth is also attributable to the development and expansion of Fort Ord Army Installation. This complex, where approximately 23,000 individuals are on active duty, has played a major role in shaping the county's economy.

Population
Between 1980 and 1984 (the date of the last quantifiable statistics), the population of Monterey County increased by 29,000 to 319,700. During that period, approximately one out of three new residents came from net in-migration (more people moving in than moving out), and two out of three came from natural increase (the difference between births and deaths).

Labor Force
Monterey County's employment rate should expand in the future with over 7,500 more residents at work . This growth, however, will not affect the unemployment rate since the labor force will increase more than employment.

Job growth is being experienced in three major industry divisions:

- Retail trade: Creating 2,100 new jobs with the largest component being in restaurants and bars.

- Services: One out of five new jobs will be in services, with tourist and business services dominating the growth.

- Manufacturing: Both sectors of manufacturing will demonstrate vigorous growth. Nondurable goods manufacturing will add 700 jobs, and durable goods 1,000 jobs.

Santa Cruz County
Industry—Occupation Overview
The unemployment rate in Santa Cruz County should register small reductions in the next two years. The unemployment rate should decrease from 8.4% to 8.0%, but the economy should expand by 6,900 new jobs. While new jobs will be an important source of employment opportunities, most openings will result from replacing personnel in already existing jobs. About one out of every five new jobs will be in durable goods manufacturing, mostly in the electronics industry.

Area Profile
The Santa Cruz Metropolitan Area comprises all of Santa Cruz County, the second smallest county in California in terms of size (439 square miles). A spectacular coastline, accessible beaches, and forested mountains all in proximity to several Northern California Metropolitan areas, make Santa Cruz an important vacation and recreational area. The southern portion of the county is a productive agricultural district with agricultural-related manufacturing—food canning and freezing.

Population
Santa Cruz County's population increased by 3.7% between 1984 and 1985, a growth rate well above the 2.2 percent rate posted for the state as a whole. This gain was atypically large for the county. The Department of Finance attributes 25% of the increase to natural increase and 75% to in-migration.

Labor Force
Santa Cruz County's employment should expand about 4% per year through 1987, increasing the unemployment rate of 8.0% by the end of 1987. Santa Cruz County should show an increase of 6,900 jobs through 1987 with manufacturing, retail trade and services showing the largest increases.

Santa Clara County
Industry—Occupational Overview
Santa Clara County should resume a steady pace of job growth. The unemployment rate which rose in 1985, is expected to drop below 5% in 1987. The

county's economy should add 53,200 jobs, mostly in professional/techni-
cal, production/maintenance and clerical positions. Growth in all three
areas is spurred by the rebound of high technology industries. The 53,200
new jobs can also be viewed from an industry perspective. A large increase
will occur in manufacturing, reflecting the growth of electronic firms. Other
large increases will be in business services and wholesale trade.

Area Profile
Santa Clara County is located below the southern point of San Fransisco Bay
and covers a total area of 1,300 square miles. Mountain ranges divide the
area into what is termed North County and South County. South County is
mainly agricultural, while North County, commonly referred to as "Silicon
Valley", is densely populated and heavily industrialized. North County
contains thirteen cities while South County has two cities.

Population
The population of Santa Clara reached an estimated 1,400,100 in July 1985,
an increase of over 105,000 from 1980. The five-year rise of 8.1% was
significantly lower than the statewide gain of 11.4% and contributed to the
slow rate of growth recorded in the Bay Area—the lowest regional growth
rate in the state.

Growth in the county is expected to continue to be less rapid in the 1980s
than during the last decade and will contribute to slower labor force growth.
There has also been a substantial drop in the numbers of persons under
sixteen years of age. During the 1970s this age group grew rapidly because
of the entrance of the postwar baby-boom generation's children.

Labor Force
The unemployment rate in Santa Clara County should decline in 1987, as
the local economic climate improves. Employment should expand by
nearly 43,000 jobs, and unemployment should fall by nearly 4,000, or a rate
of 5%.

Santa Clara County should add over 50,000 jobs through 1987. This follows
a few years in which the county lost 1,300 jobs and suffered one of its worst
periods of layoffs in the electronics industry. The county is expected to add
jobs at an annual rate of 3.3%. Only two industries are expected to register
declines during 1987—agriculture, one of the smallest employment divisions, will continue its decline, as will the construction industry.

The Total Market Area
The Central California Coast and Santa Clara County contains many dispa-
rate elements that make it difficult to define one market area. The business/
agriculture environment of one area is very different from the military/

tourist area of the Monterey Peninsula. These markets differ still from Metropolitan San Jose, which services the upscale socioeconomic population of Silicon Valley. Thus, each county we service is viewed as a separate entity. Household Bank's main customer base is in Monterey County. Therefore, our marketing programs, products, and services tend to parallel the requirements of the typical Monterey County resident.

There is no statistical information available at the bank or county level that pinpoints the characteristics of the economy or residents of Monterey County. The widely held assumption on the peninsula is that the wealth is held by a limited number of people who have a major interest in the agricultural network of Salinas Valley and the retired community of the Monterey Peninsula. This has been the assumption under which most organizations have operated for years, banks included. Without research to back up these contentions, it is difficult to present a clear picture of our market area. Serving this cross-section of population with a limited perspective of the marketplace places limits on the success we can expect to achieve.

Competitive Analysis
The competition was analyzed in the three counties that Household Bank currently serves. Each county was surveyed separately to show the variances occuring in Household Bank's market penetration in each area. The following information was obtained from the 1986 Findley Reports:

Monterey County (Salinas, Monterey, Pacific Grove only)
Commercial Banks: The four largest commercial banks hold over 72% of the total bank deposits. Household Bank ranks fourth with 9%.

• Bank of America	$299,082,000
• Wells Fargo Bank	$247,751,000
• Crocker National Bank	$101,005,000
• Household Bank	$ 96,000,000

Savings & Loans: The five largest savings and loans hold over 79% of the total deposits. Household Bank ranks fifth with 9%.

• Great Western Savings	$322,797,000
• Coast Savings & Loan	$178,193,000
• World Savings	$113,405,000
• American Savings & Loan	$111,436,000
• Household Bank	$ 96,000,000

Santa Cruz County (Watsonville, Freedom, Gilroy)
Commercial Banks: The five largest commercial banks hold over 94% of the total bank deposits. Household Bank ranks third with over 10%.

• Wells Fargo Bank	$159,198,000
• Bank of America	$ 85,441,000
• Sumitomo Bank	$ 28,560,000
• Pajaro Valley Bank	$ 27,346,000
• Household Bank	$ 40,081,000

Savings & Loans: The three largest savings and loans hold over 79% of the total deposits. Household Bank ranks third with 17%.

• Watsonville Federal	$78,968,000
• Great Western Savings	$54,590,000
• Household Bank	$40,081,000

Santa Clara County (San Jose, Los Gatos)
Commercial Banks: The five largest commercial banks hold over 70% of the total bank deposits. Household Bank ranks 25th with 0.2%.

• Bank of America	$1,329,815,000
• Wells Fargo Bank	$ 867,000,000
• Bank of the West	$ 467,964,000
• Pacific Valley Bank	$ 313,656,000
• Crocker National Bank	$ 293,785,000

Savings & Loans: The five largest savings and loans hold over 60% of the total deposits. Household Bank ranks 26th with 0.3%.

• American Savings	$ 846,016,000
• Great Western Savings	$ 350,671,000
• Sears Savings Bank	$ 259,546,000
• Home Savings of America	$ 259,117,000
• 1st Nationwide	$ 191,551,000

Market Trends
Competition from savings and loan associations is on the rise. They are becoming more involved and more creative in the area of demand deposits, as well as making aggressive moves in the consumer loan market. Total deposits for the twenty-six savings and loans total $4,428,831,000.

Competition from other financial service providers, such as credit unions are not of any real concern at this time. There are thirty-three institutions of this type with shared savings totaling $1,014,558,000.

Market Analysis
Total deposits for the commercial banks and savings and loans in the area that we service total $10,505,029,000. The four largest institutions hold over 45% of the total bank deposits. Household Bank's share is only 1%.

The two largest banks (Bank of America and Wells Fargo Bank) are market leaders in every major geographic segment in the state. Both are very aggressive in consumer services, as well as in corporate and international lending.

Internal Analysis of Household Bank—General Background

Valley National Bank (VNB), as it was called upon its inception on July 1, 1964, was the first new independent bank in Monterey County in fifty-seven years. This marked the return of community-owned banking to the area. In 1977, the assets of VNB reached over $80 million with the introduction of new services that catered to Senior Citizens and the credit card sector. In 1980, the face of banking changed forever when legislation passed that phased out Regulation Q and that allowed banks and savings and loans to pay the same rate on savings accounts. On January 1, 1981, VNB introduced its NOW Account and assets climbed to over $100 million.

The second half of 1981 brought the biggest event in the history of VNB. On July 1, Household Finance Corporation made an offer to purchase the bank. The purchase was finalized in the third quarter, making VNB a subsidiary of Household International. Even with this major change, VNB remained committed to the basic goal of serving its local communities. Since the acquisition, VNB has become one of the most progressive and successful banking operations in its service area. In late 1983 and early 1984, four branches were opened under the name of Household Bank in a new service area—Santa Clara County. This brought the branch network to eleven. In July, 1986, VNB joined the fifty-seven national branch network of Household Bank and thus changed its name. This new name identifies the bank as a part of the growing nationwide consumer bank which boasts branches in six states. During this two-month conversion period, the branches increased $20 million in deposits. The major task ahead for Household Bank is gradually conforming to the philosophy of corporate headquarters and the building of a reputation as "America's Family Bank."

Bank Resources

Household Bank is part of a six-state, fifty-three bank holding company, under the financial division of Household International. Total assets for the financial division (Household Financial Services) are $8.2 billion. Household Bank's (central California) internal resources include:

1. Eleven branches serving seven communities:
   - Monterey County—5 branches
   - Santa Cruz County—2 branches
   - Santa Clara County—4 branches

2. Employees:
   - Administrative officers—26

- Administrative non-officers—104
- Branch officers—32
- Branch non-officers—124

3. Deposits (as of September, 1986)

• Demand	$ 16,835,067
• IBA	65,296,033
• Savings (Reg. Term)	17,463,317
• Time	195,550,547
• IRAs	9,500,592
• Other	24,946,583
Total	$329,592,139

4. Loans (as of September, 1986)

• Commercial	$ 4,120,256
• Real estate	24,993,139
• Installment (w/o credit card)	13,185,002
• Credit lines	18,090,038
• Miscellaneous	191,636,327
Total	$252,024,762

BANK OBJECTIVES FOR 1987

Household Bank hopes to achieve the following four objectives in 1987:

1. Enhance and solidify the Household Bank name in all market areas
   - Create high visibility through community involvement.
   - Advertise aggressively to establish a new identity.
   - Position the bank as a retail/consumer, full-service bank.
   - Overcome resistance to the "nonlocal" perception of the Household Bank name.
   - Re-create positive image of "local," concerned, community bank.

2. Increase present market share of consumer loans and deposits
   - Consolidate the product line to position the bank more closely to the holding company's concept.
   - Assist the branch system to retain current customers and attract new customers by developing a product mix and customer service philosophy which is profitable, competitive, and meets the demands of the consumer.
   - Stimulate full-service relationships.
   - Assist senior management to identify, develop and service key markets.

- Decrease the number of lost accounts by training point-of-sale employees in product knowledge and customer relations.

- Assist the branch system in the sale of financial services by providing sales training, monitoring systems and reporting.

- Increase the combined cross-sell ratio to 3.0.

- Add to the bank's profitability by developing research to determine customer profile, market dynamics and competition.

3. Increase mortgage lending activity to become a primary lender on the central coast
   - Substantially increase awareness of Household Bank's commitment to mortgage lending.

   - Expand the loan delivery system in the present market and extend into the San Jose market.

   - Enhance the loan delivery system with faster commitments and closing times.

4. Improve the bank's total growth
   - Increase mortgage loan originations by $60 million.

   - Increase customer deposits by $40 million.

   - Increase our loan portfolio by $20 million.

   - Achieve overall pretax profit of $4 million for 1987.

STRENGTHS/WEAKNESSES
Strengths

- A strong "local community oriented" bank image

- An aggressive posture in all markets

- A strong consumer deposit base

- A healthy loan portfolio

- A competitive retail lender

- Heavy community involvement

- Extended hours, including after-hours and Saturday service

- Holding company resources

- A perfectly balanced teller program

- Sales monitoring system for customer service representatives

Weaknesses

- Inadequate ATM service

- Small mortgage loan base and a low profile in the real estate market

- Diminished community awareness due to name change

- Inadequate customer information file or software for relationship profiling

- Weak sales orientation/training for staff

- Absence of an effective, controlled officer call program

- Poor cross-selling of products and services

- No formal sales objectives

- Limited use of market research

STRATEGY AND STRUCTURE
Why Do We Need To Sell?

Most people who work in banks were not hired to be a part of the sales process. They were hired to fulfill a more technical function, that is, open accounts, process loans, take deposits, and complete all the paperwork necessary for the smooth running of customer accounts. Generally speaking, this "reactive" handling of customers and their accounts was comfortable for all parties—the customer, the bank and the staff.

Because banking was a closely regulated industry, passive behavior reaped rewards. Banking's ability to make a profit was protected by the government. It enjoyed geographic protection from other banks; product protection from potential competitors; and regulated cost of raw material (money). Thus, profit margins were relatively easy to maintain. [2]

Then came the beginning of deregulation. Suddenly, brokers, money market funds, insurance companies, department store chains and a host of others started showing bank customers alternatives to using a bank. Many people believed those alternatives were better. The banking industry was surprised and worried. Competitors had their fingers on the financial pulse of the American people and they actively began campaigning to educate the public on the "better" alternatives to banking.

Today, bankers can no longer afford to be order takers. We must assume the initiative, identify prospects, uncover needs, and then satisfy those needs. Order taking is a thing of the past, professional selling is *the* thing of the future.

Building the Sales Culture

Our task is to convert bank personnel, most of whom have never before held a "sales" position and who may have entered the banking profession precisely to avoid such a position, into capable, professional, motivated sales people. The following six characteristics, from *Bankers Who Sell*, must be present in a true sales culture.[3]

Customer Orientation

Banks with the strongest sales cultures, view sales as a way to satisfy customer needs or as a way to serve. We have made strides in instilling this thinking into our platform employees; however, we have given them neither the opportunity nor the inclination to "put the customer first." The customer service representatives (CSRs) are currently responsible for too many other duties to really be 100% responsive to the customer.

Persuasive Selling Attitude

The attitude that selling is both legitimate and important should permeate the entire institution. Even though the employees of Household Bank agree that there is a need to sell, it will be the job of this plan to give the employees the tools and the motivation to go after business instead of waiting for it.

Sense of Team

The only characteristic of a sales culture that Household Bank lacks is the cultivation of the team concept. The CSRs sales efforts are tracked individually but there is no emphasis on "team sales goals." The sales strategies discussed later will lay the groundwork for monthly sales meetings, public recognition of top sales' performers, peer pressure, and, in general, tactics designed to foster the sense of team.

Institutional Pride

It is apparent that Household Bank's administration has made several attempts to strengthen employee pride. These sporadic attempts at reinforcing employee attitudes toward the bank, however, must be deeply rooted and performed on a continuous basis. The marketing plan will provide an ongoing program designed to instill institutional pride in the sales force of the bank. The employees in turn will be more inclined to sell the bank and to sell for the bank, not just to sell for themselves.

Visible Top Management Commitment

Even if top management believes that it has a real commitment to selling, the question is: Do the employees believe that top management's commitment to selling is real? This marketing plan will establish criteria for top-level executives to set a sales example through their own behavior by making sales calls themselves, by assisting on calls, and by insisting on sales performance as a criterion for the advancement of customer contact employees. In general, "Management must bite the bullet and make necessary invest-ments for the sales program to have 'teeth.' "[4]

Faith in Employees
The final characteristic of a sales culture is that top management has a faith in the ability and willingness of its existing employees to sell.

Defining the Sales Task
The Sales Department
It is clearly important that we develop a total sales program that will enable us to maintain contact with our customers and to cultivate new business from existing customers, as well as qualified prospects. Our customers will be viewed as "clients," and the focus must be on the attraction, retention and enhancement of total client relationships. We must strive to change single-service customers into multiservice customers, and transform indifferent clients into loyal clients.

To meet this challenge, a Sales Department will be developed to pursue four primary objectives: implementation of an officer call program, develop-ment of a full-time outside sales force, sales training, and implementation and maintenance of sales incentive programs.

Tasks, Goals, and Measurement
It is important to define the special selling tasks and goals of customer contact personnel so they know what they are supposed to do. Without goals, participants in the selling program will flounder. Customer contact personnel should be able to arrive at workable goals by following these rules:

- Goals will be written down to serve as visual reminders.
- Goals will be developed from a positive perspective.
- Goals will be something the contact personnel want to do—not something they think they should do.
- Goals will be specific.
- Goals will motivate the platform personnel to work harder than in the past.
- Goals must be realistic.

Program Development
The Officer Call Program: The program must work to establish a consult-ing relationship with the bank's customers and prospects. This relationship will allow for long-term maintenance and growth on the commercial side of the bank, and will increase the deposit base and profitability.

The first six months of the program should lay the groundwork for a successful sales program. The initial Officer Call Program will involve all branch officers, lending officers, and various operational officers throughout the Bank. The entire program will be coordinated and housed in the newly developed Sales Department, which will provide support for the Officer Call Program.

The following areas of the Officer Call Program must be individually addressed:

The Client List: The classification scheme will be based on potential deposit size, which will remain consistent with the operating goals of the bank. Current accounts will be structured in a pyramid shape, with the most important accounts at the top. These key accounts will be about 5% to 8% of the total number of accounts. The next 8% to 10% of the accounts will be classified as "A" accounts. The remaining accounts, accounting for the bulk of our current accounts, can be further divided into "B" and '"C" accounts.

Since funds retention and new money are the mainstays of the bank's performance, one important goal of this program has to be the generation of new money. Prospective customers will be classified according to their potential to generate deposits and fee income and by their level of satisfaction with their current financial services provider.

Effort Allocation: Since officers have limited time available for calls, it is important to discover the amount of call time or "what is left over after the other demands on the officers' time are met."[5] Once the number of call hours that are available from the average call officer in the bank is calculated, the number of calling officers required to properly service the account portfolio and prospects can also be calculated.

Below is the method we plan to use to calculate the most efficient use of calling officers' time:

- (1 hour per call per customer) x (number of customers) +
  (45 minutes per call per prospect) x (number of prospects)
  = numbers of calling hours required

- (3 hours of call time per day) x (5 days per week)
  x (48 working weeks per year)
  = 720 call hours per officer per year

- (Number of calling hours required) divided by (720 calls per call officer per year) = number of calling officers required

The implication of this strategy is that accounts generate calling officers.

Client Files: All clients appearing on the calling list will have an information file in the Sales Department. These files will contain the following information:

- Customer/Noncustomer Information Card: This card will contain the client's name, address, telephone number, name of primary contact, names of all corporate officers/presidents, and name of closest Household branch. There is also space to log all calls, as well as to name the Calling Officer who made each call.

- Credit Report: This will be the most recent report defining the nature of the business, area served, number of employees, names of primary and secondary financial institutions.

- Current CIF Printout: This will provide information on current customers regarding prime contact, types of accounts being utilized, and account balances.

- Analysis of Client's Corporate Checking Account: This will depict by month the average daily balance, activity charges, overdrafts, and service charges.

- Copies of Prior Sales Reports: This will inform the calling officer regarding previous calls.

- Media Clippings: This will present timely information regarding the client or the industry as a whole.

Calling Assignments: All assignments will be made by the Sales Department's sales manager with input from senior management. Calling officers may request certain assignments.

Call Procedures:

- All calling officers will be given a "control card" for each assigned client at the beginning of each month. Each officer is responsible for scheduling at least two calls on each assigned client in a year's time, unless additional calls are required. All control cards are returned to the sales office and placed on a tickler file for future scheduling.

- File analysis: The Sales Department will pull the files for the clients to be contacted the following month. (For example, the files for March clients are pulled and updated in February.) At that time, the client information files will be updated and a "Call Recommendation Form" filled out. This form will list all the accounts that the client has with the bank, as well as specific items the calling officer may want to highlight, such as closed accounts, balance fluctuations, and maturity dates.

- Department memo: The month prior to the client call, the Sales Department will compile a list of customers and potential customers who are scheduled to be seen the following month. Each department head will review the list and notify the Sales Department of anything the calling officer should be aware of. This procedure should provide all calling officers with pertinent, timely client information.

- Sales Report form: A Sales Report form will be completed for all client calls. The report will be in duplicate form so copies may be distributed to the president, branch administration, marketing, and calling officers, as well as a copy for the client file.

- Progress reports: The Sales Department will prepare quarterly progress reports on each officer. These reports will be reviewed by the Marketing Department and senior management.

Business Development Officers
The current full-time outside sales force will also be expected to follow the procedures of the Officer Calling Program as it pertains to their full-time sales requirements. They will also report to the Sales Manager.

Sales Call Standards
If all calling officers are to be evaluated on the same basis, it is necessary to develop standards that promote fair evaluation.

- The calling officer will receive credit for obtaining a new customer and credit for all services sold if they are a direct result of a sales effort. The sales call that led to the new customer must be documented. All the services presented and the opening amounts of all services sold must be shown on the sales report.

- Calling officers will not receive credit for selling services to a new unsolicited "walk-in." The credit for walk-ins will be given to CSRs.

- Officers will receive extra credit for sales calls that were a direct result of a referral from a client.

- Credit will be given for unsolicited walk-ins only if the calling officer has been unable to schedule an appointment with the client. This must be documented on the Sales Report Form to receive credit.

- Credit will be given for solicited walk-ins if they are sufficiently documented on the Sales Report form.

- Credit will be given for a cold call only when account relationships or products were discussed.

- If it takes more than one call to obtain the business, credit will be given for one call only.

- Credit will be given to selling officers for new business only. Line increases and renewals will not qualify.

- All questionable new business will be reviewed at weekly sales meetings.

Sales Department Objectives

- Promote the relationship banking concept.

- Support and maintain the Officer Call Program.

- Assign our most-valued clients an "account manager" to act as their personal banker.

- Each account manager will be responsible for retaining and enhancing the accounts of assigned clients.

- Evaluate calling officer's performance on a quarterly basis, against set objectives.

- Conduct weekly sales meetings with all sales staff, including CSRs in an effort to educate and motivate them.

- Nurture relationships with area Realtors to aid in meeting the corporate growth goal for mortgage lending.

- Insure that all clients on the call lists receive adequate attention.

- Provide calling officers with accurate and timely information.

- Increase employee involvement in community activities.

- Develop and acquire sales support material for the Officer Call Program.

- Develop an in-house lead program to acquire new business.

- Develop the sales-bank concept throughout the bank.

- Incorporate the team concept.

- Implement a CSR cross-sell incentive program.

- Acquire and institute a sales training program from an outside source and continue training officers on a regular basis.

- Train noncustomer contact employees in sales support techniques.

- Regularly inspect and monitor the sales efforts of all customer contact personnel—employee shopping program.

- Monitor and maintain an automated sales support system.

- Develop and plan educational seminars that will be targeted toward our customer base.

Having the Right People Sell

Certain steps should be implemented to obtain and maintain a successful sales staff:

- The Sales Department will forecast overall manpower needed to achieve the goals set by the bank's administration. The department will determine these requirements by examining the environment, sales force objectives, and the bank's strategic plans.

- All job descriptions of customer contact personnel will be rewritten to establish what the sales people will do and why these specific duties are to be performed. The job description should leave no doubt that the job is a "sales" position.

- All present and new employees will take part in a personality profile that measures background, aptitudes, and personality traits relevant to the job. This type of profiling will be used to determine whether an employee or prospective employee meets the personal behavior criteria for sales or customer contact positions at Household Bank.

- The following rules should be applied when screening an applicant for a sales position:

Select for initiative and perseverance. Salespeople have to be self-starters since they often work largely on their own.

Insist on reliability. A salesperson must be reliable because the bank will have to trust him or her to perform the job functions.

Look for the ability to take punishment. Make sure that salespersons are able to stand up to punishment from other employees, superiors, and potential customers.

Don't pick only for selling skills. If an experienced salesperson is hired, make sure their skills are right for our bank. If an inexperienced person is considered, make sure they are trainable.

Don't pick for control of accounts. Do not hire salespeople from competitors on the theory they will bring business with them.

Don't pick only for wide acquaintance. Do not hire just because they are widely known among potential customers.

Don't expect the impossible: Even the best salesperson is only human.

If customer contact personnel do not have above-average production or performance, or achieve the prescribed performance goals after a reasonable period of time, they should be replaced or reassigned.

Preparing People To Sell

A well-trained staff is essential for attracting clients and for nurturing client relationships. Selling requires new skills, discipline and dedication. Learning how to sell is no less demanding than learning any other skill.

Sales training is ongoing and includes product knowledge, the role of sales, customer analysis, and competitive and environmental analysis. The degree of success a person may realize is dependent on how well each of these areas are addressed.

In January 1986, Household Bank developed a Training Department that was responsible for administering all training programs to customer contact personnel. All management and platform personnel who have selling responsibilities are involved in ongoing training programs that emphasize product knowledge and that attempt to provide practical experience in the basic selling techniques.

We believe it is critical for our officers and platform employees to both understand and believe in the services they are asked to sell. The "Product Knowledge Handbook" is a new tool that is currently used by the Training Department. The handbook's product profiles provide Household Bank personnel with up-to-date information on all bank products and services, such as who qualifies, the products' features and benefits, and possible cross-sell opportunities.

As important as product knowledge is learning the appropriate means of communicating that knowledge and of closing a sale. Employees are receiving adequate information on current products, but they also need professional sales training. "Sales knowledge without sales skills will mean far fewer sales than sales knowledge coupled with sales skills."[6]

Some guidelines for developing sales knowledge and introducing a sales skills development program are given below:

- The skills development program must be designed to fulfill actual needs. We propose surveys of contact personnel to identify areas in which employees would most like to improve. Product knowledge tests will be used that indicate product categories where sales people need assistance. Shopping studies will assess employees' on-the-job sales skills. This data will help reveal weaknesses to be addressed in the program and will provide criteria by which we assess the program's progress.

- Institute an outside sales program to use in conjunction with in-house training. There are numerous sales training packages available to financial institutions to aid them in developing an outside sales effort. Available training packages will be investigated and a suitable package will be chosen—one that will contribute to the bank's overall sales and marketing objectives. This will help produce the kind of professional, motivated sales force that is required. As part of the contract, Household Bank's current training officer will be trained and certified to continue the ongoing training of the employees. Sales training will be a visible, ongoing activity and will rank closely behind monetary commissions in expense. The success of our transition to a sales-oriented bank will rest on a firm foundation of training.

- Salespeople must be allowed the freedom to develop their own selling style. The Training Department will expose all platform employees to various selling approaches and techniques and will allow them to use these techniques in their own ways.

Facilitating The Selling Process
The Marketing Department, acting as a facilitator and governing body of the "sales culture" effort, will have a major role in developing the selling process throughout the bank. Facilitating this selling effort at Household Bank will call for additions and alterations to three major areas:

Organizational Structure
The bank's sales force will be reorganized to provide an effective working relationship between the sales force, the Marketing Department, and the other departments in the bank. To allow for open communication among the sales force, marketing and other groups in the organization, a sales manager position should been created. The sales manager will be responsible for the eleven branch network.

The CSR sales coordinator will actually be the sales manager of the CSRs in the system. This person will be responsible for working with the training officer to insure continuity in the training system, to conduct product testing, and to act as an all-around sounding board when the CSRs have a problem or need a question answered.

Internal Technology
Improved technology is a key improvement we must make to facilitate the selling process. In 1987, computer programs which will enhance customer sales and service as well as internal sales tracking/monitoring will be developed and implemented. When this system is completed, the bank will be able to eliminate unnecessary paperwork, to reduce costs and to increase its cross-sell ratios.

Wide Scale Use of Personal Selling Aids
Household Bank currently provides its platform employees with useful tools, such as product knowledge handbooks, flip charts, and an array of quality sales brochures. We must, however, develop other programs to make it easier for our people to sell, such as:

- A sales referral system

- A senior executive call program

- Planning forms and procedures for sales calls

- Increased internal correspondence

Rewarding the Selling Performance
The design and implementation of an effective sales reward system deserves systematic attention. A three-pronged approach will be used— direct financial awards, career advancement, and personal recognition. The following is a summary of the sales incentive program for customer service representatives and all calling officers:

- Officers meeting the quota of calls per quarter (three calls per week) are eligible for commission dollars earned through sales points.

- All products/services must be entered on the appropriate forms, which must be submitted to the Sales Department for input.

- Each officer must earn 100 points (the first 100 points are referred to as base) to be eligible for a commission.

- All commissions will be paid on a quarterly basis.

- A salesperson will participate in the incentive program after three months in the field. Any new business that is generated during the initial period will help offset the cost of training.

The products and services that are eligible for sales points are:

- Demand Accounts: Points will be awarded based on average collected balances minus reserve requirements.

- Regular Savings/Time Accounts: Points will be awarded based on the opening deposit. Time deposits must be for a minimum of three months.

- Loans: Commission will be based on the principal amount of the loan excluding the interest.

- Special Services: Points will also be awarded for special services—safe deposit boxes, automated teller, and direct deposit.

Quarterly Commission Schedule
At the end of each quarter, points will be tabulated and converted to commission dollars as follows:

> First 100 points = Base
> 101 to 250 points = $275
> 251 to 375 points = $400
> 376 to 675 points = $600
> 676 to 900 points = $850
> 901 to 1100 points = $1,150
> 1,101 points and up =$1,500

On the following page is a chart of the points awarded for each specific product sold. In the event of sales resulting from two or more officers working together, points are split evenly. Quarterly commission checks will be presented by the President at sales meetings or rallies.

Bonuses
Bonuses will be built into the annual appraisal/merit raise process. A year-end bonus will be awarded to each participant who meets the sales quota for all four quarters.

CSR Sales Development Program
The objective of this program is to increase the cross-sell ratio from 1.41% (as published on September 11, 1986) to 3.0% in an eighteen-month period.

All CSRs will participate in the training program. All current products and services will be adapted to the outside training program used.

The entire CSR Sales Development Program will be under the direction of the marketing director. Implementation of the program will be the responsibility of the sales manager and the training officer.

Not everyone in the bank will participate in the incentive portion of the program. It will be limited to eligible (having obtained a 1.60 cross-sell ratio) and certified (having completed the initial training session) CSRs. Utility staff and clerical staff will not participate in cash incentives.

The CSR sales coordinator will be eligible for override incentives for the direct supervision of branch CSRs. The CSR sales coordinator will receive 10% of the total dollars paid to branch CSRs.

Cross-sell ratios will continue to be tracked by our current tracking system (Financial Institution Services Institute—FISI) until an in-house system can be researched and developed.

SALES VALUES AND POINTS
(points awarded for specific products sold)

Demand Deposits

$0 - $999 = 4 points
$1,000 - $9,999 = 8 points
$10,000 - $49,999 = 16 points
$50,000 and up = 36 points

Regular Savings/Time Deposits

Three months to one year:

$1,000 - $9,999 = 3 points
$10,000 - $49,999 = 12 points
$50,000 and up = 18 points

One year to four year:

$1,000 - $9,999 = 5 points
$10,000 - $49,999 = 16 points
$50,000 and up = 28 points

Four years and longer:

$1,000 - $9,999 = 6 points
$10,000 - $49,999 = 24 points
$50,000 and up = 40 points

Loans

One quarter of 1% will be
earned on all lending activity

Special Services

Safe deposit box = 1 point
Automated teller = 1 point
Direct deposit = 1 point

Reports will continue to be filled out for each customer contact, verified by the branch manager, and processed in the Sales Department every Monday. Following the processing procedure, a monthly Pay-Off Report will be generated and submitted to the Accounting Department in Chicago. Individual incentive checks will be generated and distributed on a monthly basis.

Rules and Procedures

- To be eligible for any monthly bonus payout, a CSR must attain at least a 1.60% cross-sell ratio during the month as indicated on the monthly FISI tracking report.

- To be eligible for any monthly bonus payout, a staff member must be employed through the last working day on which the incentive is paid.

- The goal is multiple account sales at each encounter.

- CSRs must sell at least two accounts or services to a new (first time) customer to qualify for an incentive.

- A signature card will be attached to the tracking form for all deposit products.

- CSRs may qualify for an incentive by selling an additional service to an existing customer.

- Participants can earn a $5 bonus by initially earning $5 at the first encounter with a new customer or an existing customer.

- No incentive will be awarded for selling more than one account of the same type to the same customer.

- No compensation will be paid for accounts opened by, or for, members of the CSR's immediate family.

- There will be no incentive credit for conversion from one account to another, for account transfers from one branch to another, or for business accounts.

- Incentive credit will be awarded for all loan products when applications are verified and received by the Sales Department. The CSRs will be responsible for following the progress of all loan applications once they are returned by the customer to the loan officer. A copy of the approved credit memorandum must be attached.

Career Advancement
A key factor in this marketing plan is the use of sales performance standards for making career advancement decisions. We must make sure the link between sales performance and career advancement is evident. Household Bank will establish a dual-track system that will provide promotion opportunities within selling positions. Three levels of responsibility will be built into the customer service representative's position, which will allow CSRs the opportunity for promotion within the position. The CSR I level is the entry-level position. Employees are eligible for promotion to CSR II if they have been on the job for at least one year, have achieved performance goals, and have passed the product knowledge test. The highest level will be Senior CSR (CSR III), which will require excellent performance, passing a more difficult product test, and cross-training.

Recognition
Studies have shown that personal satisfaction, pride and recognition drive people to sell. The following recognition programs will be implemented to foster outstanding sales behavior:

- The president will send handwritten congratulatory notes to sales people who have experienced an exceptional sales period.

- A travelling trophy will move to the branch office that has experienced the most outstanding increase in loans and deposits.

- A sales rally will be held every six months, at which recognition will be given to top sales performers, including certificates of achievement and varying gifts.

- Features articles will be published in the *Household Word*, our in-house newsletter, on the top sales performers.

Measuring Selling Performance

Household Bank will use a six-part system known as management-by-objectives (MBO) to measure the effectiveness of the sales personnel. The MBO program will involve setting performance goals, measuring and evaluating sales performance and acting on the results. Three items from this six-part system follow:

1. Employees participating in the selling process will be encouraged to set their own goals. They will be informed about corporate goals for loan and deposit growth, expenses, and fee income. From there, they will be allowed to set what they feel are achievable objectives. These objectives will provide performance targets, standards and controls. This system should motivate them to reach their performance goals since they will be directly involved in the process.

2. All CSRs and selling officers will be formally evaluated by their immediate supervisor every three months through their first full year in the position. Subsequently, they will be on a biannual performance review cycle. Written reports will be given to the employee, as well as becoming a part of his or her permanent file. Additionally, the sales manager and CSR coordinator will conduct informal sales meetings on a bi-monthly basis.

   The following is a sample agenda:

   - Goals and objectives will be reviewed as they pertain to bankwide progress. Areas of weakness will be pointed out. Individuals who have made significant contributions toward the overall goals will be recognized. All individual team results will also be posted to stimulate healthy competition.

   - All members of the group will briefly discuss their current sales activities, ideas, successes and frustrations. This exercise will be a learning experience for every member of the sales force.

- Product knowledge will be reviewed.

- Role play and group exercises will encourage participation and will update selling skills.

- Meetings will conclude with the recognition and rewarding of eligible employees. A travelling trophy will be used to instill competition. The trophy will be presented to the top sales-person for the month and will be taken away by the person who outperforms the previous month's winner. Rewards and incentives will be presented by the bank's president.

3. A combination of the following quantitative and qualitative criteria will be used to evaluate the performance of all CSRs and calling officers:
   - Percentage increase of sales volume
   - Quotas obtained
   - Average sales calls per day
   - New customers obtained
   - Cross-sell ratios
   - Product knowledge test scores
   - Shopper ratings
   - Attitude
   - Team spirit
   - Motivation
   - Appearance

Developing the Sales Managers' Position

The sales managers will play a vitally important role in the success of the bank's sales program. They will be expected to plan, organize, and direct the sales staff in order to generate sales that meet the bank's objectives. This will translate into a personal goal to achieve the levels of sales volume, profits, and growth expected by upper management. The following is the job description for the sales manager's position.

Sales Manager Position Description
Under the direction of the vice president of marketing, the sales manager is responsible for managing the bank's entire sales effort to generate new business.

Sales Manager's Responsibilities
- Carry on such efforts as are required as outlined in the sales plan in order to achieve both personal and section sales quotas.

- Train and manage calling officers, business development officers and CSRs in their efforts to generate new business and retain existing business.

- Make outside calls personally and with bank officers.

- Aid in the recruiting, hiring, and training of sales personnel.

- Motivate the sales staff to perform in an outstanding manner.

- Assist in setting sales quotas.

- Monitor the sales personnel's performance in achieving of quotas and assist them in strengthening weak areas.

- Monitor the daily flow of paperwork through the sales office.

- Monitor expense reports for budget control.

- Advise the director of marketing on all field sales activities and recommend changes when necessary.

- Advise marketing of all new product or service ideas, all competitive field activity and of any special customer needs or requests.

Qualifications of Sales Managers
- College degree

- Minimum of four years experience in banking operations

- Minimum of one year management experience

- Minimum of one year sales experience

- Must be a self-starter and self-motivated

- Must be able to communicate verbally in an effective manner.

- Must be able to fulfill the following functions—planning, organizing, staffing, directing, and controlling

CONCLUSION
Making the transition from a product-oriented institution to a sales-driven one will be a long process. By implementing the programs discussed in this marketing plan, however, Household Bank will have a good start toward creating the sales culture that is necessary for success in banking today. ◆

---

[1] Leonard L. Berry, Charles M. Futrell, and Donald D. Walsh, *Bankers Who Sell* (Homewood, Illinois: Dow Jones-Irwin, 1985), p. v.

[2] Ronald M. Bentley, "Managing the Retail Sales Effort," *Bank Marketing*, (April 1986), pp. 10-12.

[3] Berry, Futrell and Walsh, p. 35-41.

[4] Ibid., p. 39.

[5] John M. Gwin. "Strategies for Officer Call Produtivity," *Bank Marketing,* (August 1986), pp. 22-26.

[6] Berry, Futrell and Walsh, p. 81.

CHAPTER 11

Enhancing the "Sales Culture"

Suzanne Iaconis
Sun Bank of Volusia County
$391 million assets

In today's competitive environment, developing and nurturing a sales culture is essential for continued success. A sales culture must permeate the entire organization, starting with top management. Every employee must receive the "sales" message loudly, clearly and continuously. Top sales performance should be rewarded, and sales champions must be recognized and promoted. Quality sales and quality service must be synonymous because the customer's needs are always the key element.

This plan builds on the "sales culture" that has already been established and enhances it for the continued future success of our organization.

SITUATION ANALYSIS
Sun Bank of Volusia County is part of a $26 billion, three-state regional banking company with almost 20,000 employees and more than 600 locations. Sun Bank of Volusia County is one of the leading banks in the Sun Bank family in Florida. There are currently fourteen branches, thirteen in Volusia County and one in Flagler County.

Volusia County
Volusia County is located fifty miles northeast of Orlando and sixty miles north of the Kennedy Space Center. The beautiful beaches and balmy weather make Volusia County a very desirable place to live. Fourteen cities and four unincorporated communities make up the Volusia area.

Volusia County is ranked as the nation's 24th fastest-growing metropolitan area. In 1986, the population was 319,018 and is projected to be 360,400 by

1990. Between 1980 and 1985, Florida's population increased by 15.8%, and Volusia County's population increased by 18.7%. The recent population surge is credited to increases in the area's working-age population. The 18-44 age group increased 110% during the last decade; the median age is forty.

The unemployment rate in Volusia is only 4.8%, compared with rates of 5.7% for Florida, and 6.7% for the United States. Wholesale and retail trade lead the employment figures with 28.5% of the work force; 26.9% are employed in service sector; 11.4% in manufacturing; 7.7% in construction and 6.2% in finance, insurance and real estate. [1]

Flagler County
Flagler County is located north of Volusia County. Palm Coast, the community where our branch is located, is a planned community. According to its planners, it is well on its way to becoming the ideal Florida city. The vision for the next century includes: a balanced community with young and older residents, industry, educational institutions, amenities, orderly growth, and an active, thriving residential environment. ITT Community Development Corporation (ITT/CDC), formed in 1971, purchased 68,000 acres to form this community. Between 1976 and 1986, the labor market experienced a significant growth in population. This reflects a 53% growth rate over the last decade. Palm Coast currently has 9,700 people, with 17,642 people residing in Flagler County. The median age is forty-two. The unemployment rate in Flagler is only 3.3%. The community is seeking industry to locate in the area and wishes to maintain a moderate cost of living.[2]

COMPETITIVE ANALYSIS
Volusia County
There are twenty-two banks and savings and loans in Volusia County for total deposits of $4.1 billion. Savings and loan institutions have historically been dominant in Volusia County.[3] A decade ago, savings and loans held 70% of the market. Currently, they have 52.8% with banks holding 47.2% of the market. Sun Bank is second in market share for banks in Volusia County and in the state.[4]

Flagler County
In Flagler County, three banks and three savings and loans hold deposits of $217,561. Savings and loans hold 48% of the market, with banks holding 52%. Sun Bank's Palm Coast office opened in December 1986, and its deposits have been growing rapidly.

Corporate Culture
Currently, our fourteen locations are run by community bank presidents in a decentralized mode. Each community has a different market area with

different needs. Community bank presidents report to a cluster manager, who in turn reports to our bank administrator. Our CEO is a third-generation Coleman, the family that founded the bank. Passed down through his family are specific customer relations values that prevail today. His father was known throughout the community for his friendliness, help-fulness, and genuine concern for the customer and the community. Thus, the quality service that is prevalent today at Sun Bank has a long history.

Bank Resources
Our CEO is dedicated to continually providing quality service to our customers and is enthusiastic in his approach to establishing a "sales culture" with support from a strong senior management team. There are currently 50 officers and 311 employees on the Sun Bank of Volusia County payroll. A board of directors and four advisory boards serve the bank and the community.

Our year-to-date average deposits are $390 million, with $322 million in interest-bearing and $68 million noninterest bearing accounts. Total loans are $330 million; $100 million in consumer loans; $43 million in commercial loans; $52 million in residential real estate loans; and $88 million in commer-cial and other real estate loans. Our loan to deposit ratio is currently 83%.

Customers
Our customer base is varied and each submarket differs slightly. We serve small business owners, retired customers, upscale customers, upwardly mobile, and mainstream customers and several of our markets have a large number of winter visitors. Our customer surveys show that our bank has a good percentage of the upscale and upwardly mobile segment and a smaller portion of the mainstream and senior market segments.

Product Line
We have several package accounts. Our All-In-One is a checking account that comes with a MasterCard or VISA that provide overdraft protection. Our Sun Horizon 55, for customers over fifty-five years old, is a checking account that comes with many options for the customer, including a credit card, insurance benefits, free checks, and many other services proven desirable to that market segment. We offer a full array of commercial, business, and personal services, including investment products, brokerage services and trusts. We have a variety of loans, including a revolving line of credit that can be unsecured or secured and is accessible by writing a check.

CURRENT PROGRAMS
We have had as many as twenty-three incentive plans, programs and pro-motions in Volusia County. Our senior management, through their expe-

rience with incentive programs, is convinced that incentives are not only effective, but essential to stimulate excellence. The description of some of our programs, which follows, shows our current position in the development of our "sales culture":

Sales Incentive Program (SIP)

Our Sales Incentive Program marked the start of our "sales culture." This program began in November, 1981 with the monitoring of the current cross-sales ratios and the selection of a sales manager. The program includes all new account representatives (currently there are fifty). Sales incentive account representatives are trained to identify the financial needs of customers, provide helpful information on the products' features and benefits that meet the customer's needs, and build a favorable impression with customers—a sense of personalized banking service. The bank rewards new account representatives who do an effective job in meeting the needs of customers.

The initial training required is thirty hours of classroom training, including product knowledge, customer relations, sales training, communication skills, role play, and the measurement system.

SIP participants receive commissions for each product and service sold according to its profitability and the difficulty involved in selling the product. A bonus is paid for each sale that is a triple (three services to one customer) or a quad (four or more services to one customer). SIP participants earn from $50 to $250 a month in commissions depending on their volume and sales performance.

Certain sales interviews are exempt for the cross-sales average: business accounts, minor accounts and duplicate sales to a single customer. SIP participants are now sometimes selling up to 10 products and services to a new customers. Existing customers are included in the sales totals to ensure that salespeople continually upgrade the products and services of our best prospects—our existing customer base.

Not only do SIP participants receive monthly commissions, they receive recognition for sales performance through prizes, awards, recognition in our monthly newsletter *SunRays*, and advanced career opportunities.

A quarterly sales rally motivates, educates, and bonds together this group of salespeople. Senior management, community bank presidents, SIP participants and professional referral winners attend this rally. Monthly and quarterly awards, prizes and trophies are delivered by a member of senior management and the sales manager to winning individuals, banks and teams.

Awards are given for top performance to individuals (based on cross-sales) and to banks (based on overall sales effectiveness, which is a weighted average based on the sale of multiple products). Team spirit is created through the team awards. The teams are divided along the Cluster Management line. Bank President of the Quarter (BPOQ) is an honored award given to a bank president based on nominations from their staff and on his or her bank's sales performance.

In May of 1987, a performance policy was instituted. It outlined the specific consequences when a sales person does not meet the minimum standard (2.00). The policy was a necessary step, since a few supervisors and community bank presidents were allowing nonperformers to remain as new account representatives. The policy was a milestone in our "sales culture" as it made clear to all that to be a new account representative you must sell. Cross-sales ratios have increased significantly since the implementation of this performance policy.

The results of the SIP program have been excellent. Benefits include customer retention, improved customer service and a cross-sales ratio increase from 1.20 (pre-SIP average) to 2.78, currently.

Professional Referral Program (PRP)
Our Professional Referral Program began in September 1986. This was a major enhancement to our "sales culture." Every employee not currently in the SIP program is eligible to participate. Officers and employees identify prospects, or customers with additional needs and refer them to a SIP participant who then cross-sells the needed services.

The referrer receives credit not only for the referral, but also for each product or service sold to the customer. The commission is one dollar for the referral and one dollar for each additional service sold. During special promotions for a specific product or service, commissions are increased to encourage additional referrals. Recognition through awards, *SunRays*, and attendance at the quarterly SIP sales rallies add extra incentives for the participants.

The success of this program has been tremendous, with 1,763 referrals resulting in the sale of 3,151 new products and services over the last fourteen months. The cross-sales ratio is 1.79. This is an excellent ratio since some referrals do not result in a sale at all. Over $6 million has been reported as new money to our bank.

The program creates a sense of teamwork within the banks, as tellers and other non-SIP participants take an interest in sales by the new account representatives. However, some problems have been identified including lack of management attention. Overall, however, the early results are extremely encouraging with over 100 of the 300 eligible employees participating. The program has helped morale throughout the bank by eliminating the idea that only new account representatives can earn commissions.

Trust Incentive Program (TIP)
This Trust Incentive Program began statewide in July, 1985, and was designed by our Trust Division. For each trust prospect who is referred to the Trust Department and results in a sale, the referer is given 10% of the first year's Trust fee. About $17 million in new business has been generated this year through the TIP program with fifty-seven awards given for a total of $13,664 paid in commissions.

Investment Referral Program (IRP)
The Investment Referral Program operates in the same way as TIP. The fee for referring a customer who purchases an investment product is $50 on certain investment products. Over $400,000 has been generated in commissions to the bank, which is attributed to this incentive program. In 1987, $12,650 in incentives has been paid to forty-five participants.

Officer Call
Community bank presidents and corporate lenders are required to make four and eight calls a month, respectively. The calls and resulting sales are reported to their cluster manager or the vice president in charge of corporate banking. These calls are an essential part of their job, however; there is no extra incentive paid currently for these calls.

Bank Telemarketing Program-Loans
This telemarketing program was started in November of 1987. Community bank presidents, lenders and SIP participants are given leads consisting of paid-out loans. The banker calls these customers, thanks them for their business, and asks for additional business. The program is too new to report results, but response to the initial training was positive. The program has potential since many indirect-loan customers have no other banking relationships with us.

Other Incentive Programs and Promotions
Our Mortgage Referral Program began in March of 1986, and gives the referer $50 for a closed residential mortgage that is salable on the secondary market. The Mortgage Department attributes the sale of many mortgages to this program.

Incentives for selling credit life and accident and health insurance on loans give extra dollars to lenders and encourage participation. The insurance agency provides awards and recognition through a monthly publication citing excellent performance.

Special promotions lasting from one month to four months have been designed for specific purposes such as increasing loan sales or sales of a specific product or service. Our loan promotions have been successful, adding loan volume when needed. A recent promotion to sign up All-In-One merchants was successful in generating new merchants who agreed to accept our All-In-One checks. This promotion also gave some participants new experience in calling on businesses.

These programs have provided us with a great "head start" in having a true sales organization.

OBJECTIVES
The *SunTrust Vision* outlines the philosophy and goals of the company.

> We seek to develop close, long term relationships with customers who put a premium on high quality, value-added service and superior professional attention.

Volusia County's specific goals are to improve profits, increase market share, provide excellent service, and have the most professional and effective employees.

To accomplish these goals, a strong "sales culture" must be present. The sales culture began six years ago with the implementation of the Sales Incentive Program (SIP). Over the past six years, the "sales culture" has grown stronger and has become a way of life for many bank employees. However, we need to continue to help this culture grow. The objectives for our sales culture marketing plan include:

- Extending the "sales culture" to all areas of the bank.
- Encouraging supervisors, middle-managenent, community bank presidents, and senior management to be more active and supportive in sales management.
- Enhancing or developing sales plans for all areas of the bank, including directors and advisory boards.
- Enhancing current sales programs to include and reward more employees and units.
- Encouraging and rewarding sales people for reaching goals and a higher level of sales ability and skills.
- Providing training sessions to develop advanced sales skills and product knowledge.
- Encouraging more participation in current training programs.

- Rewarding and promoting officers and employees who sell.

- Ensuring that community bank presidents and managers are accountable for the sales of their unit.

- Hiring and promoting only sales-oriented employees.

ENHANCEMENTS TO EXISTING PROGRAMS
The following program enhancements will help us to develop a stronger sales environment.

SIP Enhancements
The sales skills and abilities of the SIP participants have come a long way during the six years that the program has been in existence. Sales skills have become integrated and many participants are ready for the next level of sales training to obtain new sales skills.

Step 1—Financial Planning
Americans, now, more than ever, have expressed a desire for help from their banker with financial planning . Thus, the next logical step is to offer a tool for the SIP participants to use to help their customers with financial planning. Using Financial Information Products, Inc. (FIPI) to furnish single-plan financial reports and provide the initial training, SIP participants will be able to order and receive specific financial reports for their customers. These reports will be returned to the SIP participant to deliver to the customer. The reports address the consumer's need for help by showing them how different combinations of our products and services can be used to solve the issue addressed. This is called "solution selling." The customer can choose from five different reports:

- Education Planning

- Life Insurance Planning

- Household Cash Flow Control

- Retirement Planning

- Investment Planning

The SIP participants will attend two training sessions to enable them to use the plans effectively.   The first one is "Solution Selling Workshop™." The theme of this workshop is to sell solutions to customers, not products. This workshop is designed to teach SIP participants how to use our existing products to build multiple-product solutions that meet the needs of various types of customers. This workshop will enhance and reaffirm the initial SIP training. Using a different approach from the initial SIP training, this training will include using the financial plan as a tool and building block.

The next workshop is the "Comfort Zone Workshop™." The objective of this workshop is to improve the SIP people's ability to sell more professionally by increasing their knowledge of nontraditional financial products, such as mutual funds and insurance. The objective is not to turn them into financial "experts," but to make them more comfortable with discussing and selling against nonbank products.

With the completion of these two training programs, our sales people will move to an advanced level of sales skills—getting our customers the type of information that they need and request.

Step 2—Second Level of SIP
SIP participants meeting the following standards will be promoted to an advanced level of SIP:

1. Completing the "Solution Selling Workshop™."
2. Completing the "Comfort Zone Workshop™."
3. Using the information to deliver at least five plans per quarter to their customers.
4. Maintaining a 2.50 or above quarterly SIP average (for two consecutive quarters).
5. Having at least two TIP referrals per year.
6. Making three officer calls to existing customers per quarter.
7. Making six All-In-One merchant sign-up calls or revisits per quarter.
8. Having at least eight investment referrals per quarter.
9. "Shopping" four competitor banks (one per quarter).
10. Maintaining a high rating on their last performance appraisal, and maintaining a high level of operational procedures.
11. Having satisfactory or above shopping results.

For the SIP participants who complete this criteria, the incentives will be:

1. A salary grade increase and a 5% raise. The salary grade will be increased by two grades after the participants complete all standards.
2. Annual cash bonus of 1% of incentives earned through SIP, TIP, and IRP.

The continued career path of these participants should be enhanced by this additional level of SIP. This group of employees should be more knowledgeable, more professional, and more confident, thus promoting excellent customer relations and increasing sales.

These SIP participants should be more in tune with the future needs of our market. According to a recent survey, two-thirds of our customers say that they will probably save more, especially in the upscale and upwardly mobile segments, and half say that they will borrow less. This program addresses our customers' needs perfectly.

The SIP participants who choose to be in the second level will also be better prepared for advancement to positions such as consumer and commercial loan positions and community bank presidents. This group of employees has proved to be essential to the continued success of our bank. We need leaders who understand the importance of sales.

Step 3—Management Accountability
The final step is to add more line sales management to the SIP and to all sales programs through increased accountability for sales within a bank and within a cluster. Community bank presidents will be held accountable for sales results, and they will be rewarded for excellence. This is addressed later in the accountability section of this plan. Accountability is important in SIP, since banks in which community bank presidents support and counsel their staff have done well. In banks where SIP is not a priority for the community bank president, sales have eventually suffered. Sales management is a key issue and cannot be accomplished by one sales manager in a staff position. It must be supported by line management.

Benefits
The benefits to enhancing the SIP programs are numerous. Many of the SIP participants are ready for new challenges; they are accustomed to setting goals and striving to achieve them. The additional training will increase their knowledge, professionalism, confidence, and sales skills. The second level of SIP will reward those who push to achieve more. Our investment referrals and our trust referrals will be greatly increased, with increased fee income for the bank. Greater management support will take us to new levels in our "sales culture."

Enhancing Professional Referral (PR)
Although extremely successful, the Professional Referral Program is in its infancy and needs enhancing and refining.

Step 1—Awards
Currently, cash awards are given quarterly to the top four referrers in a customer contact position, and two awards are given to employees with little or no customer contact. Six awards for over 300 eligible employees,

however, are not sufficient to motivate the troops. We want to encourage participation for all levels of employees and officers. The following categories will be recognized monthly through *SunRays*, and winners will receive the following awards quarterly:

Customer Contact Officers	Customer Contact Non-Officers
$75 for first place	$75 for first place
$60 for second place	$60 for second place
$45 for third place	$45 for third place
$30 for fourth place	$30 for fourth place

A minimum of 15 referrals must be made quarterly. The current minimum is 10.

Some Customer Contact	Non-Customer Contact
(10 referrals minimum)	(6 referrals minimum)
$75 for first place	$75 for first place
$60 for second place	$60 for second place
$45 for third place	$45 for third place
$30 for fourth place	$30 for fourth place

By increasing the minimum for customer contact referrals per quarter and decreasing the amount for noncustomer contact groups as shown above, more referrals should be received from all groups of employees.

Step 2—Training

More training is needed to increase the level of participation. The initial training in August 1986 was done on-site, bankwide. Currently, in Teller Training, SIP, SIP Refresher, Product Knowledge, and Supervisory Training, the professional referral process is being reinforced. However, it needs to be enhanced significantly.

Another round of on-site training will be performed during the first quarter of 1988. PR training will be an integral part of the new employee orientation and teller training. This training includes information about the program and, more importantly, how to recognize prospects and how to encourage a sale.

Step 3 —SIP - PR Buddy System

Another way to encourage referrals, as well as teamwork, is by matching each PR participant in the bank with a SIP participant. For example, one SIP participant may have two tellers and one lender in his or her group. Together they can set referral goals and sales goals. This system will benefit the PR participants, as well as the SIP participants, in the following ways:

- SIP participants will take an interest in the performance of a teller or other PR participant.
- SIP participants will help explain prospect clues, as well as features and benefits of our products and services to PR participants.
- SIP participants will receive more prospects for SIP sales from their "group." (Referrals can be given to any SIP participant.)
- Competition can be created through these groups within the bank or cluster.
- A more intense feeling of teamwork is created in the banks.
- New tellers will feel more a part of the "sales culture" when they are coached by a salesperson.

Step 4—Management Commitment
Again, sales management by head tellers, supervisors and community bank presidents is essential to keep participation in and the results of the PR program high. Day-to-day, positive reinforcement of results is essential. Accountability at all levels is necessary to keep performance at a high level.

Benefits
Enhancing PR with more training, increased awards, the buddy system and more management attention will increase participation, employee morale and bring new customers into the bank.

Officer Call
"Building an effective sales program presents a multi-faceted challenge. Magical overnight solutions do not exist. Attempts at quick fixes will fail. To prepare people to sell but not measure their sales performance is wasteful. To measure their sales performance, but not prepare them to sell is unproductive and unfair. To speak of sales, but pay no attention to sales when appraising performance destroys credibility. All the pieces of the sales puzzle must be in place."[5]

Step 1—Identification and Goals
Calling officers will be divided into two categories—commercial business developers and retail business developers. The first category includes commerical lenders, cluster managers and some seasoned community bank presidents. The retail business developers will include some community bank presidents, loan officers, personal bankers, management associates and trust officers. Quotas will be established for each lender by corporate banking department heads, the president, the CEO, bank administrators and the cluster managers.

Step 2—Measurement System
We will design or purchase a measurement system, possibly using REFLEX. Basic information will be reported from the call reports. The monitoring and reporting of the results will be a marketing function.

Step 3—Training
Two levels of training programs—Harland's Pro Selling Program and Omega's Business Development for Bankers—will provide the needed sales information to participants, .

Harland's Pro Selling Program is a two day workshop for calling officers, that covers the basics including product knowledge, prospect sources, probing, handling objections and closing the sale. This training will be available to all calling officers, community bank presidents, and some SIP participants.

Omega's Business Development for Bankers is a training system that helps build and maintain productive sales organizations where other programs have failed. It improves business development performance at two levels:

1. A three-day class teaches calling officers skills for all phases of the business development process, including product knowledge, call planning, face-to-face calling, and account management. After completing the program, calling officers are more confident in their calling skills, make more productive calls, cross-sell more effectively and build better long-term customer relationships.

2. Managers attend a one-and-a-half-day session in which they learn the coaching skills needed to help calling officers perform most effectively. After completing the program, they are able to work with calling officers to jointly plan and execute winning calling strategies on key accounts. They will ensure that effective calling becomes part of the bank's daily routine.

This training system includes independent study, video-assisted workshops, and postworkshop field follow-up activities, as well as job aids to help organize business development performance. It is adapted to our bank's products, policies, and exisiting business development procedures. It is a practical performance-based training system that will build a more productive selling organization in our bank.

In 1988, thirty to thirty-five calling officers, community bank presidents and SIP people will attend the Harland Pro Selling Program and sixteen to twenty calling officers, community bank presidents and cluster managers will complete the Omega's Business Development for Bankers training.

Incentives
"Rewards are necessary to motivate officers to call, because business development is hard work and not all employees will want to do it. If thoses who participate are not rewarded, the effects on morale and productivity can be severe. Those who do produce and are not rewarded will stop producing (why should they call if no one cares?) or they will leave the bank and move to a job which does provide rewards."[6]

Incentives will be based on deposits received after the call quota has been achieved. Amounts will be paid as follows:

1. Checking: .0025% quarterly based on the three-month average balance of the account (1% annually).

2. Money market and certificates of deposit: .001% quarterly, based on the average three-month balance (.004% annually).

3. A $100 quarterly bonus to all who have achieved quotas.[7]

By tying incentives to deposit accounts only, lenders do a more thorough job of obtaining a total banking relationship with their customers.

Sales Management
Sales management for the Officer Call Program must be a line function to be effective. The bank administrator with help from the head of the Corporate Banking Department, will serve as the sales manager.

Telemarketing
The bank's Installment Loan Telemarketing Program will be enhanced by adding individual commissions and bank awards in 1988. The Telemarketing Program will be enhanced by giving the bank more prospect lists, such as maturing CDs. We will offer incentives for increased dollar amounts and for tying customers into longer terms.

Through telemarketing, we can reach a virtually untapped source of customers and prospects. This telemarketing will be done by the staff-operated Telemarketing Department under the direction of Marketing. The Department will expand over the next five years to become a complete Telemarketing Department, with both in-bound and out-bound telemarketing.

NEW PROGRAMS
Shopping
For years, the operational aspects of performance have been the qualities inspected within the bank. This is an extremely important part of banking, however, quality service and sales are essential to continued customer satisfaction and increased sales performance.

To inspect the quality of service and sales, we will conduct four levels of "shopping"; that is, a customer or prospect routinely making a transaction, inquiring about a service or opening an account and evaluating the service they have received.

Name "Shops"
Periodically, as part of our quality service program, customers of the bank are selected to go to the banks, conduct a routine transaction and then issue the SunBanker a card. If the SunBanker called the customer by name, smiled and said "Thank you," the card reads, "Congratulations, $50 in your next pay." However, if the SunBanker did not use the customer's name, smile, or say "Thank you," they receive a card that says "You just missed an extra $50. Please call me by name." This type of shopping done periodically with published results, goes a long way to remind everyone to call our customers by name and deliver quality service. This is an important element of a "sales culture." At least two shops per bank per quarter will be conducted.

Performance "Shops"
More extensive "shopping" will be conducted on an ongoing basis by an outside firm. A 24-question form is used to evaluate the performance of new account representatives. A separate questionnaire is used to evaluate the teller area and specific tellers. Two "shops" per bank per quarter will be conducted in 1988.

Telephone "Shop"
Telephone shopping will cover other areas of the bank, such as the Service Center, the Loan Processing Department, lending areas and community bank presidents. Customers and other SunBankers (from affiliate banks) will conduct these shops. This shopping will be done periodically or for a specific purpose such as testing the employee's knowledge of and sales approach to a new product.

Our Own "Shopping"
SIP trainees will conduct "shops" at competing banks during SIP training; and "shopping" will be part of advanced SIP training. SIP participants working on the advanced level of SIP will conduct four competitive shops per year. Thus, shoppers will learn firsthand about their competitors, including their product line and the type of service they are providing to their customers.

Awareness and Training
Through teller training, supervisory training, and SIP training, participants will learn exactly what is expected of them. Therefore, shop results will not be a surprise to anyone. Continued training will help keep the anxiety level low.

Awards and Recognition

All employees will be made aware of the shopping policy of the bank. Shopping results will be routinely published in *SunRays* and reported to senior management and community bank presidents. Recognition for excellent shopping results will be given at the SIP quarterly sales rallies. Participants not usually included will be invited to receive an award. The potential for earning this recognition will keep the employees motivated, striving for a higher level of customer service at all times.

Accountability Program

To operate at the highest level possible, accountability for all results in the bank must rest with the community bank president. Currently, community bank presidents are reviewed based on their results versus their plan. However, no incentive or bonus is given to community bank presidents with excellent results. A program to track and measure results against the plan will be developed or purchased to include non-interest-bearing deposits, interest-bearing deposits, consumer loans, controllable expenses, commercial loans, service charges, real estate loans, officer calls, PR results, SIP results, credit life and accident and health penetration, TIP referrals, shopping results, loan delinquencies, operational efficiency and market share. Points will be assigned to each category by the Senior Management Committee, and yearly bonuses will be determined every year. Sun Bank, N.A., the lead bank in the Sun Bank family, operates a plan called the Branch Measurement System that will be used as a guide in developing our plan.

Managers earning 1,000 or more points (out of 1,087.5) earn $2,500. Managers earning 950-999 points, if ranked in the top twenty, receive a $1,000 award. Our recommendation is to establish criteria, develop a monitoring and measurement system, and begin the program in January 1989. Prior to implementing this program, we recommend paying a bonus based on the percentage of plan achieved and of sales accomplished beginning in 1988. The benefits of this plan outweigh the costs. Community bank presidents will be rewarded for stretching, motivating their staff and achieving goals.

HUMAN RESOURCES AND TRAINING

The most important asset of this institution or of any company is its employees, officers, and directors. To enhance and nurture our "sales culture," we must continue to staff to sell, define sales behaviors, prepare people to sell, make it easy to sell, measure and reward sales performance, and turn supervisors into sales managers.

Staffing To Sell

"Training, incentives and other critical factors in developing a sales program are of limited value if the wrong people are placed in sales positions.

One key to building a sales program is factoring criteria relating to selling potential into hiring decisions. Financial institutions that give short shrift to hiring decisions involving entry-level positions, that entrust these decisions exclusively to the Personnel Department, that hire just about anyone to fill open positions—these institutions inhibit from the start their ability to become successful in selling. Holding out for the best people is one of the most important things to do in developing a sales program. Input shapes output." [8]

The best salespeople are assertive and empathetic. They have the drive to take control in selling situations, yet are sensitive to the customer's needs. They are enthusiastic about the sales role, are professional, have good interpersonal skills, are self-motivated, are goal oriented, are entrepreneurial, and are team players within the organization. These attributes should be considered when interviewing candidates for all sales positions. [9]

The teller trainer will interview candidates for teller positions, along with Personnel, the community bank president, and the head teller. For SIP sales positions, the sales manager will interview the candidates to determine sales ability by using a sales role play. The training officer should be involved in all phases of the hiring process. Calling officers, community bank presidents and corporate lenders should possess a high degree of sales ability and should be hired and promoted for their sales skills. Every job, directly or indirectly, is a selling job.

Defining Sales Behavior
"Sales task clarity is a crucial element in a salesperson's motivation." [10] Sales behavior should be in the job description of every position. Sales task clarity should begin during the interviewing process and should be reinforced continually throughout the employee's career. New employee orientation should be conducted on the first day a new hire reports to work. During that day, sales task clarity, no matter what position the new employee is in, should be stressed. It will be explained that Sun Bank of Volusia County is a sales organization and that sales are expected at every level of employment.

Preparing People To Sell
Preparing people to sell is a continuous process. Once they have been prepared to sell, sales ability must be upgraded and reinforced. The programs that will be used to prepare and reinforce sales ability have been discussed in previous sections of this plan.

In addition in product knowledge sessions, employees will learn about features and benefits of our products and services. Teller training gives new tellers skills in teller operations, customer relations, and sales. Customer relation and banking fundamentals classes are offered to all employees. Each employee will receive the training/career path best suited to his or her immediate and long-term goals.

Making It Easy To Sell

Unfortunately, it is not as easy to sell as we envision. Office automation will relieve the new account representative of much of the tedious paperwork that is now essential. In the meantime, we will look at every activity that is done in the bank by salespeople and consider having it done centrally.

> Bank people don't have time to sell, their responsibilities cover too broad a spectrum of administrative, operational, and customer service activities to allow them sufficient time to sell. Obviously, this is a critical area and one of the major obstacles that must be overcome to implement a sales environment. [11]

We need to regularly ask our salespeople what will make selling easier and then followup on the suggestions. Having the right products and services to sell is essential. We must be a market-driven, customer-oriented bank as opposed to a product-driven institution. We must see through the customer's eyes.

Timely and effective advertising can help the sales process and can develop interest in a specific product to get people to come into the bank. An effective and uniform internal signage program can make the banks look more attractive and enhance the sales atmosphere by presenting products to people who do not want to go through a presentation. "The crux of retail marketing is the use of effective, action-oriented in-bank advertising."[12]

Measuring and Rewarding Sales Performance

Measurement systems will measure, track, and report results for all the programs discussed. In addition, all departments should set clear-cut standards for employees and for the department, measure results and reward accordingly. Dollar incentives are extremely important for continued success and must be distributed generously, but they must be accompanied by recognition from supervisors and top management. The use of recognition enhances team spirit among employees, banks, and clusters.

Turning Supervisors into Sales Managers

Supervisors on all levels need to feel as if they are a part of the management team. In turn, they must coach, nurture, and lead their employees to high sales results. Many supervisors do not feel that they are part of the management team. Employees should be carefully selected for supervisory positions; and when they are promoted to a supervisory position, it should be a memorable occasion for the new supervisor. They should:

- Receive a letter from the president saying "welcome to the management team."

- Receive a *Supervisor's Handbook*. (Currently, they have to borrow one from their community bank president or a department head—many do not know these books exist.)

- Promptly be enrolled in supervisory classes (if not before the promotion).

- Be included in officer's meetings and in decisions affecting their bank or department.

Supervisors are key to producing high sales results. In supervisory classes, sales management is one of the main issues addressed; they must be accountable for the sales results of their unit. "Rewarding supervisors, when the sales performance of those they supervise is good, is an effective way to reach supervisors with the sales message."[13]

Employee Segments
Certain groups of employees are currently not receiving the desired training or attention needed to complete the sales loop. Attention should be directed at increasing sales involvement from the following groups:

Support Areas
More training and more support is needed in some staff areas, in sales management and about understanding the importance of sales and quality service. The "old-time banking thinking" still prevails in several staff areas of our bank.

Management Associates
Currently, management associates report to Personnel and are typically on a one-year schedule. Management associates feel that much of their time "in training" is not beneficial. They are frequently given copy-machine and envelope-stuffing duties.

This group of future leaders needs to have more supervisory training and to be coached extensively in the sales management process. They need to understand market share and effects of advertising and promotion along with the departmental and credit training that they currently are receiving. For these reasons, they should report to the training officer who has the resources to get the most out of their training time. We feel that this would be an investment in enhancing the "sales culture" now and in the future.

Boards
Currently, our board of directors and four advisory boards are not as involved in the sales process as we would like them to be. Beginning in

January, each boards' meeting will include a short training session on a product or service. Board members will make referrals using the PR system and make occasional joint calls with commercial loan officers or community bank presidents and participate in the Officer Call Program. This will enhance our image in the community and further the education of an important resource—our board of directors.

IMPLEMENTATION

The implementation of the enhancements just described will take teamwork and coordination. For the Officer Call Program and the Accountability Program, task forces will be formed to ensure that all areas involved understand and participate in the planning and implementation stages. Each stage of the development process will be assigned to a specific banker to ensure that timely action is taken. The Marketing Department and the bank administrator will coordinate the initial meetings with the approval of the respective task forces.

Estimated Costs

The cost of the suggested programs, which are shown on the following chart, are misleading because the increased sales results that the proposed programs should produce are difficult to measure.

BENEFITS

The benefits of having a true "sales culture" far outweigh the costs. To survive and prosper in the competitive marketplace of today, we must face the future and strive to build a sales environment. Having the right people selling, the right products to sell, and the right environment for selling will keep us a step ahead of our competition.

With the enhancements outlined for SIP, PR, the Officer Call Program, and the new programs — bank accountability, shopping, new training sessions, and improvements in staffing—we will be well on our way to having a true "sales culture."

"The branch of the future will be a highly developed, disciplined selling center, not merely a convenient spot for customers to bring deposits or make loan deposits to an order taking, reactive staff."[14]

With hard work and strong management commitment in a proactive environment, our goals can be accomplished to make Sun Bank of Volusia County ready for the customers of today and of the future.

ESTIMATED COSTS

Program	1987	Incentives 1988	1989
• SIP commissions	$42,000	$45,000	$50,000
• SIP second level bonus	- 0 -	8,000	10,000
• PR incentives	5,000	10,000	15,000
• PR cash awards	1,000	3,360	4,500
• Telemarketing incentives	- 0 -	1,000	5,000
• Officer call incentives	- 0 -	- 0 -	55,000
• Bank accountability bonus	- 0 -	- 0 -	28,000
• Shopping	1,000	1,000	1,000
• Other costs	- 0 -	4,088	8,500
		Other Costs	
• Shopping	- 0 -	5,000	5,000
• Training:			
• Omega Business Development Fin. Plan. (Comfort Zone™)	- 0 -	6,000	600
& Solution Selling™)	- 0 -	6,000	600
• Internal Signage	- 0 -	10,000 (5 yrs.)	10,000 (5yrs.)

CONCLUSION

Creating a "sales culture" is hard and tedious work. It takes years to accomplish and involves many elements. This plan marketing will not solve all the problems of our bank, or change it miraculously, overnight. It will be a long process, but a process well worth exerting all our efforts and resources to accomplish. ◆

---

[1] Volusia County Business Development Corporation, *County Data Profile 1987-1988*, p. 1.

[2] ITT Land Corporation, A Development Resource Group, *Palm Coast, Florida Data and Demographics: A Business Relocation Guide*, (October 1987), p. 1.

3 Volusia County Business Development Corporation, pp. 21, 22.

4 Florida Bankers Association, *Office Level Report on Florida Bank Deposits, June 30, 1987* (Orlando, Florida) pp. 1, 475.

5 James H. Donnelly, Jr., Leonard L. Berry, and Thomas W. Thompson, *Marketing Financial Services—A Strategic Vision* (Homewood, Illinois: Dow Jones-Irwin,1985), p. 194.

6 E. Laird Landon, "Creating a Commercial Sales Culture," *BMA Alumni Newsletter,* Vol. 11, (September 1987).

7 *Sun Bank of Polk County Business Development Plan.*

8 Donnelly, Berry and Thompson, p. 186.

9 Ibid., pp. 186-187.

10 Benson P. Shapiro and Steven X. Doyle, "Make the Sales Task Clear", *Harvard Business Review,* (November-December, 1983), pp. 72-76.

11 Robert Caira, "Deeply Rooted Obstacles Must be Overcome to Put New Selling Priority into Effect,"*Bank Marketing,* Vol. 18, No. 9, (September 15, 1986), p. 40.

12 John C. Ryan, "In-Bank Merchandising Fosters Sunny Retail Sales Climate", *Bank Marketing,* (July, 1987).

13 Donnelly, Berry and Thompson, p. 193.

14 Jack Whittle, "Sales Culture Needed When Spreads Decline," *The American Banker,* Marketing Management, (March 12, 1986), p. 4.

Market Segmentation Strategies

CHAPTER 12

Private Reserve:
An Upscale Program for the Bank of Stockton

Angela D. Brusa
Bank of Stockton
$527 million assets

HISTORICAL POSITION OF BANK OF STOCKTON
Background/Corporate Personality

The Bank of Stockton (BOS) was founded in 1867, under the principle of "with the safety of the depositors in mind." This philosophy is still adhered to today, as the bank continues to be one of the largest independent banks in Northern California. Despite only eight branch offices in the San Joaquin Valley, Bank of Stockton is classified as a medium-size institution, with assets of $527,236,962.

Each department's expertise, combined with its highly experienced management personnel, work together to achieve the bank's goals. A dedication to excellence and a strong commitment to the families and businesses of the community have characterized the bank for 120 years. Generations of families have placed their funds in this institution known for its strength, stability and community involvement.

Internal Strengths and Weaknesses on a Macro Level
Internal Strengths (Macro Level)

- With 120 years of strength and stability, the Bank of Stockton is the oldest bank in California still operating under its original charter. It has a history of capable and conservative management.

- Its cohesive top-management team receives direction from the CEO and the executive vice president.

- Its image conveys trust and credibility. Public relations and community involvement make BOS the "Community Helper."

- Both local management and senior management are accessible, with a visible CEO and executive vice president. Decisions are made locally.

- A personalized service approach has characterized BOS since its inception.

- We have a strong and stable asset base of $527,236,962 and have eight offices. Our 350 employees are loyal, with only a 3.33% turnover rate.

Internal Weaknesses (Macro Level)
- Communication of the bank's goals flow well throughout the upper levels of management; however, the department head/supervisor level often neglects to inform subordinates (customer service representatives, tellers and new accounts representatives) of the bank's goals. This key weakness contributes to a lack of team effort in meeting the bank's objectives.

- Tasks are assigned without clear direction. This slows implementation and decreases the effectiveness of potentially successful ideas.

- Many offices insist on doing things their own way, rather than in accordance with a total bank perspective.

- BOS is more "reactive" than "proactive." Because of its cautious and conservative approach, it often misses opportunities in the marketplace.

- Many employees lack product knowledge and sales skills (cross-sales and suggestive selling), especially at customer-contact levels. Employees are often only order takers.

- More education must be given to employees on all levels regarding product knowledge, sales functions, and personalized service. The main factors differentiating BOS are not familiar to most employees.

- There is no accountability, with little incentive for those who achieve beyond the call of duty.

External Opportunities and Threats (Macro Level)
External Opportunities

- Deregulation and the expansion of the financial services industry has led to growth. Great opportunities exists for the development of products and services to further differentiate BOS.

- Opportunities to gain increased market share through cross-sales, suggestive selling, business development, and market segmentation are virtually untapped in BOS's local market area.

External Threats (Macro Level)

- As a result of deregulation, competition has become fierce. Professional salespeople (brokers and insurance agents) have an advantage over bankers, who traditionally have not been "sellers." In addition, the professional's productivity is directly related to his or her income; as most banks exist today, productivity is not directly related to income.

- Larger institutions are more progressive. Their resource base allows them to risk being first in the marketplace to offer a new product or service. Smaller banks, such as BOS, take a back seat in product innovation.

- The San Joaquin Valley has experienced a depressed agricultural economy over the last five years, resulting in an overall depressed local economy.

- The city of Stockton, California, is in a "no-growth" state, brought about by the implementation of Measure A in 1986. This has slowed both residential and commercial growth.

DEVELOPING THE PRIVATE RESERVE PROGRAM

Today's affluent market is very different from this population group in the past. A new breed of individuals is joining the ranks of the upper class. An oil rigger, a business executive or a promising entrepreneur[1] can now be affluent. The upscale are no longer one set of stereotyped demographics; rather, they are a diverse group of people. This fact makes the upscale market difficult to identify; nevertheless, the quest for this new customer base has created tremors throughout the banking industry. Statistics reveal that nine out of ten banks are now trying to market some type of private banking program in hopes of gaining this market. The key to pulling the affluent away from competitors is through unique products and services. Traditional banking, however, may not entirely appeal to this segment. Therefore, financial institutions must have a game plan as they seek this new and very powerful market.

Statistics

The affluent market is growing in size and importance. In 1980, about 8.4% of households were affluent. By 1990, that percentage will climb to 13.8%. In addition, the affluent group is growing at a rate almost four times that of other segments of the population. The affluent market is also becoming younger, so it will be in the marketplace for a longer period of time. Banks that achieve success with affluent customers now will be likely to secure and hold their business, and thus reap the rewards of this profitable segment.[2]

A Need for the Program

Although various competitors are offering products that can potentially attract upscale individuals, none are aggressively seeking the market with a "package" of benefits and services that will act as a true incentive to generate deposits. Our goal is to design a program for BOS, based on the wants and needs of the upscale market. We want to retain BOS's present upscale customers, while seeking a larger share of this market.

SITUATION ANALYSIS

This situation analysis will concentrate specifically on the ability of BOS to offer an upscale program for the untapped upscale market of San Joaquin County.

BOS Internal Strengths and Weaknesses (Micro Level)
Internal Strengths for Offering a Program to Existing Upscale Customers

- The BOS has a significantly larger profitable customer base than the typical bank, with 43% of the customers holding accounts considered to be profitable. Based on a recent industry cost study, accounts that have a minimum balance of $1,000 or more can be considered as adding resources rather than costing resources. Under this criteria, 96% of the bank's accounts are considered profitable. In addition, 20% of the bank's customers who hold deposits of $10,000 or more constitute 82% of the bank's deposits. A breakdown of accounts of $100,000 or more reveals 819 accounts; $75,000 or more, 1,109 accounts; $50,000 or more, 1,760 accounts; $25,000 or more, 3,597 accounts; and accounts $10,000 or more, 8,606 accounts. The BOS has a fertile customer base for an upscale program.

- From BOS's inception, service has been a priority. With proper training, the bank's employees would be able to make the transition for implementing an upscale program, along with its service requirements.

- Flexibility on the lending side of the bank will serve as an attribute for this program. It allows BOS to meet each customer's needs on an individual basis.

- With proper training and adherence to guidelines, BOS has the personnel to serve this segment.

- The longevity of BOS makes it a natural for an upscale program; a large portion of the old money in town is already in the BOS. BOS carries the credibility and image (strong and stable) that this segment of the market demands.

Internal Weaknesses for Offering a Program to Existing Upscale Customers
- The BOS has eight offices in San Joaquin County. The upscale who want ready-access to the bank despite their location, might not choose BOS. BOS is not a nationwide bank. This, however, is also a problem experienced by the other local banks in our community.

- In offering such a program, BOS's service must be exceptional to retain "upscale" customers. Training on all levels will need to be conducted to introduce the program, discuss service requirements, and meet customer expectations.

Internal Strengths in Offering the Program (On a Micro Level)
Internal Strengths for Generating a Larger Market Share of the Upscale
- The BOS image is appealing to those who consider their money special. BOS is involved in the community, and invests in it.

- BOS has influential social and political ties throughout the communities it serves. This makes name identification an asset for the upscale customer, who is often involved with these same groups.

- BOS's flexibility in addressing customers' needs and its flexible lending policies are strengths upscale customers appreciate.

- The local, quick-decision making capabilities of BOS's lending staff differentitates the bank from its competition.

- Due to a low employee turnover rate of 3.33%, customers see familiar faces. This is important in developing a banking relationship on a first-name basis, thus promoting trust and credibility.

- The upscale base that BOS currently possesses can serve as a valuable referral source to generate more market share if the program is properly implemented and meets expectations.

Internal Weaknesses for Generating a Larger Market Share of the Upscale
- The mode of thinking at BOS is conservative and reactive; whereas, this program entails progressive thinking in terms of the upscale customers' wants and needs, and of truly fulfilling them.

- Accountability is not in the nature of BOS, but will be necessary if the program is to succeed. Customer follow-up, attention to problem-solving and personal attention are demanded by upscale customers. Unfavorable comments from upscale customers because of unmet expectations will ruin the bank's program.

External Weaknesses for Generating a Larger Market Share of the Upscale
- Most of the potential upscale customers are presently banking with other banks or financial service organizations. Pulling them away will be difficult.

- The professional salesperson has an advantage over the banker. The professional salesperson is a primary competitor for the upscale market.

- As the upscale market continues to gain importance, the possibility of market saturation exists. However, if the program offered by BOS is superior, it will have a jump on the market and a greater likelihood of success.

- Economic trends as a whole may reverse. Consumers are presently in a growth market. If the economy regresses, consumers will feel the effect. In addition, new tax laws could affect the upscale market and the financial service companies involved with these markets.

Competition
This section is separated into two parts: local, community banks, that compete with BOS on a comparable, direct level, and the regional banks. Both will be analyzed on a general basis.

Local Competition
Strengths and Opportunities. The strengths and opportunities of the local banks are very similar to those of BOS. They are independently held and also share the community bank image. However, BOS's longevity, flexible lending policies, and secure deposit history should differentiate it from the local competition when considering an upscale program.

Weaknesses and Threats. Threats and weaknesses of the local banks are also very similar to those at BOS. The local competition could offer a program geared to the upscale, but research indicates that none of them are currently pursuing this market. Although competitors agree that this market is important, none are planning, at the present, to aggressively pursue it. For now, they are content with the products and services they provide. This makes the upscale market untapped on the local level.

Big Banks
Strengths and Opportunities. Size is the most obvious asset of the big banks. These banks are nationally known and have a ready market because of name recognition. Customer convenience is addressed by the use of technology to a greater extent by larger banks. These banks are proactive; usually being the first in the marketplace to introduce new programs and products.

Weaknesses and Threats. Consumer perception of big banks is less favorable on the local level because these banks invest outside of the local communities. Bigger banks suffer from bad public relations. They are viewed as impersonal when compared to local banks. The perception of a lack of personalized service makes people feel that they are not special. A big depositor might think that his or her deposit is considered less important at a big bank than at a smaller bank such as BOS. Few decisions are made locally; decision making is less flexible than at a local bank.

Given this competitive situation, we believe BOS is in a good position to offer a program for upscale customers. The need for such a program is clear, since these customers are not being fully targeted by competitors.

Benefits to the BOS in Offering an Upscale Program

1. This program will maintain and increase the deposit base and/or overall banking relationship of upscale customers.

2. It allows the bank's image of personal service to be magnified.

3. It facilitates cross-sales, tying the bank more closely to the customer.

4. It enhances the bank's competitive edge in the marketplace.

5. New products and services will be developed as we address the needs and wants of this market.

6. Given that implementation meets customer expectations, BOS will be looked upon as more progressive, and as an expert in the field of financial services. Referrals based on satisfied customers will create a growing market share.

Risks to BOS in Offering an Upscale Program

1. Expectations on the part of the consumer must be met. If these expectations are not met, word-of-mouth will destroy the image of the program and the credibility of the bank. Further, it will give competitors an opportunity to win over the customer whose expectations were not addressed properly.

2. Those customers that cannot quality for the program must be carefully handled if we are to maintain their existing relationship with the bank.

3. In offering this program, it is essential to consider those customers who qualify initially and do not qualify at a later date. The manner in which these customers are disqualified from the program is important so that their original banking relationship is maintained.

LOCATING AND IDENTIFYING THE UPSCALE MARKET

A key aspect of this program is understanding the upscale market. This is necessary for the bank to directly pursue the affluent. The goal is to identify customers whose deposit relationships make them profitable and to not lose them to waiting competitors, while increasing market share of the upscale market. The creation of this upscale base will focus on both existing and new customers, drawn to BOS by the program.

Problems with Identification

Realizing that the upscale market is comprised of many segments is critical to the development of this program. The 20/80 rule within the banking industry reflects the fact that, typically, 20% of a bank's retail customers are responsible for 80% of all retail deposit dollars. Identifying that 20% is the key to identifying true upscale customers. There is something to be said about the 20/80 rule. Most banks recognize that deposit accounts with less than $1,000 minimum balances are not generally profitable; however, individual deposit relationships are insufficient in determining profitable or unprofitable customers. While 80% of all deposit accounts may be minimally profitable or unprofitable, it is not necessarily true that 80% of all customers, after examining their total bank relationship, are minimally profitable or totally unprofitable.

To find profitable customers, customer files from the retail, corporate, and trust areas must be integrated. Without a complete relationship management system, knowing which relationships are truly profitable is impossible. Deposit analysis by itself only determines which accounts are profitable or unprofitable. The solution is a customer information system that integrates by division (retail, commercial, trust), all available information for each customer.

This identification is important: Effective access to resources depends on the ability to know what the present total customer relationship is, as well as what the relationship has the potential of becoming.

Segmenting the Upscale Market

When a deposit analysis is done, generally the 20% that hold 80% of the deposits are segmented into two groups. Forty percent (40%) of the 20% (who retain 80% of all deposits) are referred to as Personal Banking Customers (PBC). PBCs are those who retain minimum balances of $10,000 or more in a single-deposit account. About two-thirds are retirees, while one-third are two-income families with white-collar jobs. All PBCs are not considered upscale, but they are a distinct segment, that, as a whole, can be further segmented to determine hidden upscale customers.[3]

The other 60% of the 20% who maintain 80% of all deposits are referred to as Semi-Personal Banking Customers (SPBC). SPBCs maintain between $1,000 and $9,999 in a single-deposit account. Given the current industry cost structure, an account with a minimum balance of $1,000 is considered profitable. Thus, SPBCs represent a profitable segment of our customer base. SPBCs are often young professionals, recent college graduates or two-income blue-collar families. This segment can also be segmented further to locate hidden upscale.[4]

Assuming a retail deposit base of 100,000 accounts. PBCs would constitute 8,000 account, or 8% of the total customer base. SPBCs would constitute 12,000 accounts, or 12% of the total customer base. Using this formula for BOS's current customer base, one would expect approximately 5,504 accounts to be PBCs and 8,256 accounts to be SPBCs. In fact, however, of the 68,800 retail accounts at BOS, 12.5% of the total customer base, or 8,606 accounts are PBCs, and 31% of the total customer base, or 20,880 accounts are SPBCs. In our case, 43% of the accounts contribute 96% of all deposits. Based on BOS's breakdown of deposit accounts, the bank has significantly fewer unprofitable accounts than the typical institution.

BOS's customer base, therefore, is more profitable than the typical bank's. This would seem to indicate fertile ground for offering an upscale program. Excluding the profitable customers in the $1,000 to $9,999 range would mistakenly eliminate potential hidden upscale (HU) customers; therefore, for the purpose of this study, the model used for segmentation purposes was based on 43% of the customers comprising 96% of the deposit base.

Segmenting the Hidden Upscale
Only a small percentage of current PBCs and SPBCs will actually be upscale. The hidden upscale (HU) among the PBCs include the affluent, who, for whatever reason, retain a portion of their holdings in high-deposit , low-yield accounts. Approximately 12.5% of the bank's current PBCs are expected to fall into the HU category.

Similarly, approximately 8.3% of a bank's SPBCs are expected to fall in the HU category. These might be physicians or career professionals who are managing their financial resources for personal gain and choose not to place funds into the highest-interest-yielding investment.

Given these beginning statistics, a bank with a deposit base of 100,000 retail accounts can be expected to have 1,000 HU among its PBCs (12.5% of the 40% PBCs, of the 20% who maintain 80% of all retail deposit dollars) and 1,000 HU among its SPBCs (8.3% of the 60% SPBCs of the 20% who maintain 80% of all retail deposit dollars).

Since actual accounts of PBCs ($10,000 or more) are 8,606, representing 29% of the 43% who hold 96% of the deposits, the HU market in BOS should constitute 1,076 customers. SPBCs, representing 71% of the 43% who hold 96% of all deposits should generate a HU base of 8.3% or 2,610 customers. Thus, the estimated HU market, among our current customers, is 3,686 accounts.

CRITERIA TO QUALIFY FOR THE PROGRAM
The bank will adhere to a strict set of criteria to choose individuals for the program. The criteria will be as follows:

- Net worth must exceed one year's gross income
- Liabilities must be less than 50% of assets
- Debt must be less than 35% of gross income

Loan pricing policy will be tied to a compensating balance philosophy. The best loan rates will be given to those customers who maintain a compensating balance in a demand account equivalent to one-third the amount being borrowed. Thus, a customer with a $30,000 demand deposit account could potentially borrow up to $90,000 at prime or prime plus one-half percent. The exact rate would be determined by the criteria outlined in this paper, as well as:

- Length of customer relationship
- Depth of total customer relationship
- Evaluation of customer integrity
- Risk of loan purpose

OBJECTIVES
The objective is to effectively segment the 43% of the retail customer base whose deposit relationship make them profitable customers. A major goal is to retain existing profitable customers while increasing profitable market share.

Program Goals: Qualitative & Quantitative
The qualitative goal is to retain existing profitable customers while increasing profitable market share by tapping the hidden upscale market held by the competition. The bank will aim to obtain as many of these customers as possible.

Quantitatively, the goal is to increase BOS's total deposits over a one-year period by 2%, based on the implementation of this upscale program. This goal should increase deposits by $9,557,597.

$477,879,830 (Total deposits BOS, 12/86)
x_____.02% (Goal of increase)
$9,557,597 (Deposit generation, 1-year period)

Over a one-year period, the number of accounts, based on a 2% increase would be approximately 811.

$9,557,597 (Goal of program in deposits for 1 year)
$11,790 (Average deposit size of HU)
811 (Accounts pulled from market in 1 year)

In addressing the goal above, the asset and liability side of the bank must also be addressed. It was established earlier that one of the customer benefits of the program was a loan up to three times the amount held in a demand deposit account. Using the $9,557,597 as an annual deposit increase goal of 2%, BOS could potentially increase loan volume by a total of $28,672,791 over a one-year period. Some customers will not take advantage of the credit incentive, or will not use the total amount of funds they qualify for. However, for the purposes of the study, the above growth figures should be considered by the Asset/Liability Management Committee of the bank.

UPSCALE PRODUCT DEVELOPMENT: "THE PACKAGE"

In addition to the deposit incentives via credit, five products will also be introduced. When considering the following list, it is important to note how each product is designed to appeal directly to the needs of the upscale. The list is by no means exhaustive, however, it does detail a package for the program that can be easily implemented by BOS and is designed around the concept of meeting the unique needs of the upscale.

Executive Line of Credit

This is a personal line of credit ranging from $10,000 to $100,000 or more. This product makes a statement to upscale customers about their ability to leverage personal assets for business investments. [5]

Special Access Automatic Teller

Customers would be granted a daily access amount between $500 and $1,000 (as compared to the usual $200 limit). [6]

Executive Hotline

The executive hotline would provide twenty-four hour communication with the banker at the customer's convenience. A constantly available two-line answering/recording service would be installed for the customer to communicate directly with their banker. This product reduces perceptions that banks don't function for customer convenience. Access to the line is exclusive, and the cost to install such a system is minimal. [7]

Financial Hotline

By adding a second line to the 24-hour customer phone, the bank can maximize the cost efficiency of both. This line could give the Dow Jones; the price of silver and gold; and quotes on euro-dollars, commercial paper, and large CDs. [8]

Guaranteed Check Cashing Card

The guaranteed check cashing card will guarantee a check in any BOS branch. The customer will have to credit-qualify, as well as be a signer on the demand account for which the card is issued. A limit of $200 a day would be sufficient for most customers, especially if dollar access to the ATM is increased. Tellers will not have to ask for identification and waiting time for customers will be reduced substantially.[9]

Special Seminars

Seminars dealing with profit realization, and tax planning are good vehicles to reach the upscale. They are excellent for referrals, giving present customers the opportunity to bring a friend.[10]

The above products are inexpensive to implement although they add substantially to fulfilling the convenience, ego and status needs of upscale customers. Any one of the services offered by itself would not make a great impact on how upscale customers perceive the bank; however, when the entire package is offered, the bank is making a clear statement that it plans to meet the unique needs of these customers more fully than its competitors.

MARKETING AND ADVERTISING

The marketing mix of price, product, promotion, and distribution will position the product to appeal to the upscale market discussed earlier.

Product and Price

The criteria established result in a three-tiered program. Price (loan rates) are tiered according to compensating balances. The customer, in return, receives red carpet treatment, preferred rates, and a package of exclusive benefits.

Promotion

Promotion will be generated by word-of-mouth and by referrals. The marketing approach that generates profitable customers is the goal: quality of customers versus quantity of customers. A subtle form of communication via direct mail will be used. All correspondence will be on "Private Reserve" stationary.

Distribution

Once the upscale segment is identified internally, direct mail will be used. Studies indicate that direct mail is the best means of communicating with the upscale market because the qualifications are so strict. This results in cost-efficiency as an added benefit.[11] An initial letter from the CEO of the bank will introduce the program and its benefits. This will also be used for referrals.

Positioning

The image the program will aim to project is exclusivity as well as flexibility. The "Private Reserve Program" will position itself as unique, prestigious and exclusive, and continue to maintain the strong and stable image of Bank of Stockton.

STRUCTURE

The Private Reserve Department will be structured so that lenders have different levels of responsibility and sufficient support staff to handle noncredit decision matters. Structure is important in allowing lenders the time required to analyze special credit requests. Time is necessary to analyze and determine the appropriate pricing of a loan. Attempting to hire less support employees initially or combining staff jobs are ways to lose credibility from the beginning. Lenders have to have the time to deliver quality service to customers while generating customer referrals. Unless the quality is superior, present customers will not make referrals. A proper structure assists the efforts of the department to encourage a total relationship with one bank.

To provide the flexibility needed to make this department unique, the initial structure will provide for three levels of lenders, each with sufficient loan authority and support staff to let them function in an efficient manner. In addition to the three levels of lenders, a secretary, loan closer and market associate will be hired to perform necessary functions that the lenders do not have the time to perform.

IMPLEMENTATION

The proper implementation of the Private Reserve Program will involve several important phases to ensure a quality program.

Phase 1: Develop of a relationship management system
Integration of the customer information file to link customer relationships in different divisions (commercial, retail, trust) and to determine the total customer relationship, as well as profitable and potentially profitable accounts. This will locate and identify profitable accounts internally.

Phase 2: Designate key platform officers of Private Reserve Program

- Education on upscale customer wants, needs, and statistics

- Program orientation

- Product development, discussion, and education

- Intensified program training

- Revamp customer contact personnel
  - Sales training
  - Customer profiles
  - Personal selling

- General employee orientation to the program
  - Service training
  - Identification of upscale at all levels of customer contact
  - Training on program benefits and product knowledge

Phase 3: Formally organize department
  - CEO, executive vice president, senior loan administrator and branch administrators choose officer(s) for Private Reserve Department

  - Hire/choose closer, market associate, and secretary

  - Decide on the logistics of department (location, decor, and image)

  - Establish department

Phase 4: Develop and cultivate upscale customer base
  - Internal

  - External market (generate and seek referrals)

  - Direct mail/calls

  - Continual monitoring of percentage objectives of customer base

Phase 5: Maintain and service existing upscale
  - Aggressively seek new market share

  - Add business development officer(s), with an emphasis on new business from upscale consumers

  - Maintain existing accounts

  - Develop new products, based on wants and needs customers

CONCLUSION

The key to success of the Private Reserve Program depends heavily on a commitment from top management in the bank. Although the program has tremendous profit potential, the service and coordination aspects cannot be overlooked. The analysis recognizes the fact that the needs of all consumers are not the same. Certain retail customer segments are sufficiently profitable to warrant special attention in meaningful product development. The program will allow the bank the opportunity to focus attention on the profitable and potentially profitable, high-deposit segments. BOS's large number of profitable customers makes them a prime candidate for offering the Private Reserve Program. Based on the competitive analysis of San Joaquin County, the need for such a program is evident. ◆

---

1 Author Unknown, "Firms Urged to Update Corporate Identities in a Push To Attract Changing Upscale Customer," *Financial Services Week*, Vol. 2., No. 9, (March 4, 1985).

2 Donald F. Howard, "Planning for the Affluent Market," *ABA Journal of Personal Financial Services for the Affluent*, Vol. 1, No. 4 (Summer 1985), p. 6.

3 Marilyn MacGruder Barnwell and Jerome R. Cori, *A Banker's Pragmatic Approach to the Upscale*, (The MacGruder Agency, Denver:1982), p. 9.

4 Ibid.

5 Ibid., p. 55.

6 Ibid., p. 56.

7 Ibid.

8 Ibid.

9 Ibid.

10 Ibid., p. 57.

11 Diana Wendt, "Florida's Park Bank Makes 'House Calls' on CMA Customers," *Trust Marketing Resource*, (November-December), 1985, p.4.

CHAPTER 13

Product Proposal for the "Up and Comer" Market Segment

Scot Ferris
Old Kent Financial Corporation
$5.5 billion assets

PREFACE

In January of 1986, Old Kent Bank - Kent's management commissioned a market research study to determine its perceived image in the communities it serves. Briefly, the research findings indicated that the bank was perceived by consumers (both customers and noncustomers) as being relatively undifferentiated from its competitors. The research indicated that consumers ranked the bank fifth on a scale of six banks (six being the worst ranking), based on twelve evaluative criteria. This was particularly alarming given that Old Kent has the largest share of the market at 37%, while its nearest competitor has a 21% market share.

In light of the severity of the bank's image problem, its management identified three critical actions in its 1987 strategic plan which in sum, will be effective in improving the bank's image. These actions, defined in broad terms are (1) product development, (2) an image/positioning advertising campaign, and (3) an aggressive customer relations program.

This market plan is intended to partially address the bank's product development needs. The rationale for focusing on this strategy is to ensure that the products and the accompanying service provided are representative of the image that the bank wishes to project to consumers.

Enhancement of the bank's image will entail the creation and articulation of an image that reflects the bank's strengths and cultural philosophy and that is believable and deliverable to the consumer. The market plan presented here, focuses on increasing the bank's penetration into the "up and comer" market segment. Briefly, "up and comer" households are defined as those households whose annual income is at least $25,000 and whose primary wage earner is between twenty-five and forty-nine years of age. This program is intended to enhance the Bank's image by actualizing or "delivering the goods" to the market's largest group of consumers—the twenty-five to forty-nine years olds. Coincident with enacting strategies related to penetrating this age group will be implementation of an ad campaign with the slogan, "Old Kent Bank, Common Sense—Uncommon Service." The proposed market plan should help the bank meet consumer expectations created by the campaign and should, in time, improve consumer perceptions of the bank and our performance.

SITUATION ANALYSIS
Current Position of Old Kent Bank
Old Kent Bank - Kent is an affiliate bank of Old Kent Financial Corporation (OKFC) and is located in Kent City, Michigan. This report is the result of a request submitted by the bank to OKFC for assistance in the product development area.

Financial Information (December 31, 1985)

- Total assets $96,577 M
- Total deposits $87,941 M
- Total loans $55,412 M

- Return on assets   1.02 %
- Return on equity   13.67 %
- Leverage   13.4 x

- Deposit market share   30.70 %
- Loan market share   35.00 % *

* This market share figure was derived based on the assumption that Federal Savings and Loan experienced a 60% loan-deposit ratio in 1985.

The bank's five-year loan growth (1980-1985) was 7.8%. Bank of Sparta and NBD-Kent exhibited growth rates of 20.5% and 18% respectively, for the same period. Deposit growth at Old Kent was 32.9% (1980-1985) compared to 42.1% for the market.

Organizational Information
The bank has eight branches within Kent County, with a full-time staff equivalent of 84 employees. Old Kent has one ATM which is located in Kent City. In 1984, the bank changed its name to Old Kent, and a new president/CEO was appointed to the bank in 1985.

Significant Market Segments

Since this plan focuses on the retail segment of the market, commercial segments have been ignored. A portion of Old Kent Bank's market is found in the following areas:

- Hughes State College: 10,000 students, 500 faculty members
- Spring Lake: Represented by a relatively older, more sophisticated market with good potential for residential mortgages and a growing, stable deposit base.

The market has the following characteristics:

- Thirty-three percent of the Kent County's population is between twenty-five to forty-nine years of age compared to 24% in 1980.
- The median age of the county's population was twenty-two in 1980, and is currently twenty-seven years of age.
- Old Kent's penetration of the 25-34 year old segment is 21.9%, its penetration of the 35-49 year old segment is 22.7%

The relatively large market potential that exists in the twenty-five to forty-nine years old segment both in terms of absolute size and in economic strength underscores the need for the bank to capture a greater share of this segment's financial patronage. As these consumers grow older and their lifestyles change, their financial needs and habits will change as well. Due to the aggregated economic value that this segment represents, the bank must position itself to meet their financial needs now and in the future.

This plan is focused on addressing this target market's current financial needs with the intent of fostering long-term banking relationships, as these consumers move through their financial life cycles.

CRITICAL ASSUMPTIONS

The following assumptions, by no means conclusive regarding the environment that the bank operates in, are deemed appropriate for this proposal.

Economic

The bank's market area will continue to experience economic growth estimated to be 2% to 3%, annually. This growth rate is approximately 50% less than that experienced in Michigan general.

Regulatory/Legislative

New federal tax laws will become effective January 1, 1987. The liberalization of interstate and intrastate banking laws have prompted consolidation and acquisition activity both locally and nationally.

Social
Consumer awareness and understanding of financial services will increase, but at a much slower rate relative to the increasing number of financial services being offered and the various types of firms offering these services. As a result, product differentiation will continue to be difficult, and many products can be expected to have shorter life cycles. Consumer fascination and confidence in the stock market will continue to be strong; and the emphasis by the consumer on quality and value will continue to be prevalent. Bankers can expect increased public concern regarding the stability of the banking industry.

STRENGTHS AND WEAKNESSES
The bank's strengths and weaknesses are presented below and focus on issues which are pertinent to the proposed product and the bank's perceived image.

Strengths/Opportunities

- Thirty-three percent of the population is between 25-49 years of age.

- Resources are avaliable to offer a broader range of financial services than our competitors.

- The bank has a countywide distribution system.

- Old Kent is a market leader relative to share of deposits and loans.

- Old Kent has a reputation as a financially strong institution.

Weaknesses/Threats

- The bank is relatively weak regarding penetration of the 25-49 year old age group.

- Old Kent has a declining deposit market share.

- The bank has a relatively poor image rating.

- The Bank of Sparta currently offers a "package" account.

- The growing presence of the local credit union poses a threat.

- Depressed interest rate conditions have caused consumers to seek alternative investment programs, that is, stocks, bonds, and mutual funds which are outside the Bank.

- There are limited commercial loan and commercial deposit opportunities.

- Old Kent is in a "slow growth" local economy.

OBJECTIVE

Old Kent's main objective is to increase penetration of the 25-34 year old and the 35-49 year old market segments by 23% and 13%, respectively, by January 1988.

Specific steps to meet this objective (to be accomplished by January 1988) include the following:

- Enhance the bank's image as a provider of quality products and quality services.

- Create multiple account relationships (DDA, savings, credit card, installment loan) to increase the longevity and profitability of each customer's association with the bank.

- Increase deposits (demand deposit and statement savings) by 5% ($400,000).

- Increase retail credit outstandings (nonmortgage) by 6% ($1 million).

STRATEGY

By December 1986, the bank will introduce a "package product," called the All-in-One-Plan, to be targeted at the 25-49 year old market segment. The underlying reason for recommending a package-product strategy is found in market segmentation.

The proliferation of financial services and financial service providers has increased exponentially within the past five years. Given this environment and the consumer's limited capacity to assimilate the volume of related information, the need for a bank to differentiate or position its products and services apart from its competitors is critical to its long-term viability. The package product concept proposed here is one tactic that reflects a market segmentation strategy.[1]

Research conducted by Burnett and Chonko found that four general market segments exist as distinguished by product usage patterns.[2] This further substantiates that a package product concept or a segmented approach toward the development of bank products is logical. The tactical issues presented in the subsequent sections are based on this premise.

Product Development

Market Research

Secondary market research information obtained from ACCOUNTLINE regarding product usage by age category and by non-mortgage credit balances is presented below.[3] Please note that this information is for Grand

Traverse County. Similar information was not available for Kent County but this will suffice for inferring usage patterns to the targeted population.

PRODUCT USAGE

Product Utilized	Average Age
DDA	39.0
Savings	39.3
CDs	43.7
Auto loans	35.6
Personal loans	35.3
Credit cards	40.0
N = 500	Average Age = 38.8

Nonmortgage Credit Balances

Balance	Average Age
Non-users	40.0
Less than $1,000	46.7
$1,000 - 2,499	34.9
$2,500 - 4,999	34.1
$5,000- 9,999	37.8
$10,000 +	36.1

The average age of individuals using credit-oriented products declined by 3.2 years with the exception of credit card users. As shown above, there is little deviation in average age in usage of savings accounts and checking accounts.

There is a strong correlation between age and outstanding credit balances, confirming the assertion that the younger market has a greater need for leverage-oriented products. The sampling indicated that the average age of an individual having nonmortgage credit balances is forty. Outstanding nonmortgage credit balances increase as the average age declines, for balances between $1,000 and 4,999. Even more significant is the fact that the average age of the consumer who has less than $1,000 in outstanding credit balances is 46.7 years, almost seven years higher than the sample average age of forty. Again this underscores the declining use of leverage among older consumers.

In conclusion, it is clear that the twenty-five to forty-nine year old segment has a substantial need for credit or leverage-based products. Also, the ACCOUNTLINE data indicates a general need for warehousing (savings) and transaction (DDA) oriented products that is consistent among all life cycle segments. Therefore, the twenty-five to forty-nine year old segment can generally be characterized by a strong demand for consumer credit; thus, the evolving product concept should incorporate attractive credit features as a unique way to differentiate the product to the target market.

Proposed Product Features/Customer Benefits
The proposed features of the All-in-One Account are delineated below:

Pricing: It is recommended that a $6.50 monthly fee be assessed for each account. If a $1,500 minimum balance is maintained, or if a $2,000 average collected balance is maintained, the $6.50 service charge would not be assessed. If the $2,000 average balance is met, the account would earn a rate of interest approximately twenty to forty basis points below the current rate paid on the Money Market Checking Account. The rationale for this strategy is primarily to differentiate the proposed product's interest-bearing checking account from the Insured Money Market Checking Account that the bank currently offers, and the minimization of interest expense associated with the proposed product. The fixed monthly fee is intended to provide consumers with a simplified pricing structure that is easy to understand and easy to budget for.

Unlimited Check Writing: The customer would not be limited in the number of checks he or she issues per month, thereby eliminating potentially high service charges while meeting the customer's need for a transaction-type product.

Free Check Orders (specified style only): Customers would not be assessed a fee for check orders of a designated check style. This would eliminate an additional cost of a checking account typically incurred by a DDA customer.

Discount of 1/2% on Installment Loans: A 1/2% discount would be offered to qualified customers on auto, boat, recreational vehicle, personal, and home improvement loans. This feature minimizes associated interest expense for the customer, and effectively addresses the customer's need for leverage-based services.

Discounted Credit Card: A discounted credit card of the customer's choice—VISA or MasterCard—would be offered as a feature of the proposed product. The "current" and "proposed" credit card pricing structures are summarized on the next page. The "current" category represents Old Kent's standard credit card pricing policy. The "proposed" pricing category reflects the recommended credit card pricing policy for the All-in-One Account.

PROPOSED CREDIT CARD PRICING

	Current	Proposed
• Annual fee	$15.00	$ 0
• Annual percentage rate	18%	15%
• "Grace period" (purchases only)	30 days	15 days

The rationale for this credit card pricing structure is fourfold:

1. It addresses the target market's need for leverage while providing tangible representation of the discounted nature of the overall product.

2. It's contended that the All-in-One customer base will have as a group, a much smaller percentage of delinquencies related to outstanding balances, thus decreasing associated credit risk and allowing a more aggressive pricing strategy.

3. Interest-rate risk would be minimized by decreasing the grace period on purchases from thirty days to fifteen days. This would increase the cash flow or collection cycle of the credit card base. Therefore, the net cost of the 300-basis-point discount is somewhat less relative to the current pricing methodology.

4. Mounting consumer pressure and potential legislation regarding regulation of "exorbitant" credit card interest rates has created an environment which would be receptive to the discounted credit card feature. This may be a primary catalyst in stimulating demand for the product under current rate conditions.

Buying Service: A buying service offered by FISI allows customers to purchase thousands of items via a toll-free phone number, often at a substantial discount from suggested retail prices. To the customer, this is a convenient and cost-effective method to shop for an array of durable goods.

"No-Fee" Savings Account: Customers who open the proposed package account would be allowed to fall below the designated minimum balance requirement for savings accounts thereby avoiding the quarterly maintenance fee. This feature will help meet the customer's need for the basic warehousing of funds and minimization of service charges.

ATM Card: Each customer would be issued an ActionBank 24/CIRRUS ATM access card that effectively provides the customer with greater convenience.

Combined Monthly Statement: All DDA and savings account activity will be incorporated into a single, monthly statement. This will provide the customer with a consolidation, or synopsis of his or her basic account activity.

Market Potential/Projected Sales
Market potential for the proposed product is estimated to be 6,993 households. Projected sales of the product are estimated to be 1,117 accounts by January 1988. This projection is based on the following four assumptions:

- The bank currently has 887 and 668 households represented by the 25-34 year-old and the 35-49 year-old segments, respectively.

- Thirty percent (467 customers) of the current customer base who are 25-49 will open the proposed product.

- The product will attract approximately 300 (5.5%) additional households of the noncustomer portion of the 25-49 year-old segment by January 1988.

- Five percent of the current DDA base (those not included in the target market) will open the proposed product.

Profitability
The profitability aspects of the product discussed here are based on projections derived by using incremental or marginal analysis. It is contended that this methodology is appropriate for this situation in that representative cost data is not available for the bank. Thus, the following three assumptions evolved:

- Cost data, either from the Federal Reserves' Functional Cost Analysis, or from Old Kent Bank and Trust is inappropriate for Old Kent Bank of Kent.

- The infrastructure required to produce, distribute, and maintain the product is already in existence. It is assumed that excess capacity exists, thereby, enabling the bank to accommodate the additional volume created by the product without creating additional direct and indirect expenses.

- Current services, as they are now priced on an individual or "unbundled" basis, provide the bank with a net profit or, at the very least, contribute to fixed costs. Therefore, any incremental or marginal income produced by the product will enhance the bank's profitability by that margin.

Based on estimated accounts generated and on pricing structure, the following financial projections can be made:

Incremental Revenue (per account, per annum)

Service fee	$36.60
Investment income	$51.40 *

* Assumes an average net interest margin of 2.57%, based on a $2,000 average collected balance.

Incremental Expenses

Credit card (waived annual fee)	$ 7.50
Free check orders	5.69
Buying service	1.80
Loan discount	9.00 *
Total Incremental Expenses	$23.99

* It is assumed that 50% of the product's customer base will use the 1/2% loan discount at any specified time.

Projected Incremental Profit (per account, pretax, per annum)
Accounts that fall below the $1,500 minimum balance requirement should have a profit of $12.61. Accounts that maintain at least a $2,000 average balance requirement should have a profit of $27.41.

Note that both deposit and credit balances associated with this product are excluded from the analysis. This approach is consistent with the assumptions stated at the beginning of this section regarding the application of marginal analysis to this product, although additional deposits will likely be general, it is the difficult to project balances with confidence.

Total Incremental Revenue
Assume that 80% of the projected number of new accounts will be assessed the monthly service charge.

$$1,117(.8) \times \$12.61 = \$11,268 \text{ (incremental fee income)}$$

Assume that 20% of the projected customer base maintains a $2,000 average balance and therefore, is not charged a service fee, but provides the bank with an interest margin.

$$1,117 (.2) \times \$27.41 = \$ 6,123$$

Total Incremental Income
The total incremental income projected for 1987, pro rata basis of 65%, is $11,300. The $11,300 does not include incremental   advertising, promotional, or incentive expenditures (shown in the "Budget" section of this report). Additionally, cash flow created by fee income or investment income will increase as more accounts are added throughout the year, hence the basis for the pro-rata of 65%.

Communications
General Objective
The bank's general objective for comunications is to effectively position the product to appeal to the 25-49 year market segment while minimizing cannibalization of the Advantage Fifty prospect base (those consumers who are age fifty or older).

General Strategy
Three general strategies will be used to create the desired perceived image of the product.

Product name: The name, *All-in-One Plan* is recommended for this product. This recommendation is based on the positive reception of All-in-One by focus group participants during the "Gold Kent" research. Participants felt that the name All-in-One Plan implied an account which would encompass, "all the basic financial services that I would utilize." Licensing for the use of the name through First Hawaiian Bank is contingent upon the approval of the proposal by the bank's management. Costs associated with obtaining the rights to this name will be absorbed by Old Kent Bank and Trust.

Communication of benefits: The advertising will focus on the benefits afforded to the customer by the All-in-One Plan. Basically, the focal point of both print and radio advertising will be on the value that the All-in-One Plan provides the customer primarily through its discount oriented features,such as the 1/2% interest rate discount on instalment loans, discounted credit card, no-fee savings account, and unlimited check writing. The message will attempt to emphasize value without increasing the consumer's consciousness of the bank's pricing policies.

Advertising: The presentation of the advertising (graphics, copy, placement) must be done with consideration given to both the emotional and rational processes of the consumer in order to create a perception of value, that is, price and quality. This perception is founded on three factors: the benefits offered, the price of the service, and the image of the bank portrayed in the ads. These general factors will create a price-quality relationship (perceived value) for the service.

Development of advertising materials will be referred to Sefron Associates Advertising Agency. Production costs will be allocated to each participating bank within the holding company, dependent upon the modifications requested.

External Communications
The media campaign for the All-in-One Plan will be delayed until after the Christmas and New Year's holiday, because of the volume of seasonal

advertising that typically occurs during this time of the year. External communications will include newspaper, radio, advertising, brochures, direct mail, and statement messages.

Newspaper
1. Ad production (one ad): All advertising materials, including both print and radio ads will be produced for Old Kent Bank and Trust. Old Kent Bank-Kent will not absorb any production costs other than those related to altering the ads for use in the bank's market.

2. Ad placement
   * *Pioneer* (daily) and *Pioneer East* (weekly)

   * 35 column inch ad (5x7)

3. Frequency of ad
   * Initial six weeks
     --2x per week (*Pioneer*)
     --1x per week (*Pioneer East*)

   * Maintenance (on going)
     --1x per month (*Pioneer* only)

   * Frequency: 35x

   * Estimated budget: $1,922

Radio
1. Ad production (two ads)

2. Selected Stations
   * WBRN-AM: Modern country/crossover 25-49 year old adults

   * WBRN-FM: Adult contemporary, 18-49 year old adults

3. Total Schedule
   * 90 spots in total initial six weeks, budget $1,255

   * 78 spots maintenance rotating through the year, budget $765

4. Estimated budget: $2,020

Promotion
1. Develop point-of-sale brochure with an estimated budget to be absorbed by Old Kent Bank and Trust.

2. Direct mail: The direct mail campaign will be initiated approximately six weeks subsequent to the introduction of the product.

3. Statement messages
   - DDA and TDA
   - To be included on statements during the initial 12 weeks

Internal Communications
Employees will be informed of the All-in-One Plan program during training sessions described in the Distribution/Sales section that follows.

Distribution/Sales
Product Training: Product training will focus on assisting personnel in articulating the the benefits afforded the customer by the All-in-One Plan. All employees should receive training regarding the All-in-One Plan. The level of training should depend on the frequency of customer contact and whether or not sales opportunities exist with a given position. The training seminars should be designed with the following attendee profile.

Classification	Level of Training
Branch managers	Maximum
Tellers	Maximum
General info. telephone operator	Medium
General management (non-retail)	Medium
All other personnel	Low

Employees should receive an outline describing the product's features and underscoring the associated benefits. The bank's Marketing Department should conduct a formal telephone "shop" of employees to determine the effectiveness of training. This should occur approximately two weeks after the introduction of the product. Additional training, or modifications in the training techniques should be initiated depending upon the findings of the "shop."

Sales: It is essential that sales opportunities be defined and exploited. A brief listing of potential opportunities is presented here and illustrates a sales orientation toward fulfilling customer needs via the All-in-One Plan. This listing is not intended as a conclusive menu of sales tactics, but merely to illustrate situations where opportunities exist.

- Review and discuss with the prospect his or her current level of monthly checking account service charges. The flat-rate monthly fee of the All-in-One Plan might prove a strong incentive.

- Cross-sell to prospective installment loan customers at the point of sale (at a branch office or during a phone inquiry) emphasizing the 1/2% discount on the loan if the customer opens an All-in-One Plan.

- Target newlyweds, newcomers, and mortgage applicants as prime prospects for the All-in-One Plan. Points of distribution and sources of information include the local Welcome Wagon, Realtors, the local newspaper (wedding announcements), and the bank's mortgage department.

- Tellers should be prepared to refer customers to the platform area who: 1) express displeasure with DDA service charges, 2) make frequent payments on their credit cards or installment loan, 3) are reordering new check forms, or 4) inquire about interest bearing accounts.

- Customers who will be paying off their installment loans within one to three months are good prospects to receive direct mail regarding the All-in-One Plan. A letter would be mailed to these customers thanking them for their patronage and introducing them to the benefits of having an All-in-One Plan when applying for their next installment loan. The letter would briefly mention, but emphasize the 1/2% loan discount available with the All-in-One Plan. An All-in-One Plan brochure would also be enclosed. The intent here it to use our current customer base as a source for new accounts.

- The 1/2% installment loan, interest rate discount afforded by the All-in-One Plan will be mentined in the installment loan and credit card brochures.

- It is recommended that $1,000 be budgeted for employee incentives related to the All-in-One Plan.

MONITOR
Identified below are several methods that should be used to monitor and assess the status of the All-in-One Plan program. Furthermore, as this information is reviewed, tactical adjustments should be initiated as needed to ensure that the stated objectives are achieved and that the basis for the success or failure of a strategy or tactic can be documented. This procedure will aid in future decisions related to the product.

Monthly Product Reports
A monthly product report should be developed and should contain the following information:

1. Number of accounts

2. Number of new customers versus the number of existing customers who converted to the All-in-One Plan

3. The average opening deposit balance (savings and checking combined)

4. Average opening loan balance

5. The number of customers utilizing the discounted interest rate on installment loans

6. The number of accounts opened during the current quarter

7. Balance stratifications (DDA only)

8. Information regarding the source from which the customer first obtained information regarding the All-in-One Plan (to be obtained from new account forms)

9. Competitor pricing (reaction)

Employee Quality Control Evaluations
Employee quality control evaluations ("shops") will be conducted via phone approximately two weeks subsequent to the introduction of the All-in-One Plan.

One or two customers will be given a questionnaire from which to read and record responses. Approximately thirty shops will be executed. "Shoppers" would be paid $2 per completed questionnaire. Potentially, all employees could be "shopped."

Market Research
A less extensive market research study than that which was conducted during the first quarter of 1986 will be designed by the Market Research Department and administered during the first quarter of 1989.

Specifically, the research will attempt to establish whether or not 1) the bank's image has been enhanced by its product development, communications and customer relations efforts; 2) penetration into the twenty-five to forty-nine market segment has increased; and 3) competitors have made any significant gain on the designated perceptual criteria that were defined in the initial study.

Budget
A summary of the budget for the proposed All-in-One Plan is shown on the following page.

ADDITIONAL RECOMMENDATIONS
The environmental analysis conducted to support this plan revealed the need for the bank to establish a more formal pricing mechanism than is currently in place. It appears that the bank has lagged behind the market in initiating pricing changes. Additionally, the relationship between the

BUDGET SUMMARY

Projected 1987 incremental income		$11,300
Communications		5,965
Newspaper	$1,922	
Radio	2,020	
Direct mail	2,023	
Employee Incentives		(1,000)
Monitoring		
Customer quality control program		(60)
Market research (deferred until 1989)		-0-
Projected Pretax Net Incremental Income		
1988		$4,275
1989		$20,000

pricing structures of various related products does not appear to be synchronized. Therefore, the following actions are recommended:

1. Formulate a formal pricing committee to review pricing policies and strategies on a regular basis.

2. Increase fees on Personal Checking.

3. Increase fees on Thrift Checking.

4. Introduce a fee on "low-balance" savings accounts.

CONCLUSION

This proposal for the All-in-One Plan evolved as one of the actions, identified by Old Kent Bank 's management, required to enhance the bank's image and, in the end, its long-term growth.

The All-in-One Plan is intended to attract consumers in the twenty-five to forty-nine year old segment, but it is quite probable that consumers from all segments could be drawn to this product. Because of its credit orientation, however, the majority of demand should be from the target segment.

The projected incremental income of $4,275 (pretax) for 1987 may appear insignificant relative to other sources of income, but as with any type of relationship pricing strategy, the entire value of the account relationship must be assessed. In this analysis, the profitability of the product was completed using incremental analysis, thereby assuming that the bank will benefit long-term by guaranteeing an expanded account relationship with each All-in-One Plan consumer. Therefore, the projected net income for 1987 is a very conservative estimate of the benefit that the bank would realize as a result of this product offering. ◆

---

[1] F. D. Reynolds and W. D. Wells, "Life Style Analysis: A Dimension for Future-Oriented Bank Research," *Journal of Bank Research* , (Autumn 1978), pp. 181-184.

[2] John J. Burnett and Lawrence A. Chonko, "A Segmental Approach to "Packaging" Bank Products," *Journal of Retail Banking*, Vol. 6, No. 1 and 2, (Spring/Summer 1984), p. 10.

[3] ACCOUNTLINE - Compendium, "Life Cycles: Charting the Tide of Service Use, Deposit and Credit Balances, and Above All, Profits," Vol. 3 and 4, (August/September 1982), pp. 2-9.

CHAPTER 14

The Mature Market Program

Jamie E. Logan
National Bank of Detroit
$15 billion assets

INTRODUCTION
As federal financial deregulation proceeds, competition among the region's financial servicers is increasing and intensifying, and consumers are becoming more knowledgeable and demanding. In the past two years National Bank of Detroit (NBD) has been losing market share.

To help NBD maintain market position, recapture lost market share, and increase its customer base and profitability, NBD proposes a program for the mature market—a two-tiered set of packages of financial products and services designed to meet the special needs and desires of older consumers (ages fifty-five and up).

This group of consumers has the resources to demand special treatment from financial institutions—and to make that special treatment worthwhile to the institutions.

OBJECTIVES
Corporate Mission Statement
To paraphrase NBD's "Retail Strategic Plan for 1985-1989," our corporate mission is: To remain a leading marketer of valuable and convenient financial products and services, and to respond to the demands of our market with clearly superior and innovative new products and services.

Corporate Objective
National Bank of Detroit is the leading provider of consumer banking services in southeast Michigan. It has earned this position by providing

expert financial advice and products of high quality, by locating branch offices conveniently, by developing efficient banking operations, and by quickly adopting and applying technological advances in consumer banking—from individual teller terminals to automated teller machines.

However, as federal financial deregulation proceeds, competition among the region's financial servicers is getting more intense. In the past two years, another local bank, Comerica, has become a major competitor, cutting into our markets and taking market share away from NBD in several product areas.

In order to maintain market position, recapture lost market share, and increase our customer base and profitability, NBD must become more sensitive to consumers and develop innovative financial services and marketing strategies for these new services.

Our five-year corporate objectives are the following (to protect the confidentiality of NBD's real strategic plan, all figures listed on this page are hypothetical):

- Manage the products of NBD's Regional Banking Division on the basis of meaningful profit and loss statements, balance sheets and customer relationship profitability.

- Increase NBD's retail deposit base in southeast Michigan at a rate greater than our historical natural growth rate.

- Double NBD's commercial loan portfolio, while maintaining the high quality of assets.

- Develop an NBD Marketing Management Database by December 1985 (this has already been accomplished).

- Improve NBD's image with consumers in southeast Michigan, in order to help the bank:
    —Increase new account acquisition rate from 12.6% to 19% by the end of 1986, and to 29% by the end of 1989.

    —Improve cross-sell ratio of current customers from 5.4% to 5.7%, and of new customers from 6.0% to 7.2% by the end of 1989.

    —Maintain NBD's present positive image with our customers.

Objectives of the Mature Market Program

The objectives of NBD's "mature market" program are to increase deposits by current customers who are over fifty-five years old, and to encourage those who bank at other institutions in addition to NBD to consolidate their balances at NBD. In addition, we want to attract new customers from this age group, using an integrated package of products and services to improve cross-sell ratios and depth of customer relationships with NBD.

The mature market program will directly support several objectives of NBD's five-year strategic plan, including the following:

- Relationship profitability
- Increased deposit growth
- Increased new account acquisition
- Improved cross-sell ratios

MATURE MARKET SITUATION ANALYSIS
Background: National Bank of Detroit
National Bank of Detroit is the primary subsidiary of NBD Bancorp, the largest bank holding company in Michigan. NBD has total assets of over $15 billion, employs more than 6,000 people, and has more than 11,000 stockholders.

Assets and Liabilities
Deposits for the corporation total approximately $9 billion: $2.4 billion in demand accounts; $2.5 billion in savings and time accounts; $1.4 billion in certificates of deposit; and $2.6 billion in money market accounts. NBD also has $4.4 billion in commercial loans, $958 million in mortgages, $64 million in real estate construction loans, and $687 million in consumer loans.

Technology
NBD is a leader in electronic banking services including ATMs (over 100, at both branch offices and off-branch sites), a pay-by-phone bill payment system, and is test marketing of video banking. NBD is also a member of the CIRRUS ATM network, which gives participating customers access to over 6,500 ATMs across the country. Branches in the United States use an online Computer Response Inquiry System to process customer transactions and a central information file to access customer account information.

Marketing Department Structure
The Marketing Services Division includes three departments: Market Management and Product Development, Marketing Communications, and Market Planning and Research. In 1984, the Market Management and Product Development Department was divided into four groups corresponding to major market segments, including the mature market.

Background: The Mature Market
This excerpt from Senior Achievement, Incorporated's video teleconfer-

ence, "Communicating With The Mature Market," describes the potential profitability of the mature market:

> The mature market consists of 61 million prospects, 44% of all households. It is the fastest-growing demographic segment of society, growing to 80 million in the next fifteen years, and doubling by the year 2020.

> The over-fifty customer has over half a trillion dollars on deposit, controlling more than half of America's disposable income. Typically high-balance, they can become your most loyal and most profitable customers.

> They have the greatest need for guidance and specialized services, and they want and deserve personal attention.

NBD's Market Share

In October 1985, Lincorp Market Share Research, a financial research company based in Detroit, published a study of market shares and share changes in the Detroit area. The study covered the period from the end of 1983 through the first half of 1985, and concluded that 14% of the people in the metro Detroit tricounty area (comprising Wayne, Oakland and Macomb counties) considers NBD to be their "primary financial institution." Of the Detroit area's three major banking competitors, only Comerica Bank showed higher market penetration, at 15%. However, NBD has dropped three percentage points of market share since 1982, while Comerica has picked up points. The table below traces recent changes in NBD's market share.

NBD SHARE POINT CHANGE

82-83	83-84	82-85	Net Change 84:4-85:2
-2	-1	-4	-1

General Changes
The changes in regional banks' market shares are not uniform; they break down in the following ways:

- NBD's heavy advertising of loans has helped increase penetration in the consumer loan market. However, customer erosion has taken place in savings products, which (excepting IRAs) have not had advertising support. NBD's credit card portfolio suffered a dramatic loss of market share in the first half of 1985.

- Comerica has had the greatest increase in overall market share; it gained two share points in the first half of 1985.

- The collective share of community banks has dropped dramatically over the first half of 1985, from 19% to 14%. Large banks other than NBD have seemed to have gained most from the community bank's losses.

Changes in the Transaction Accounts Market

- NBD's share of the total checking account market dropped from 20% in the last quarter of 1983 to 18% in fourth quarter of 1984, where it has remained since.

- Credit unions' share of the total checking account market has not changed significantly over the past year.

- The proportion of customers maintaining regular, noninterest-paying checking accounts has declined steadily since 1982; the proportion using interest-bearing accounts has increased.

Changes in the Savings Account Market

- The proportion of consumers using certificates of deposit has fallen, along with rates of return, since 1983. NBD's share of the long-term certificate market dropped from 19% to 12% in the survey's measurement period.

- Comerica increased its share of the long-term certificate market from 14% to 22% over the same period, during which Comerica heavily advertised CDs.

- All financial institutions in the region, except credit unions, lost some of their regular savings and money market account market share. The perception of savings and loans as less secure financial institutions may have contributed to their decline.

Changes in the Consumer Credit Market

- NBD showed both gains and losses in consumer-credit market shares, thanks largely to heavy advertising.

- Auto and personal loan shares have increased, despite a decline in consumer demand for both.

- Despite a rather depressed mortgage market in the region, NBD increased its share from 4% to 9% of the market.

- NBD's share of charge card households fell from 24% to 17%.

Demographic Analysis

The tricounty area's mature market is estimated at about one million people; NBD's share of this market is 18%. When compared to other banks in the region, NBD has an older customer base. NBD and its major competitor, Comerica, share a similar base of older and slightly upscale customers. Mature consumers' use of interest-bearing checking accounts and savings certificates exceeds that of the general population. In contrast, they are less willing than younger or less affluent customers to use electronic banking services such as ATMs, and pay-by-phone bill-paying services.

There are also distinctions to be made among mature market consumers. Consumers fifty-five to sixty-four years old are more financially sophisticated than consumers over sixty-five. They use a greater variety of investments and types of financial institutions. They are less likely to automatically turn to commercial banks for CDs, life insurance, money market funds, stocks and bonds, and mutual funds. Customers over sixty-five are more likely to turn to a bank than to specialized, novel or unconventional sources for these financial products. Of course, both groups say that the most important criteria in choosing a bank are the efficiency of the service the staff's helpfulness, service charge levels and the quality of financial advice. The table below ranks these criteria for both groups within mature market.

MOST IMPORTANT FACTORS
IN CHOOSING WHERE TO BANK BY AGE GROUP
(Source: 1980 U.S. Census)

55-64	**65 and older**
1. Helpful staff	1. Helpful staff
2. Low service charges	2. Efficient service
3. Efficient service	3. Low service charges
4. Good financial advice	4. Established relationship

In choosing an investment the most important factor was a guaranteed competitive rate of return. In general, CDs are the most attractive savings instruments for this group of consumers. A major concern of the mature market, attributable to the experience of the Great Depression, is financial safety.

MOST ATTRACTIVE SAVINGS INSTRUMENTS, RANKED
(Source: Senior Achievement, Inc.)

55-64	**65 and older**
1. Certificates	1. Certificates
2. MMDA	2. Passbook savings
3. IRA	3. MMF

Consumers 55 to 64 years old are more rate-sensitive than older consumers but apparently would respond only to very high rate differentials, about 2 percentage points.

Mature Consumers' Financial Attitudes

Urban Data's Detroit subsidiary, Market Resource, prepared a study, *A Comprehensive Assessment of Financial Lifestyles and Attitudes Among Consumers Over 54 Years of Age,* for NBD. It was based on a telephone survey of 500 financial decision-makers over fifty-four, who were asked questions about potential products and services in a mature market financial package, and what they would be willing to pay for such a package.

The tested package features were: various minimum balance requirements for free service; monthly service charges; free travelers checks; certified checks and cashiers checks; safe deposit boxes; and reduced membership fees for Automobile Association of America (AAA) and American Association of Retired Persons (AARP).

The study reported little price-sensitivity with respect to three proposed minimum balance requirements for checking, savings, time deposits, and money market certificates; it concluded that the minimum balance requirement would make little difference in market penetration. However, the study's data show a difference of 9% in potential market penetration depending on minimum balance requirement. This difference will be considered significant enough to affect the strategies for the mature market, found toward the end of this plan.

Age was reported to have little significance in acceptance of a mature market package. However, respondents from fifty-five to fifty-nine, inclusive, are significantly more receptive to a $10,000 minimum balance (or a monthly $7.00 service charge) than older respondents, who responded best to the $5,000 minimum balance.

Different minimum balance requirements made no significant differences in potential rates of use of "additional services." Fifteen percent of the respondents would be "very likely" to change financial institutions and meet the minimum balance requirements of $5,000, or more simply to get the additional features tested. Research support for additional services was slim—"less than one in three," the study stated, are "very interested" in them.

Among the additional features tested, the reduced yearly fee for AAA membership proved most attractive. However, adding AAA and AARP discounts and a free safe deposit box in a package would, according to the study, have "minimal impact" on the level of market segmentation. Those customers who are now AAA or AARP members are no more likely to sign up for the tested mature market package than are those who are not members. The most common reason for lack of interest in all of the additional services is the belief that they are already available to the respondent through present financial packages. Uninterested respondents also said the following:

- They were satisfied with their current institution, 20%.

- They were already using the services, 15%.

- They needed more information on the institution, 6%.

Effects of Communication Strategies on Mature Consumers' Financial Service Decisions

In 1985, NBD purchased a study by Senior Achievement, Inc., entitled *Communication with the Mature Market*, which measured the influence of different advertising media, as well as the impact of other factors, on mature consumers' financial service decisions. The study included a telephone survey conducted by Yacoubian Research. For this study *mature consumers* were consumers in the United States of 50 years or older. From a universe of approximately 60 million consumers, 1,323 persons were interviewed, randomly selected from thirty-five states and the District of Columbia. Although the study was slanted somewhat toward urban mature consumers, interviews were conducted with rural consumers, as well. The final sample of 1,323 is geographically balanced and generally representative of the mature market. The sampling error is about 3% at the 95% confidence level.

It is interesting to note that of five industries tested— banking, real estate, health insurance, investment services, and travel and leisure—mature consumers feel that the banking industry does the best job of informing them about its products and services.

Factors Influencing Checking Account Decisions

Nearly nine out of ten mature consumers (89.4%) said they have a checking account. Four out of five (81%) have their checking accounts with banks, 12% have them at savings and loans, 4% have them with credit unions, and 3% have them at brokerage firms. Furthermore, half (49.4%) said that their accounts pay interest. Male respondents and those with annual incomes of $25,000 or more are slightly more likely to have interest-paying checking accounts (52% and 53%, respectively) than female respondents and those with incomes below $25,000.

Mature consumers cited "convenient location" as the most important factor in choosing the institution at which they had their checking accounts. Of the remaining five choices, one-fourth of the consumers (24.7%) cited "recommendations from relatives or friends" as the most important factor in choosing their checking account institution; "recommendations by friends or relatives" was also cited frequently as influential on product choices. This shows that a good reputation for customer service is a major reason for a bank's selection by consumers shopping the financial services market.

Factors Influencing Savings Decisions
More than eight out of ten (81.6%) mature consumers said they have savings accounts. Of these, 58% have their savings account with banks. Fifty-six percent of the savers have only regular savings accounts, 21.7% have money market savings accounts, and 17% have both.

Nearly 45% of the mature consumers in the sample said they have CDs. Of this group, 60% of those respondents with annual incomes over $25,000 said they have CDs, and 61% of those have their CDs with banks.

Among CD holders, 45.8% cited interest yield as the most important factor in choosing the issuing institution.

Use of Financial and Tax Planning Services
Although 58% of the mature consumers said that their primary financial institution offers financial and tax planning services (one-third didn't know), only 15.8% of the consumers said that they use financial planning services—from *all* sources. Of those who do, 50.6% consult banks, 21% consult brokerage firms, 20% consult CPAs or lawyers, and 9% consult savings and loan institutions.

Focus Group Findings
Yacoubian Focus Groups
In conjunction with the telephone surveys for Senior Achievement, Yacoubian Research conducted four focus groups dealing with the mature consumer. Participants were shown ten television commercials, nine sets of magazine ads, five sets of newspaper ads and four sets of brochures. None of the advertising was for financial products or services, but all of it was aimed at the mature market.

The mature consumers participating in the focus groups generally felt (87%) that advertising improves the chances of selling a product. Seventy-six percent of the participants watch television every day, 76% read newspapers "regularly," 61% read magazines regularly, 24% listen to the radio regularly, and 37% said they carefully read direct mail brochures.

Although they seem to identify with mature-looking people in advertising, a majority of the participants said the ages of models in advertising made no difference to them. Participants would rather see someone who is sincere and articulate, regardless of age or gender.

And although two-thirds of the participants said they believe that older consumers should not get better deals or preferential treatment from retailers, four-fifths did say that they are more likely to use the products or services of companies that provide special prices for older consumers.

NBD Focus Groups

NBD conducted focus groups in February 1985 to measure the appeal of mature market banking packages. Four sessions were held, two with groups of 55-to-64-year-olds and two with groups of people at least 65 years old. All participants had liquid assets of at least $5,000.

Participants received two sample packages provided to NBD by outside vendors, one by Financial Institution Services, Inc., (FISI) and one by Madison Financial Services (MADISON). The packages were quite similar and included products and services such as insurance benefits, emergency cash services, hotel discounts, an identification card, car rental discounts, free checking and check imprinting, free travelers checks, free safety deposit box, free Preferred MasterCard, free (or reduced fee) AAA membership, newsletters, and seminars. Although the packages were quite similar, participants generally preferred the FISI package. The seminars and newsletters were judged by participants to be the most attractive and important nonbank features of both packages.

Testing the bank services that NBD would add to the FISI or MADISON packages led to the conclusion that these would be more popular with mature consumers than the additional nonbank features would be.

Participants generally believed that $5,000 was the best minimum balance requirement for free service, and would tolerate a monthly service fee of $7.00 if balances fell below $5,000. However, none of the participants paid, at the time, for checking on a per-check basis, and they were not attracted to a package with a monthly fee. In fact, resistance to a higher minimum balance and to monthly fees was very strong. Note that this is in sharp contrast to Market Resource's interpretation of the data in its study. Complicating the picture even more was the participants' agreement that too low a minimum balance requirement for free service would make them skeptical of the package; they believed that a lower price meant a less valuable and less exclusive program. (Fairly high prices—premium prices—are routine in the marketing of many upscale or luxury products, for example, alcoholic beverages, clothes, and even financial planning services.)

The NBD focus groups also indicated that while outside vendors' packages may offer interesting services, the banking services are the ones that are specifically attractive to mature consumers. And participants agreed that training of branch personnel would be important in promoting a mature market package.

Current Mature Market Competitive Situation
Many financial institutions have recognized the attractive market mature consumers represent, and have put together special programs to take ad-

vantage of this potential. This has already been indicated by the FISI and MADISON vendor packages. Outlined below are a few mature market programs offered by financial institutions in Michigan and in other areas of the country.

Michigan
A local competitive study, conducted by NBD's Market Research and Planning Department, showed that mature market packages in the tricounty area are limited to simple packages of just a few traditional banking services, primarily free checking and check printing. Only one bank in the region, Michigan National Bank, has promoted its account.

Michigan National has also introduced a special fund, called the Independence for Life Fund, for research, education, and recreation programs for the state's senior citizens. Whenever a checking, VISA or MasterCard account is opened at Michigan National, the bank puts fifty cents into the fund; it also contributes one cent for each transaction completed at Michigan National ATMs. A fifteen-member committee on aging established by the bank will determine the fund's spending distribution. However, Michigan National has not advertised this fund, and we have no information on how well it is working out.

Outside-Michigan
In February 1985, **Sun Banks, Incorporated** in Florida, introduced "Sun-Horizon 55," a package of services for consumers fifty-five and over. It gives customers several free features, provided they maintain a minimum balance of $1,000 in a money market account, regular savings account, or a CD, or in a combination of account balances. If the minimum balance requirement is not met, a monthly service charge of $11.00 is assessed. The account features include the following:

- Choice of regular or interest-earning checking accounts
- Check imprinting
- Notary public services
- Travelers and cashier's checks
- MasterCard
- $10,000 accidental death insurance coverage
- Up to 15% discount on Sun Investor Services' brokerage commission
- Guaranteed check acceptance of up to $200 at more than 12,000 Florida businesses

Sears, Roebuck and Company's "Mature Outlook" program offers people fifty-five and older several financial, insurance, travel and entertainment benefits. The program, with an annual fee of $7.50 includes the following:

- Low interest rates on auto financing
- Travel and accident insurance plan
- Health and Medicare insurance guide
- Insurance-value review
- Discounts on homeowner and auto insurance
- Personal data organizer
- Personal investment portfolio evaluation
- Personal investment booklet
- Investment seminars
- Relocation assistance
- Film development discounts
- Sears catalog
- Membership card

Commercial Federal Savings and Loan (CFS&L) in Nebraska offers a program called the "Leisure Years Package," which includes the following:

- Market rate investment (short- and long-term)
- Free Statesman's Club membership, with qualifying deposit
- Direct deposit of Social Security benefits
- Investment counseling through CFS&L's brokerage service
- Leisure loans
- Free no-minimum-balance checking

National Westminster Bank (New York) offers the "Prime Benefits Club." To become a member of NWB's "Prime Benefits Club," customers fifty-five and older must open a regular, NOW, or money market checking account; and must maintain a minimum balance of $10,000 (in any combination of personal, NOW or money market checking account; money market, passbook, or statements savings; or CD balances). The club's benefits include the following:

- An additional half-percentage-point of interest on all CDs of more than thirty-one days in maturity

- An automatic preapproved $1,000 cash-reserve line of credit
- Up to a 10% discount on safe deposit box rentals
- A premium ATM access card with higher limits for ATM access and check cashing through the branch system
- No maintenance fees on personal, NOW, and money market checking accounts
- Free check imprinting
- Up to $1,000 in free travelers checks per year
- Direct deposit of Social Security benefits

STRATEGIES FOR THE DETROIT MATURE MARKET
NBD's Positioning and Image in the Regional Market

Traditionally, NBD has positioned itself as a solid, conservative financial institution; advertising has been aimed at their older, security-conscious customer. To this end, the positioning has worked well; the tricounty region's older consumers generally think well of NBD, and NBD is the top bank in the region.

There is a downside to such "conservative" positioning, however. NBD is also perceived as less innovative than its competitors. This view was succinctly summarized by a young man participating in an NBD focus group who said, "Comerica is a red Corvette, and NBD is a Cadillac sedan." Indeed, NBD's advertising has seldom been aimed at younger consumers.

Senior Achievement's research shows that mature consumers of financial services depend heavily on the advice and recommendations of friends and family members, who are often younger and who may not bank with or recommend NBD. Younger consumers tend to feel that NBD is less likely than other banks, especially Comerica, to extend credit or give the best interest rates.

Still, though NBD could profitably improve its image with younger consumers, its established reputation with older consumers does give it a strategic advantage for attracting mature consumers through a special, integrated mature market package.

General Strategy

For the purposes of this plan, our target market is consumers fifty-five and older living in Detroit's tricounty area. The primary target will be currently employed consumers fifty-five to sixty-five years old; the secondary target market will be retired consumers, fifty-five and older.

We will offer mature consumers a package of services that will be free when a minimum deposit balance requirement is met. We must develop a support system at NBD to provide the VIP treatment that these older, more affluent consumers expect.

Products and Pricing
We would recommend two packages, one for consumers who can maintain minimum balances of $5,000, and another for those who maintain minimum balances of $10,000. The latter package offers more products and services.

We recommend two packages because the Market Resource, Inc., study shows a potential increase of 9% in market penetration, with a $5,000 minimum balance requirement as opposed to a $10,000 requirement. This increase seems significant enough to warrant two packages.

The packages would include such services as free travelers checks and free cashier's checks. Market Resource's study concluded that the mature consumer uses them infrequently. However, since the number of benefits is part of the attraction of any such plan, regardless of whether or not they are used frequently, they do improve the program and cost the bank very little.

Offering two packages also promotes our corporate objectives. In itself, introducing a mature market package might improve NBD's image; however, offering only the package with a minimum-balance requirement of $10,000 could create the misconception that, NBD is a "rich person's bank." Offering two packages will allow mature consumers with lower balances to participate and will encourage them to build their deposits with NBD to qualify for the premium package. It should also encourage consolidation of balances from other financial institutions.

Furthermore, for customers who meet the $5,000 minimum, the two-tiered program would create an incentive to increase their balances to the $10,000 minimum, as the three nonbanking services (a newsletter, seminars, and travel packages) in Package Two are the most attractive features of the package, according to representatives of Sun Banks in Florida, Central Fidelity Bank in Missouri, and other banks.

Both packages are checking-based products; the Senior Achievement study showed that mature consumers are more likely to need and use a checking account than any other financial service. Customers may choose one of two types of checking. In addition, they may choose from two savings plans (or they may choose both). Giving customers options is recommended by the experience of the SunHorizon 55 plan of Sun Banks. Sun Banks has found that mature customers like to make choices; they want a money-managing program, but they also want to feel in control of important decisions.

Package One

Eligibility requirements and fee structure: To qualify for Package One, a customer must be fifty-five years of age and maintain a minimum of $5,000 in any combination of personal, NOW, or Super NOW checking; passbook or statement saving; Money Market Bonus; or certificate of deposit account balances. If this $5,000 balance is not maintained, a monthly fee of $7.00 will be charged.

Products and services in Package One include the following:

- Interest-bearing or regular checking (with no minimum balance requirement)
- Money Market Bonus account or regular savings
- Free check printing
- Free Travelers Checks
- Free cashier's checks
- Free bond coupon processing
- Free payment line service
- Free copying service
- Free notary service
- Direct deposit of Social Security checks
- Postage-paid, bank-by-mail envelopes
- 15% discount on NBD brokerage services
- ATM card
- Special member ID card

Package Two

Eligibility requirements and fee structure: To qualify for Package Two, a customer must be at least fifty-five years of age and maintain a minimum of $10,000 in any combination of personal, NOW, or Super NOW checking; passbook or statement savings; Money Market Savings; or CD account. If this balance is not maintained, a monthly fee of $11.00 will be charged.

Package Two includes all the products and services of Package One, plus a free safe deposit box (small size), as well as three important nonbank services: periodic newsletters, periodic seminars on topics of particular interest to the mature consumer, and special travel tour packages. NBD has many unused, small safe deposit boxes; adding boxes to the package would make good use of our resources and cost us very little. In the NBD focus groups, seminars and newsletters were judged to be the most attractive nonbank services. This is confirmed by representatives of other banks who offer a package for the mature market.

In addition, many bank representatives mentioned a travel package of some kind as crucial to the success of their program; without exception, every bank consulted described the travel feature as the most popular feature of mature market packages.

Because mature consumers want high quality customer service, five "thank you" cards will be included in each account kit. Customers will be asked to give these cards to any NBD employee who they feel has given them extraordinary service. When an employee has accumulated five cards, he or she can redeem them for $150 (NBD will take care of any taxes associated with this money), and a letter of commendation, signed by the appropriate regional director, will be placed in the employee's personnel file.

We should also conduct intensive branch training programs, explaining this package and how these customers should be treated. Mature market "specialists" will be trained for each branch, and the training will include lectures by a professor of gerontology. These specialists will then be called upon to explain this program to customers at their branch, and will also be able to advise them on matters concerning retirement and investments.

Advertising
Advertising should be based on the premise that this program is special recognition for a special group of people. These customers have reached maturity, not just in age, but in financial position and security.

The advertising strategy, product name, and product positioning will be developed in consultation with our advertising agency.

The advertising buy should be focused on newspapers and radio spots. Yacoubian's focus group study concluded that 76% of mature consumers read newspapers "regularly," and 24% listen to the radio "regularly."

The Senior Achievement study showed that our target audience is heavily influenced by family and friends, so NDB should include informational stuffers in DDA and savings statements mailed during the first month of our program. A brochure will he distributed in the branches. The Senior Achievement study found that mature consumers like "conservative" colors, such as dark green, grey, burgundy, and gold. The Senior Achievement study also found that too many inserts make a bad impression, because the are hard to use and easy to lose. Thus, the brochure should be bound like a book with a table of contents.

Other promotional materials could include birthday cards to participating customers; a financial-planning guide; a retirement-planning checklist; and counter cards, posters, and desk plates for branch personnel.

Research
The Market Research and Planning Department should conduct a competitive analysis on a semiannual basis.

Six months after the program is introduced, the department should determine how many accounts have been opened and how often each feature of the program has been used.

After the program's first year has been completed, the department should conduct a study to determine the level of consumer awareness of NBD's Mature Market Program, to determine customer attitudes toward the packages, and to see how customers think these packages should be modified.

CONCLUSION
NBD's plan to offer two financial packages to mature consumers (ages fifty-five and over) should help the bank increase its customer base and profits. Surveys have shown that mature consumers desire the financial products and services that are featured in each of the two packages. By successfully marketing these packages to this expanding and affluent market segment, NBD's image should improve and its market share should increase. ◆

Chapter 15

Marketing Plan for Targeting
Small Health Care Establishments

Sherry L. Constanzo
First Pennsylvania Bank
$5.7 billion assets

INTRODUCTION

First Pennsylvania Bank is a regional bank with $5.7 billion in total assets. It is the nation's oldest commercial bank serving five contiguous counties in southeastern Pennsylvania.

> First Pennsylvania Bank's mission is to be a leading regional bank, a bank of recognized quality, known for profitability and professionalism in each segment of banking in which it is engaged. [1]

One of the niche market segments that First Pennsylvania has chosen to target is health care. A special health care unit has been formed within the Corporate Banking Department to service large health care related firms. Smaller health care firms including private practices, small group practices, and medical and dental labs are being targeted by the Consumer Group through the branches. This plan will focus on the needs and opportunities for developing relationships with these smaller firms.

SITUATIONAL ANALYSIS
External Analysis
1. Market Profile
   a. Current Branch Trade Area
      First Pennsylvania's trade area includes the Pennsylvania counties of Bucks, Chester, Delaware, Philadelphia and

Montgomery. The Philadelphia Metropolitan Statistical Area is
the nation's fourth-largest metropolitan area, also known as the
Delaware Valley. Like other major metropolitan centers, the
area is experiencing a trend toward suburbanization. Much of
the residential and commercial growth is occurring in outlying
suburban areas, particularly within Bucks and Chester Counties.
Between 1980 and 1985, population in these two counties has
grown by 7% and 5.6%, respectively.[2] The Philadelphia SMSA is
expected to experience a moderate 2% gain in population by the
end of the century, with a continued shift of 11% from the city to
the suburbs.[3]

The Delaware Valley is at the center of an area that is the most
comprehensive "medical belt" in the nation. It boasts the second
highest concentration of health care facilities in the country.[4]
Greater Philadelphia has six medical schools from which graduate over 10% of the nation's physicians, and two dental schools
that produce 7% of the nation's dentists. Nearly 10% of the
region's work force is employed in health care.[5]

b. Target Market
    Offices of physicians and dentists of all specialties are included
    in the target market. The distribution by county is as follows:[6]

	Bucks	Chester	Dela.	Mont.	Phila.	Total
Offices of Physicians	318	220	455	889	1,246	3,128
Offices of Dentists	218	147	257	435	498	1,555
Total	536	367	712	1,324	1,744	4,683

c. Market Needs
    Health professionals represent a distinct market with distinct
    needs. In attempting to serve this market, bankers should
    understand these professionals' psychological needs as well as
    their financial needs.

    Psychological Needs: The most basic psychological need is the
    need for "respect." The typical health professional wants to be
    respected not only as someone with a lot of money, but as
    someone who has earned a position of status through the
    exercise of intelligence and responsibility.[7]

    Time is their most precious commodity, so convenience is of the
    utmost importance.

Health professionals are also looking for a personal relationship with their banker. They want a banker who takes a special interest in them and their needs. Their account officers should have some knowledge of the medical practice as a competitive business and should understand what equipment the practice needs to be successful.

In addition to their needs for respect and acknowledgment of their valuable time, medical professionals want to have a hand in the management of their investments. [8]

Financial Needs: Most health professionals run their own practices and do their own banking. At larger group medical practices, there is usually one associate responsible for the firm's financial decisions. Few medical and dental schools offer courses in practice management, so professionals generally rely on their accountants, attorneys, and stockbrokers for advice.

SOURCE OF INVESTMENT ADVICE
(Source: Survey by Beta Research Corporation)

Accountant	45.6%
Attorney	32.8%
Stockbroker	29.2%
Publications	17.6%
Banker	12.4%
Financial advisor	9.2%
Self	7.2%
Friends	4.8%
Other	1.2%
Don't know	2.4%

Banks can provide and/or coordinate many of the services provided by these many counselors and save professionals precious time by doing so. However, medical professionals do not think of banks first when seeking financial advice. [9]

The health professional's financial needs will change over the course of his or her career. The typical professional's financial needs can be grouped into at least two distinct phases.

Phase I: The types of services needed in the early part of the health professional's career include basic business checking and savings services, start-up loans, a moderate credit line, and equipment leasing. It is important to support the professional who is just starting out in order to build a mutually beneficial and long-lasting relationship.

Phase II: Once the individual or group practice is established, the financial needs become more sophisticated and may include investment services, tax shelters, real estate, expansion financing, an expanded credit line, pension plans, trust services, and payroll.

Credit Needs: Depending on the size and type of practice, financing needs vary from firm to firm. Typical financing needs include equipment purchases, leasehold improvements, commercial real estate (professional office building/condominium), practice buy-in or buyout, and establishing a satellite office.

The success of a medical practice depends on the principal. In determining credit worthiness, the lender should evaluate the medical professional as a business manager. [10]

d. Services Used
    According to the bank's 1985 Small Business Benchmark Study, the most used financial service was business checking followed by a business money market account and a money market fund.

    Checking Pattern: The majority of doctors and dentists have business checking account balances below $50,000, write fewer than 100 checks a month, and deposit 100 or more checks into their account each month.

    Business Savings: Forty percent (40%) of the doctors and dentists surveyed had a business money market account at a bank, 27% use a money market fund, and 22% use other business savings accounts.

    Savings and Investments: A third of the medical/dental professionals surveyed had an average combined business savings and investment balance of less than $25,000, 13% had average balances between $25,000 and $49,000, 19% fell into the $50,000 to $99,000 range, and 11% were in the $100,000 to $249,000 range. A higher proportion of doctors than dentists had combined savings and investment average balances greater than $50,000.

    Doctors and dentists are relatively the same in the deposit services that they use, with one apparent exception. Fewer dentists appear to use business money market accounts than doctors.

Credit: Forty percent of the doctors and dentists surveyed had business loans outstanding while another 10% have had business loans in the past two years. A term loan and line of credit were the most-used types of credit followed by a commercial mortgage. The majority of loans were secured. A slightly higher number of those loans were secured by personal assets than by corporate assets. Also, a slightly higher number borrowed at a fixed rate rather than at a variable rate. Forty three percent (43%) of the doctors and dentists with loans outstanding reported their loan balances to be between $10,000 and $50,000, 17% had loan balances between $51,000 and $100,000, and 10% had balances between $101,000 and $250,000. Dentists appear to have proportionally more loans outstanding and to have had more loans in the past two years than doctors. Dentists have a greater need to borrow money for equipment purchases since many doctors have the use of equipment at the hospital with which they are affiliated.

Pension Plans: Slightly more than half of the doctors and dentists surveyed offer their employees a pension or retirement plan. Of those that do not currently offer a pension or retirement plan, 20.3% are planning to in the next year; and 14.5% in the next two years. The plans used by over 90% of the doctors and dentists are a company retirement plan (pension, profit-sharing, or thrift plan) and a Keogh plan. A higher percentage of doctors than dentists offer such plans to their employees.

Leasing: Just over a fifth of the doctors and dentists currently lease cars or equipment; three quarters of them spend $10,000 or less. The financing is split evenly between banks and leasing companies.

Merchant MasterCard: Approximately one fifth of these professionals accept bank credit cards for payment.

Direct Deposit: Seventeen percent (17%) of the doctors and dentists surveyed used payroll direct deposit services.

2. Competitive Factors
   a. Major Competitors and Their Market Share
      Using our 1985 Small Business Benchmark Study, which included interviews with 150 physicians and dentists, we were

able to measure market share by bank. The major competitors
and their share of the market are as follows:

Fidelcor (Fidelity/IVB)	24%
Provident	15%
Mellon	14%
Continental	14%
Meridian(American/Central Penn)	10%
First Pennsylvania	8%
Philadelphia National	7%
Philadelphia Savings Fund	7%

b. Size of Major Competitors
All of these competitors have been involved in mergers and
acquisitions, and all have established ATM networks. Ranked
by deposit size, First Pennsylvania and its major competitors are
as follows:

COMPETITOR RANKINGS
(In Millions)
(Source: Philadelphia Business Journal Book of Lists, 1986)

	Total Deposits	Total Assets	# of Local Branches
Mellon	$18,582	$33,406	72
Provident	11,826	18,777	61
Philadelphia National	7,838	11,080	68
Fidelcor	7,103	8,995	135
Meridian	4,851	6,230	59
Continental	4,042	4,718	60
First Pennsylvania	3,861	5,652	70

c. Major Competitor Strategies
Fidelity Bank: Fidelcor is the current market leader serving
almost one quarter of this market. In addition to effective target
marketing, the recent merger of Fidelity and IVB, which had
shares of 14% and 10%, respectively, also contributed to its
leadership position. According to a former Fidelity lender, the
bank has been working to reestablish its health care specializa-
tion. A special product package has been developed for health
care professionals.

Fidelity is following Provident's strategy of locating banking
facilities on hospital premises. Both ATMs and minibranches are
located in Philadelphia hospitals.

Provident Bank: A First Pennsylvania Bank Officer formerly employed with Provident confirmed that the bank had a separate division within its Private Banking Department charged with serving health care professionals. A complete package of financial services was developed and is marketed to medical students, residents, and doctors with a good deal of success.

This effort sought primarily to attract the younger, developing individuals in the health care market, in addition to cultivating relationships with more-established doctors.

A variety of services are offered to subsegments of the medical professional market. Charge accounts and tuition loans are directed toward medical school students; start-up loans are heavily marketed toward residents; and financial planning seminars are conducted for established doctors, on topics such as tax shelters and other investment options. To attract physicians to seminars, Provident uses the following techniques:

- Hosts seminars on the hospital premises.
- Finds an inside contact such as the director of student services to present the seminars.
- Targets business managers of group practices, rather than the physicians themselves.
- Hosts the seminars in their branches located within hospitals.

In addition, Provident offers free checking and unsecured lines of credit to established physicians, has several ATMs located in hospitals, and has print advertisements targeting physicians.

d. Other Competitors
Several small regional banks compete for the health care market within First Pennsylvania's trade area. Banks targeting medical and dental professionals include Atlantic Financial, Royal Bank, Commerce Bank, and Constitution Bank.

In addition these competitors, nonbank financial service providers are attracting larger amounts of deposit dollars from medical professionals by offering higher rates than commercial banks.

Economic/Regulatory Issues
a. Increased Competition
Physicians: Until recently, the health care industry has been operating under certificate-of-need (CON) regulations. These

regulations served as a "barrier to entry" for health care providers. Strict standards had to be met before health care facilities could open their doors to the public. With the elimination of CON regulations, health care providers are overexpanding and new facilities are being located in areas already served sufficiently. [11]

According to federal estimates, by 1990 there will be 150,000 more doctors than are necessary to service the country's health care needs. More attractive areas already have surplus physicians, making it difficult to establish economically viable medical offices. [12]

Dentists: Better dental care habits, an overall orientation toward prevention rather than repair, fewer cavities, and more dental school graduates have forced many dentists to actively pursue patients. Peter Sanchez, associate professor of marketing at Villanova University and a marketing consultant to many dentists, said recently, "There's a glut of dentists right now. It was an attractive profession a few years back, with good money to be made, and a long waiting list of patients. But today there just aren't enough patients to go around."[13]

b.   Increased Pressure to Reduce Cost of Care
A significant regulatory change in this industry was the adoption of DRG (diagnosis-related groups) legislation. This new legislation changes the payment method for Medicare patients. Instead of cost-based reimbursement, the physician now receives a lump sum payment per diagnosed illness. Many industry observers expect private health insurers to adopt a DRG system as a cost-containment measure. Health care providers must now be more aware of cost accounting principles since payments for the delivery of service now reward the efficient and penalize the inefficient. In the long run, inefficient providers will be squeezed out of the overall health care system.

With the increased pressure to contain costs, we will see more alternative systems emerge, such as outpatient delivery systems, health maintenance organizations, and home health services.[14]

In the dental industry, the oversaturated market is also working toward reducing the cost of care. "Chain store" dental shops are becoming popular as more and more locate in malls and high traffic areas. Group practices are also becoming popular since the expenses of opening an office can be shared. [15]

Internal Analysis

1. Branch Responsibility

   By definition, the bank's Branch Department is responsible for developing and maintaining relationships with companies in the five-county area with annual sales sizes under $35 million. An exception is that any loan request for over $1 million received in the branches from a health care establishment is referred to the Health Care Division of Corporate Banking.

2. Bank Resources

   a. Branch Network and Calling Officers

      The bank's distribution network consists of seventy full-service branches and thirteen remote service units. Forty-six percent of these facilities are located in Philadelphia County. Account officers include seventy branch managers and forty-two lenders.

   b. Market Potential/Bank Penetration

      In 1986, First Pennsylvania Bank commissioned Dun and Bradstreet to determine the potential bank penetration of this market in the five county area. The results are presented below:

Offices of physicians	# of Establishments	2,386
	Clients	65
	% Penetration	2.7%
Offices of dentists	# of Establishments	1,564
	Clients	31
	% Penetration	2.0%
Offices of osteopathic physicians	# of Establishments	265
	Clients	7
	% Penetration	2.6%
Offices of chiropractors	# of Establishments	151
	Clients	1
	% Penetration	.7%
Offices of optometrists	# of Establishments	124
	Clients	2
	% Penetration	1.6%
Medical laboratories	# of Establishments	69
	Clients	5
	% Penetration	7.2%
Dental laboratories	# of Establishments	90
	Clients	4
	% Penetration	4.4%

According to the 1986 Dun and Bradstreet records, there are 4,649 offices of physicians and dentists in the five-county area. The 1984 County Business Patterns shows 4,683. Of these, the bank can identify at least 115 clients. Since this information is a result of a match between the bank's commercial DDA records and the Dun and Bradstreet records, it is only an estimate. The actual number of clients with a medical practice is probably slightly higher. Private and small group practices not included in the Dun and Bradstreet study could not be matched against the bank's client base. [16]

3. Strengths and Weaknesses
    a. Strengths
        First Pennsylvania Bank recently hired Dr. Stuart Shapiro, former health commissioner of Philadelphia, to head up a specialized Health Care Division in Corporate Banking. Though he is primarily responsible for developing and maintaining relationships with large health care firms such as hospitals and nursing homes, he is a valuable resource for branches targeting smaller health care firms. Being an M.D. himself, he can provide insight into the financial and psychological needs of physicians.

        In addition, the bank is currently in the middle of an image campaign. The campaign focuses on providing personal, responsive and efficient service to clients. Top management is fully committed to making this claim a reality. Several changes have been made to benefit the customer. For instance, lending teams have been established to handle portfolios of commercial clients. In the event that the assigned lender is not available to respond to a client's inquiry, a team member can act as a backup to answer questions or handle any problems arising.

    b. Weaknesses
        First Pennsylvania's branch locations are not numerous enough to offer the convenience several of our larger competitors can offer, particularly in the suburbs. In addition, insufficient attention has been paid to time-saving delivery systems for this market. Physicians and dentists bank where its most convenient. ATMs and minibranches on hospital premises seem to be working well for our competitors.

GOALS AND OBJECTIVES
Purpose
The purpose of this plan is to provide a set of guidelines for management which, if followed, will help us to achieve the Consumer Group's goals and

the bank's mission. The need for this plan was determined after analyzing the following:

- The bank's long range goals and 1987 objectives

- The results of the Business Market Analysis which identified the health care industry as one of the fastest growing and most profitable market segments in the Philadelphia area

- The results of the 1985 Small Business and Professionals Benchmark Study which showed that doctors and dentists don't perceive any one bank as a specialist in serving their financial needs

- Increased competition

Consumer Group Goals

1. Be a profitable servicer of the financial needs of small and lower-middle market businesses (including professionals) in the eight-county area, while maintaining a significant market share.

2. Systematize sales efforts to increase market share in growing and profitable industries.

3. Increase sales to clients by cross-selling and by upgrading relationships.

4. Retain clients through recognition.

5. Reinforce First Pennsylvania Bank's image as a personal, responsive, and efficient institution genuinely interested in meeting the financial needs of small business owners and professionals.

Consumer Group Objectives

1. Differentiate First Pennsylvania as a bank committed to understanding and serving the financial needs of medical and dental practices.

2. Increase our primary market share in this market from 8% to 10% by 1988.

3. Uptier existing medical client relationships by increasing the services used by at least one.

4. Increase average loan outstandings by 15%, deposits by 10%, and fee income by 15% per year.

STRATEGIES AND TACTICS
Strategy
Medical professionals are practicing in an environment very different from the environment three to four years ago. A great deal of pressure has been

added to their already hectic lives as a result of cost containment, alternative delivery systems, malpractice suits, professional advertising, and a surplus of providers. According to Murray Simon, DDS, of D.R.S. Healthcare Consultants, "Marketers who position themselves as sensitive to physicians' or dentists' needs with products or services committed to helping them improve the quality and profitability of their practices will profit during these changing times." [17] Considering this and the opportunities identified in the situation analysis, the following strategy has been developed for targeting this market.

1. Cut into weaker competitors' share of the market by developing "alternative delivery systems" for financial services that would make First Pennsylvania Bank the most convenient institution with which to bank.

2. Position the bank as a provider whose account officers understand how a medical practice runs and can offer services to improve the efficiency and profitability of the practice.

Tactics
1.   Alternative Delivery Systems
   a.   Bonded Courier Service
        Hire or establish a bonded courier service to pick up deposits at group medical practices and deliver them to the bank's ten regional offices for processing on a daily basis. Medical practices should be receptive to courier service since they already have them through lab service firms, and pharmaceutial companies.

        Group practices with a sufficient volume of deposits could sign up for this service for a nominal fee if an outside courier is used. If the couriers were employees of the bank, the service would be offered at no charge. Clients will be required to open a deposit account at First Pennsylvania with minimum balance requirements to be determined by the product manager. The estimated cost for the courier service is $40,000.

   b.   Commercial MAC Cards
        Issue commercial MAC Cards to principals of existing medical practices, which will enable them to make deposits to commercial accounts through First Pennsylvania Bank MAC machines. This service is offered as an alternative to night vault service. Unlike the night vault, a receipt for the deposit is issued immediately, and there is no need to drop by the bank the next day to pick up a night bag. During regular banking hours, long teller lines can be avoided. This service can be offered without any cost to us.

2. Product
    Develop and offer a credit card product to professional partnerships.
    With the new tax laws, more and more medical professionals are
    switching from professional corporations to professional partner-
    ships. At the present time, MasterCard can only be issued to indi-
    viduals or corporations.

    Medical professionals traveling to medical conferences and symposia
    must rely on their personal credit cards to cover their expenses and
    later be reimbursed. Cards issued to partners in a partnership, or to
    solo practitioners, would improve recordkeeping for the practice and
    save time for the professionals. The system is already capable of
    handling partnerships and proprietorships. The only additional cost
    would be the cost of new forms.

3. Communications
    a. Direct Mail
        Develop a direct mail program to communicate our interest in
        serving the needs of medical and dental practices; to introduce
        the "alternative delivery system" for financial services (bonded
        courier service); and to ask for an appointment to discuss
        services that can help to increase the practice's profitability. A
        similar program will target existing medical clients stressing the
        commercial MAC Card rather than the courier service.

        The theme of the letter will compare the changing environment
        of the health care industry with changes in the financial indus-
        try, such as surplus delivery systems, alternative delivery
        systems, slimmer profit margins and the need for specialization.

        The direct mail package will contain a letter from the regional
        vice president, a separate piece to describe the bonded courier
        service, and a reply card. The whole package will be sent first
        class to financial decision makers at group practices only. The
        estimated cost of the direct mail program is $10,000.

    b. Telemarketing
        Telemarketers will be hired to call group medical practices to
        find out who is responsible for making their banking decisions.
        The resulting list will be used for the direct mail program. The
        estimated cost of the telemarketing program is $2,000.

    c. Advertising
        In general print, radio and television advertising are not cost-
        effective for this market. Medical professionals are inundated

with publications that they have little time to read on a regular basis. The only advertising recommended for this market is an ad placed in the Special Health Care Section of the *Philadelphia Inquirer*, which is published twice a year at $3,300 a placement. The estimated cost of advertising production and placement is $7,800.

d.   Trade Shows

For the past several years, First Pennsylvania has participated in local Chamber of Commerce business expos. More recently, the Bank has started to participate in local medical and dental conferences. FPB was the only bank to participate as an exhibitor at the 1985 and 1986 Liberty Dental Conference sponsored by the Philadelphia County Dental Society. The bank was offering a 1% discount on a commercial loan for three months beginning the day of the show. The results of our participation in this conference have been very favorable.

First Pennsylvania Bank will be participating in the 1987 Liberty Dental Conference. In addition to exhibiting, two of the bank's experienced lenders will be conducting a two-hour session on financing alternatives for established dentists. In the past, the seminars have been directed toward students. A special slide presentation has been prepared. The estimated cost of participating in this dental conference is $2,000.

In December 1986, FPB participated as an exhibitor at a medical conference sponsored by the Philadelphia County Medical Society. Even though the show did not draw the number of physicians anticipated, we left the show with approximately fifteen good leads. Dr. Stuart Shapiro of the Bank's Health Care Division began the luncheon presentations with a short talk on "The Banker and the Physician." Several doctors stopped by FPB's booth to ask for Dr. Shapiro's card. The general consensus among the bank officers who staffed the booth was to plan to exhibit again next year. With the bank planning to participate in future medical related conferences, new artwork for the trade show booth is recommended. The message on the booth will read "All the Bank a Professional Practice Will Ever Need" and will have a back-lit photograph of a physician and a dentist. The estimated cost for the new booth and participation at this medical conference is $2,800.

e.   Seminar

A seminar on pension plans is planned for the fall of 1987 for medical and dental professionals. According to the 1985 benchmark study and a recent survey of *Insights* readers (the bank's newsletter for business owners and professionals), the topic of greatest interest to this market was pension plans. A seminar co-sponsored by an independent pension consulting firm and First Pennsylvania Bank is recommended. The seminar will include breakfast and will be limited to one hour. A mailing to medical professionals who bank with First Pennsylvania will invite them to attend the seminar and will encourage them to bring an associate. A mailing to medical prospects in the Philadelphia area is also recommended. The estimated cost of the mailings and the seminar is $3,000.

f.   Public Relations
To round out the bank's communication plans, a public relations program is recommended. After each seminar or presentation, an article would be prepared and submitted to local business publications and trade journals. In 1987, there are three presentations/seminars on the agenda:

- Financing Seminar for Established Dentists. Liberty Dental Conference—March 1987.

- Pension Plan Seminar for Physicians and Dentists. Co-sponsored by FPB and an Independent Pension Consultant—Fall 1987.

- Luncheon Presentation to Physicians: Rx for Survival—December 1987.

First Pennsylvania Bank's Public Relations Department will handle the writing and placement of the articles. This program can be accomplished at no additional cost to us.

4.   Training
To build product knowledge and improve cross-selling ratios, Richardson Training should be continued through 1987. This training, provided by the Richardson Group of Philadelphia, focuses on sales skills and product features and benefits.

In addition to in-depth product knowledge, managers and lenders would benefit from seminars on professionalism and consultative selling techniques, particularly with the medical market.

Bank salesmanship should be done in a consultative manner where communications and needs identification always precede the sales pitch. This role should be crystal clear in the minds of our managers

and lenders. The estimated cost of this new training program is
$50,000.

5. Market Research
In 1988, as part of the Small Business Benchmark Study, include
interviews with 200 financial decision makers at medical practices.
By including this market, we will be able to measure the effect of our
strategies and of our competitors' strategies by changes in market
share. Greater emphasis will be placed on measuring satisfaction of
bank delivery systems and other key strategic factors in gaining and
retaining medical practice clients. The estimated cost of the medical
market portion of this study is $15,000.

Tracking
Each tactic will have a tracking mechanism to measure its results. The direct
mail pieces will be coded; advertising leads will be tracked by the telephone
banking department; contacts made at trade shows and seminars will be
checked periodically against the bank's customer information files to track
new business.

Use of the new service and delivery systems could be monitored through
existing systems. Results of training will be measured via the Benchmark
Study proposed for 1988.

BUDGET
A summary of the budget for this program is shown below. The figures in
this budget are estimated costs. Actual costs may vary by as much as 15%
in either direction, due to unforeseen circumstances.

BUDGET

Alternative delivery systems	$40,000
New product	-0-
Communications	27,600
Direct mail	
Telemarketing	
Advertising	
Trade shows	
Seminars	
Public relations	
Training	50,000
Market research	15,000
Total	$132,600

CONCLUSION

The strategies and tactics outlined in this report are feasible only if the required funds for a bonded courier service and training on consultative sales techniques are available. Under the existing organizational structure, the cost of these tactics would not come from the Small Business marketing budget. The cost of remaining tactics are within the existing research and promotional budgets. ◆

---

[1] First Pennsylvania Corporation, *Annual Report*, 1985.

[2] *Annual Planning Information Report*, prepared by Labor Market Analyst Office of Employment Security, (Philadelphia PMSA, September 1986).

[3] Anne L. Hearn, *Survey of Community Assets and Needs*, (November 1985).

[4] Philadelphia County Medical Society.

[5] "Philadelphia: Special Advertising Section," *Fortune*, (April 29, 1985).

[6] U.S. Department of Commerce, Bureau of the Census, "1984 County Patterns."

[7] Evan Eisenburg and Aryen L. Rubin, "Tips for Reaching Health Professionals," *Bank Marketing*, (November, 1984), pp. 18-21.

[8] Ibid.

[9] Ibid., p. 19.

[10] Daniel B. Keohane, Stephen S. Matthews, Steven J. Popovich, and Theodore G. Widmayer, "Lending to the Health Care Industry," *The Journal of Commercial Bank Lending*, (December 1985), pp. 13-18.

[11] Ibid., p. 16.

[12] Robert Morris Associates, "Financial and Credit Characteristics of Selected Industries," *Credit Considerations*, (January 1986).

[13] Mike Hughes, "This Drill for Hire: Being a Dentist Today is Nothing to Smile About," *Business Digest of Delaware Valley*, (March 1986), p. 4, 20.

[14] Reed Abelson, "Reimbursement Rules Changed," *Philadelphia Business Journal* (November 17-23, 1986), pp. 1, 37.

[15] Mike Hughes, p. 20.

[16] Dun and Bradstreet Match with FPB Commercial DDA Client Records, 1986.

[17] Murray Simon, DDS, *Marketing News*, (January 30, 1987), p. 21.

$P_{ART\,6}$

Building Relationships with Commercial Customers

CHAPTER 16

A Marketing Plan for Implementing a Market-Driven, Results-Oriented Business Development/Retention Program

Robert M. Zubella
Bank of Sturgeon Bay
$153 million assets

INTRODUCTION
The days when bankers could merely stay at their desks waiting for business to walk in the door are gone. With competition continuously increasing, bankers are being forced to seek business or else watch their institutions be acquired by more aggressive banks. It is no coincidence that financial institutions are finding that they must be more effective sales organizations.

The purpose of this plan is to organize the thought processes and philosophical changes necessary to develop Bank of Sturgeon Bay's business banking area into a market-driven sales division and to address the specific strategies and tactics that will be used to orchestrate this change.

SITUATION ANALYSIS
General Market Area
Bank of Sturgeon Bay serves a geographic marketplace in Wisconsin known as the Door County Peninsula. Door County is located in the extreme northeast corner of the state. The peninsula juts out into Lake Michigan and has 250 miles of shoreline on Lake Michigan and the bay of Green Bay. The closest major metropolitan city is Green Bay, which has a population of approximately 90,000 and is located forty miles southwest of the city of Sturgeon Bay.

Of the approximately 500 square miles of area within the county, 54% is classified as agricultural (including many cherry and apple orchards), 28% forest, 11% residential/commercial, and 7% public recreational. [1]

The area has eighteen small municipalities and a total year-round population of 26,900. The largest single municipality is Sturgeon Bay. With the return of summer residents during May through October, the county's total population is estimated to expand to over 50,000. During this same period, Door County also hosts an estimated one million tourists, of which 57% are overnight guests. [2]

The Door County market area relies very heavily upon two major industries—shipbuilding and tourism. At the present time, both are stable, however, neither is guaranteed future success.

The Bank

Bank of Sturgeon Bay is a wholly owned subsidiary of Baylake Corp., a one-bank holding company. Since its establishment in 1889, Bank of Sturgeon Bay has developed a branching system of six year-round, full service offices and two limited-service summer facilities. It has also expanded its product line beyond traditional commercial bank services to include separate divisions for trust services (1940), financial services—investments/discount brokerage (1984)—and insurance services (1985).

Over the years, Bank of Sturgeon Bay has enjoyed consistent growth (an average of 8% to 10% per year) in deposits. Normally, the bank is very liquid in the summer and fall seasons because of the tourism industry. In the winter, we tend to draw from that built-up liquidity to service commercial demands in construction and inventory areas—while at the same time off setting some deposit outflows.

One of our major strengths is our strong level of core deposits. Much of our deposit base is tied to market rates, but we have adapted our asset strategy allocation to prevent major income fluctuations in falling or rising rate environments.

Since the Bank of Sturgeon Bay is located in a growing area, our loan demand remains strong as evidenced by our high loan-to-asset ratio of 62.45% (our target is 54%-65%). During the current weak bond market, loans have been our best investment alternative. However, a weakness in the future may be in attracting the additional deposits needed to fulfill these loan demands.

As of June 30, 1987, Bank of Sturgeon Bay had reported total assets of $153 million and deposits of $135.5 million. Year-end projections for return on average assets is 1.25% and for return on equity, 15%. Current deposit levels and loan volumes are as follows: [3]

	$ Million
Savings/time deposits	90.6
Demand deposits	36.8
IRAs	7.9
Real estate loans	25.0
Instalment loans	11.9
Student loans	1.5
Agriculture loans	3.9
Commercial loans	56.2

Bank of Sturgeon Bay's overall share of the Door County marketplace is currently estimated at 56.7%. However, a closer examination of our commercial loan market share as of June 30, 1987, reveals an area in which the bank has demonstrated an exceptionally strong performance, and currently services an estimated 62.4% share of the market.

Competition
Until recently, the Door County marketplace was not classified as an attractive market by outside competition. The area is serviced by two commercial banks, two savings and loans, one credit union, three stockbrokerage firms, and all of the major auto finance companies. This concentration of financial services firms, combined with the fact that the county is surrounded by water on three sides thus limiting overlapping geographic markets to only one county (Kewaunee) to the south, has helped keep outside competition at bay.

The traditional lack of aggressive market share penetration efforts by local competitors is fast disappearing. Pressure from larger outside financial institutions from Green Bay, Manitowoc, and Milwaukee (commercial services), and from the super-regional and national organizations (consumer credit services), have finally forced local institutions to take an aggressive approach toward protecting and increasing their respective market shares.

Conclusion
Not unlike many medium-size commercial banks, Bank of Sturgeon Bay is experiencing changes in its marketplace. Consumers are better educated, less loyal as yield spreads widen, and more easily attracted away from traditional bank services. The influx of major competitors with aggressive marketing and pricing continue to erode bank deposits. Real estate and auto loan demand remain weak. Strong demand for commercial loan and deposit services continue to be bright spots. Fortunately, they are Bank of Sturgeon Bay's most competitive offerings.

The value-added aspects of quality, service and reliability have helped set Bank of Sturgeon Bay apart from the competition. There is little doubt, however, that we must seek more effective ways to remain competitive, especially in the area of commercial services.

EXISTING CALL PROGRAM

Bank of Sturgeon Bay made its first attempt to establish a formalized officer call program in 1984. Unfortunately, the program was tailored to accommodate the bank's existing operating structure and personnel.

Emphasis was quickly directed to demonstrating some semblance of an organized calling plan with an immediate short-term goal of increasing the number of client contacts. Effectiveness was measured in terms of call quantity rather than call quality, and calls were viewed as a means of developing positive relations rather than as a method of developing new business.

The program's structure offered further evidence that success would be limited. Under the structure, all of the bank's officers (excluding the president, senior vice president, and a select few other officers) were enlisted to participate in the program. To stimulate competition, two teams were established. Each team was headed by a captain who was given the responsibility of establishing monthly call quotas and of developing methods to motivate team members into action. The problem, was that neither the team captains nor the team members received any formal sales management or sales skills training.

To support the calling effort, client/prospect sheets were developed; and calling officers were encouraged, not required, to complete the forms prior to making a call. The officers never fully understood the value of precall research; and obtaining client information was difficult. As a result, the client/prospect sheets were seldom used.

Use of a call reporting system was encouraged but also not required. The written call report forced structured thinking, was time consuming, and, thus, never developed into an effective reference or management tool.

When the sale of a product or service did occur, a tracking sales sheet was to be completed. Again, the practice was only encouraged, not required. Since no real value had ever been placed on making a sale, there was no incentive to sell—let alone complete the form.

Was the program a failure? Not completely. In fact, in many ways it was a success. Bank officers received their first introduction to selling, and several demonstrated that they had the "right stuff" to succeed in sales. The bank's commercial clients experienced a new interest in their businesses as a result of increased officer contacts. And, bank management tasted enough success to want to develop a long-term call program.

BUSINESS BANKING RESEARCH PROJECT

During the third quarter of 1986, Bank of Sturgeon Bay contracted with an independent, outside research firm to conduct a business banking research project to determine whether the bank's perceived business banking image, structure, products, and delivery system were meeting needs of the marketplace and were consistent with overall bank management objectives.

The results of the research were to be used to help develop specific action plans, strategies, and goals for our Business Banking Division.

Research Objectives

- Analyze the current business banking posture and image of the Bank of Sturgeon Bay, as well as its competition.

- Analyze the market needs of customers and prospects to confirm the bank's current product offerings and/or to determine the need for new product development.

- Uncover cross-selling opportunities with existing clients and prospects.

- Gather the raw material necessary to give clear direction to future business banking strategies to develop a formalized business banking marketing plan, and/or confirm the bank's current plan.

- Analyze current business banking personnel, procedures, and management information systems.

- Demonstrate a market-driven approach to the Door County business community.

Research Methodology

The data was acquired through personal interviews with seventy-two individuals who interact with the bank's Business Banking Division. These individuals were selected from groups of business customers, business prospects, professionals, outside directors of the bank, senior bank management, and business bankers. Through personal interviews we were able to obtain honest reactions from this diverse but representative group of contacts. Each participant was guaranteed confidentiality.

Research Analysis (Synopsis)

The market research study demonstrated a need to address certain internal structures and systems, as well as specific styles and procedures involved in externally interfacing with business customers and prospects in our marketplace.

Generally, the business market wanted a more hands-on, creative, and advisory approach to banking that involved the development of a close, stable, and caring relationship between the business customer (owner/manager) and the bank's client relationship officer. This officer is responsible for using the total bank's resources to maximize opportunities with the business client. Businesses wanted the bank to demonstrate interest in their operations—that is, call on them—and be committed to helping them grow and prosper.

Regarding Bank of Sturgeon Bay's business banking image, the following perceptions were uncovered in the study:

- Positive perceptions were size, stability, conservative, safe, reliable, responsive, imaginative, innovative, well run, friendly, interested in the community, professional, knowledgeable, quality service, fair and honest, with good changes in last few years.

- Negatives perceptions were that the bank was not for the little guy, makes people jump through hoops, takes its place in this market for granted, lacks expertise and experience, should give more advice to customers, does not price competitively, and does not call on customers enough.

The report also reconfirmed our knowledge about the increased activity from outside competitors who were positioning themselves as "experts" and keying on "price" in an effort to penetrate our market.

PRIMARY GOAL
The bank's primary goal is to:

Build a long-term market-driven sales culture within Bank of Sturgeon Bay's Business Banking Division, and to develop the systems and procedures that maximize penetration into our overall business market.

The initial phase of this effort will involve only the Business Banking Division. Later, other appropriate divisions will be included. However, the business banking system will be developed immediately so that all the bank's divisions recognize the importance of systems and procedures in the development and building of a long-term sales culture.

The cornerstones of this objective are:

- The market will drive our system, procedures, and product development.

- The market desires, and is willing to pay for, quality products that are professionally delivered by a caring and nurturing high-touch relationship.

- The market wants sincerity, consistency, and long-term bank commitment to the above philosophies.

OBJECTIVES, STRATEGIES AND TACTICS
Management Commitment
Commitment from all levels in the bank is the single most important ingredient in ensuring the future success of Bank of Sturgeon Bay's business development efforts. Commitment, however, must begin with senior management.

Senior management must be willing to hold the appropriate people accountable not only for the development of the program, but also for the achievement of its stated objectives. This accountability must be balanced by appropriate compensation, incentives, and career development opportunities.

Management's commitment will become evident when support of the program's development and implementation is provided, and when a new corporate culture evolves that is sincere, consistent, and long-term in nature.

The following objective and its strategies and tactics are aimed at securing senior management's commitment to this program:

Objective: Ensure that senior management and the members of the senior business banking team are totally committed to taking the necessary steps to achieve the overall objective of building a quality business developing program.

Strategy A: Communicate the finding of the business research study to senior management and senior business banking team members.

Tactics, Responsibility and Completion Dates:
1. Analyze and assemble the research into an understandable, meaningful, and presentable format. To be done by the marketing officer and commercial division manager, and completed by September 30, 1987.

2. Make a formal presentation and recommend course of action. To be done by the marketing officer and commerical division manager, and completed by October 1, 1987.

Strategy B: Jointly define *commitment* and management's role in adding teeth to the program's development and implementation.

Tactics, Responsibility and Completion Dates:
1. Establish senior management's level of involvement and participation in the program. To be done by the senior management team, and completed by October 15, 1987.

2. Assign responsibilities for researching compensation, incentive, career development, and nonperformance issues. To be done by the senior management team, and completed by October 15, 1987.

Strategy C: Communicate senior management's commitment to all key business banking personnel who will be responsible for actively participating in the business development program.

Tactics, Responsibility and Completion Dates:
1. Present research findings to all division officers and support staff and issue a statement of management's support and cooperation. To be done by the marketing officer, CEO and commercial division manager, and completed by October 21, 1987.

2. Outline program development plans and business banking team members involvement in the development. To be done by the marketing officer, CEO and commercial division manager, and completed by October 21, 1987.

Resources Required: Business banking research data; availability of senior management team members; successful external business development, compensation, incentive and nonperformance program research data.

Synopsis of Results: A broad definition of senior management's role in the program is one of providing assistance to the key players and jointly setting overall program goals and objectives with them. They are also responsible for assisting where appropriate in goal achievement, monitoring, rewarding successes, and dealing with nonperformance. Management has agreed to interact with both clients and prospects through joint calls with the responsible officers, and to do so in such a way as to not diminish the officer's line credibility with the client. It is also understood that it is the business banking management team's responsibility to carry out the day-to-day activities necessary to achieve the program's objectives—for which they will be held accountable.

Mission Statement

An overall strategic plan has been developed to guide the future direction of Bank of Sturgeon Bay. The key, now, is to develop a strategic business banking plan that supports and parallels the bank's overall strategic plan by tapping the planning skills of our management team.

As with the organization's overall plan, our Business Banking Division must develop a core strategy that reflects how we intend to approach and exploit the business marketplace with our products and services. This core strategy will become the final test against which all major business banking decisions are made, and it will serve to indicate where our resources should be concentrated.

Ultimately, a mission statement that captures the essence of our new strategic priorities must be developed and communicated in order to ensure that our future efforts are clearly focused.

Job Description Analysis

To ensure the maximum success of our business development program, it is vital that management recognize the existing abilities and potential of key employees and develop job descriptions that appropriately reflect these abilities, including proper time allocations.

All business bankers, support personnel, and management team members must jointly participate in the analysis and the development of new job responsibilities. The main objectives of this analysis are to create sufficient time for account management at appropriate levels, push responsibility to all levels in the organization, and allow sufficient time to service clients and develop new business for the bank. More specific objectives for this analysis follow:

1. Identify the business banking team and support staff members who should be included in the analysis.

2. Conduct a time-expenditure analysis and build an awareness of expenditures of time concentrations.

3. Develop "ideal" work performance responsibilities, with an emphasis on the percentage of time to be devoted to business development.

4. Determine the current ability level of each member of the business banking team and support staff.

5. Develop individual job descriptions that have the right people involved in the right task and in the right proportion of the business development effort.

Organizational Structure

Examining Bank of Sturgeon Bay's current business banking organizational structure is as important to the development of a sales culture as is the examination of individual job responsibilities. The structure must clearly show management's areas of responsibility; extend individual responsibilities to all levels in the organization; promote upward, downward, and lateral communication; and allow for effective business development activities. If the current structure is not operationally efficient enough to support new business development efforts, a structure must be developed and implemented that is. The following steps are recommended to achieve an efficient organizational structure:

1. Examine all areas of the existing Business Banking Division organizational structure to determine the necessary changes.

2. Develop an initial pro forma Business Banking Division organizational structure that represents the "ideal" desired structure.

3. Implement the necessary structural changes.

Client/Prospect Analysis

Bank of Sturgeon Bay has never conducted a complete analysis of its current business customer with regard to total loans, total deposits, profitability contributions, servicing time, or contact frequency requirements; nor have business prospects ever been officially identified, their desirability established, or their possibilities of development quantified.

Before responsibilities for cultivating current accounts and for prospecting for new business can be appropriately assigned to our business development officers, this type of market analysis must be completed. The information provided by such an analysis will serve as a logical basis for establishing relationship assignments.

The two main objectives, and their strategies for conducting a market analysis follow:

1. Conduct a thorough analysis of Bank of Sturgeon Bay's existing business client relationships.

Strategies:
- Compile all available internal resource data.

- Develop an analysis worksheet that will provide an effective overview of each client's account relationship to assist in determining servicing time and assignment requirements.

- Complete the appropriate portions of the analysis worksheet using clients' data.

- Estimate increased potential business from each client.

- Where applicable, use current loan information to establish complexity and risk.

- Determine the experience level required for business bankers to service clients.

- Estimate the frequency of contact necessary to build client relationships.

- Estimate the number of hours required to adequately service each client's needs on an annual basis.

- Make preliminary account assignments.

2. Conduct a thorough analysis of the key business prospects in our marketplace.

Strategies:
- Identify all prospects will potential of converting to client status.

- Establish a system for ranking prospects based on desirability and likelihood of conversion.

- Make initial assignments of these prospects to business banking team members.

Account Assignments

The fact that Bank of Sturgeon Bay's business customers and/or prospects have never been officially assigned to specific business banking team members has, over the years, repeatedly caused communication, workload, and relationship problems.

At this stage of the program's development, each member of the business banking team will have played an active role both in the job description and client/prospect analysis, and in the initial preliminary assignment effort. The intent, at this point, is to assign all current business clients and prospective clients to a specific business development officer to develop a more thorough understanding of the client's/prospect's business and needs, to develop better communications and cross-selling opportunities, and to create a more solid, hands-on relationship.

Objective: Make final assignments of business banking team members to clients/prospects.

Strategy: Use the combination of established time allocations, client needs, complexity standards, preliminary assignments, and any comfort levels previously developed to make final assignment modifications.

Sales/Call Planning and Management Tools

To be effective, this program has to include appropriate tools for planning and objective setting. These tools should assist business banking team members in analyzing their portfolios, determining client profitability contributions, targeting contacts, and planning the actual number and timing of their annual calls. In addition, appropriate tools must be developed to facilitate interdivision communication and management of the business banking team.

The following objectives have been set for this part of the business development plan:

1. Develop a Service Analysis Form and appropriate usage guidelines that will assist business development officers in analyzing current client service usage, service gap identification, and cross-sell objective setting.

2. Develop a Services Analysis Summary Form and appropriate usage guidelines that will allow business banking team members to get a grasp on their portfolios, as well as allowing supervisors to assist in maximizing portfolio potential and in measuring results.

3. Develop a Targeted Call Form and usage guidelines that will assist business banking team members in planning the total number, and timing, of their annual calls, and that will provide a method of recording actual calls made, as well as provide supervisors with a method of monitoring and measuring results.

4. Develop a Department Call Summary Form and usage guidelines that will assist supervisors in the monitoring and measuring of the division's planned versus actual call performance.

5. Develop a Client Profitability Worksheet and appropriate usage guidelines that will assist each business development officer in determining client profit contributions and servicing requirements.

6. Develop a Client Profitability Summary Form and usage guidelines that reflect the total current profitability of each business development team member's portfolio, as well as, measures future contribution increases.

7. Develop a Department Profitability Summary Form and appropriate usage guidelines that will assist in determining the division's current profitability and trends, in measuring division productivity, and in setting future individual and division goals.

8. Provide each member of the business banking team with appropriate training regarding the usage and the purpose of sales/call planning and management tools.

Management Information Systems (MIS)

Any successful program aimed at achieving long-term, business development and sales objectives must not only be well organized, but must also
address critical communication, monitoring, and feedback issues.

Management information systems have to be designed to facilitate a smooth
flow of business development activity information and promote ongoing
interaction. Data originating from contact with clients must be collected,
assembled in a meaningful format, channeled through appropriate management levels, and disseminated throughout the sales force.

If the systems are properly structured, overlapping effort will be eliminated, sales opportunities will be prevented from falling through the cracks,
communication lines will become continuous, and managers will be in a
better position to effectively manage the program.

The following objectives have been set for the development of business
banking management information system:

1. Develop an input and reporting system that will effectively inform
   management of current business-in-progress—activity that business development officers have in the "pipeline."

2. Develop an input and reporting system that will effectively report
   and record business that is booked from the "pipeline."

3. Develop an input and reporting system that will effectively report
   business turndowns from the "pipeline," as well as the reasons for
   the turndowns.

4. Develop an input and reporting system that will effectively report
   lost (nonbooked) business from the "pipeline," and record the
   reasons for the losses.

5. Computerize and test the input and reporting system.

Call Reports

The importance of building proper communication systems into the business development program cannot be overstressed. The proper management of information can be a key competitive advantage. A great deal of
information is uncovered and produced from client contact that is crucial
to the business development program's success. A procedure for recording
and communicating that information must, therefore, be developed. This
procedure must be adaptable to each development officer's personal style.
It must be immediate, encourage information accuracy, provide for additional input from management and from fellow business development
team members, and give direction for future follow-ups.

The two objectives for this part of the program follow:

1. Develop a first class, streamlined call reporting system that is immediate, simple to use, accurate, and saves time; and that improves the overall internal and external communication of the business development program.

2. Provide each member of the business banking team with appropriate training regarding the methods and procedures associated with the call reporting system.

Central Processing Support System

When the actual business development efforts, an immense amount of information will be generated. Information such as call data, lead generation, development activity (pipeline, business booked, business turndowns and business lost), and the resulting MIS reports will have to be processed. If this information is to be properly channeled, a central processing support system must be developed.

Sales Management

In this program, the sales managers will, in effect, wear two hats. They will determine the volume, profits, and growth objectives, as well as bear the responsibility for managing the sales efforts of the business development team in order to achieve those objectives. That they are key senior management members will lend support to the total effort, plus they will possess the power necessary to make immediate decisions affecting standards of performance.

Two objectives have been set for the sales management part of the program:

1. Identify the most-logical candidates who would, and could accept the responsibilities of managing Bank of Sturgeon Bay's bank-wide business development sales teams.

2. Obtain senior management's support of the plan, as well as acceptance of the responsibilities by those identified as top sales management candidates.

Training

One of the single most important ingredients necessary to ensure an ongoing successful business development program is training. Without it our ambitious objectives would be unattainable, our well-planned systems rendered useless, and our efforts wasted.

Determining who, what, how, and how often to train is an ongoing process that involves assessing abilities, determining needs, researching resources, designing and implementing programs, and monitoring effectiveness.

In order to meet the objectives of our business development plan, training has to be prioritized based on immediate and long-term needs. Our aim is to build a solid structure from which our program can be launched, plus develop an ongoing training plan that will successfully drive our program into the future. The following training objectives have been set:

1. Develop and implement appropriate training to explain the necessity and the mechanics of the business development program's systems and procedures; and solicit support for using this training.

2. Develop and implement a program that will prepare business development team members with a level of sales-skills training necessary to launch the program; and outline plans to build long-term, ongoing sales-skills training.

3. Develop and implement an ongoing sales management training program aimed at developing and refining the management skills of our program's designated sales managers.

4. Develop and implement an ongoing product training program that emphasizes the features and benefits of both existing and new bank products.

5. Develop and implement a training program that will introduce our board of directors to sales and their role in the overall business development program.

Enhancing Success (Internal and External)

After we have successfully built the necessary structure for a long-term business development program—a committed management, an analyzed market, operational systems, and a trained sales staff—we can turn our efforts to enhancing the total effort and communicating our market-driven philosophy, both internally and externally.

Enhancing success is an ongoing promotional process aimed at building enthusiasm, supporting development efforts, projecting the desired image, and most importantly, improving communications. The objectives and strategies for enhancing the success of our program follow:

1. Build internal direct-communication system(s) that will keep sales staff members informed and energized.

   Strategy: Develop ways to communicate recognition, feedback, performance updates, and program changes in a timely fashion.

2. Develop methods to communicate Bank of Sturgeon Bay's market-driven, business banking approach to the business community.

Strategy: Based on sound marketing and public relations practices, develop external communications tactics as part of the overall 1988 marketing plan.

Incentives And Compensation

Incentive and compensation programs must be based on performance and reward systems, and must adequately blend the appropriate monetary, achievement, and recognition elements. Our aim is to address each of these elements in order to build a sales performance reward system that gives selling performance credibility without sacrificing customer service.

Two objectives have been set for the incentives and compensation portion of this program:

1. Design and implement a visible, tangible, and continual perform-ance-based reward system that will motivate Bank of Sturgeon Bay's business development team to sell.

2. Design and implement a performance-based bonus system to reward sales managers for directing Bank of Sturgeon Bay's business development teams to high sales levels.

Program Review

On a day-to-day basis sales managers will regularly review and inspect the business development efforts of sales team members. As a result, slight program modifications and/or systems and procedures improvements, can be expected. However, there are much broader dimensions to the program that must be routinely reviewed.

The progress of the business development sales efforts must be consistent with overall corporate objectives; and the image that is projected and the level of service that is provided through the program must meet desired corporate standards. In order to determine whether or not strategies need to be modifed, a review system must be designed. The responsibility for guiding this system must be assigned to senior bank management. Thus, we must develop a program review system that addresses business development progress, impact and future direction issues.

CONCLUSION

This plan will help Bank of Sturgeon Bay accomplish its stated objective of building a long-term, market-driven sales culture within our Business Banking Division; and it will ensure that we maintain and improve our leadership position in this market. ◆

[1] Door County Chamber of Commerce, *Community Profile Report*, (July 1987).

[2] Door County Chamber of Commerce, *Guest Study*, (August 1986).

[3] Bank of Sturgeon Bay, *Call and 10Q Report*, (June 30, 1987).

CHAPTER 17

BusinesSystem Banking: A Plan for Building Commercial Customer Relationships

Catherine M. McCloskey
Delaware Trust Company
$1 billion assets

SITUATION ANALYSIS
Delaware and Its Economy

Delaware, the second smallest state in the nation with land area of only 1,982 square miles, has three counties: New Castle, Kent, and Sussex. New Castle, the northern-most and smallest county, is the industrial, urban-suburban center of the state and the most densely populated of the three counties. Kent and Sussex counties are largely agricultural (one-half of the state's land acreage is used for farming), with poultry accounting for over two-thirds of agricultural receipts. In this state of approximately 613,000 people, manufacturing is the largest source of state employment and income. Within the manufacturing segment, the chemical and automotive industries dominate all others.[1]

Delaware has fashioned a corporate tax structure favorable to business. The state has no tax on inventories, and no tax on process machinery or equipment. There is no sales tax, no personal property tax, and no state-level real property tax in Delaware. Although Delaware levies a corporate tax on net income, partnerships and sole proprietorships are not subject to this tax. Instead, partners or sole proprietors are liable for personal income taxes only on their proportionate share of the business's income. Also exempt from state corporate income tax are investment and holding companies, which maintain and manage intangible investments and collect and distribute income from these investments or from tangible property outside Delaware.[2] As a result of this favorable corporate tax treatment, more than half of the Fortune 500 companies are incorporated in Delaware, and *Inc.*

Magazine ranked Delaware sixteenth in the nation in its fourth annual report of favorable climates for small business. Delaware improved thirty-three positions in two years.

In 1984 alone, the number of firms incorporated in Delaware grew by over 2,000, to a total of 160,000; the value of commercial construction increased by 60%, compared with 23% for the nation; and the value of building-construction contracts grew by 27%, compared with 12% for the nation.[3] In 1985, the value of all construction contracts in Delaware increased 42%, compared with 8% in the United States.[4]

The Commercial Market in Delaware

According to the University of Delaware's Bureau of Economic and Business Research, Delaware had 14,241 firms in 1984. The services industry segment had the largest share of all firms, with 30.9%; followed by retail trade, with 26.0%; construction, with 14.9%; wholesale trade, with 8.9%; finance, insurance, and real estate (F.I.R.E.), with 8.6%; transportation, communications, and public utilities, with 4.6%; manufacturing, with 4.6%; and agriculture with 2.0%.

Because the state of Delaware levies no sales tax, firms need not report sales information, making it impossible to obtain public information about sales volumes for Delaware firms. Neither is this information available from any reliable secondary source. Delaware Trust therefore hired Dun's Marketing Services to analyze firms in the state and to provide a market profile of sales, along with various other data. Dun's field work was completed late in 1983 and analyzed in 1984. It revealed that most firms in Delaware had annual sales of less than $1 million. However, 8.2% of all firms had annual sales of $1 million or more. Delaware Trust's management was particularly interested in these firms, which will be called "large firms," as prospects for commercial lending. Large firms were therefore analyzed in greater detail.

By combining information from the proprietary Dun research with data from the previously cited University of Delaware statistics, Delaware Trust's marketing research department was able to project the concentration of large firms within each industry segment. The results reveal that the manufacturing and wholesale trade industry segments have relatively high concentrations of large firms, with relatively low concentrations are found in the services and F.I.R.E segments.

The state of Delaware's Department of Labor provided data from which we were able to calculate industry growth rates. Based on the percentage of change in the number of Delaware firms between 1975 and 1984, the services segment had the highest growth rate in the state, an increase of 54%, followed by agriculture (44.5%), wholesale trade (41.6%), construction

(39.5%), transportation/communications (31.9%), F.I.R.E. (31.0%), retail trade (17.7%), and manufacturing (10.4%).

A late 1985 study of commercial banking services in the mid-Atlantic region supplied additional information. The study, conducted by Trans Data Corporation, collected data via a telephone survey from a random sample of firms in Pennsylvania, southern New Jersey, and Delaware, having over $5 million in annual sales and headquartered in the region. From this data, we developed a profile of credit use within industry segments, based on the number of firms that had borrowed within the previous two years. Results yielded an estimate of the relative propensity to borrow within industry segments for firms in Delaware with annual sales greater than $5 million. Firms in the construction industry were more likely to borrow than firms in any other industry segment (91.5%), followed by agriculture (82.4%), wholesale trade (82.3%), retail trade (79.3%), manufacturing (77.1%), services (74.5%), transportation/communications (62.9%), and F.I.R.E. (52.6%).

Delaware Trust's Competitors

In addition to Delaware Trust, there are four major banks competing for a share of the commercial market in Delaware. In order by asset size as of June 30, 1986, they are Wilmington Trust Company, with assets of $2.5 billion; Bank of Delaware, with assets of $1.5 billion; Wilmington Savings Fund Society (WSFS), with assets of $1 billion; and Mellon Bank of Delaware, with assets of $846 million.[5]

All competitors used print advertising in the past year to communicate to the commercial marketplace. In general, the messages stressed the expertise, commitment to business, and individual attention provided by the sponsoring bank. All competitors used visuals featuring their commercial lenders. In most ads, the text focused on lending, with the intent of attracting businesses in the market for a commercial loan.

Wilmington Trust pictures its commercial loan officers in print advertising that describes them as "experienced" and "professional."

Bank of Delaware calls its commercial loan officers "relationship managers" and pictures them with customers in pseudotestimonial print ads bearing the headline "Looking for Delaware's business connection?"

Mellon Bank pictures its "Mellon business officers" and tells readers they are ready to help businesses of all sizes with an array of business products.

WSFS uses a case history, showing a member of its "commercial lending team" with a customer, in a print ad targeting real estate development and construction.

A tracking report compiled by Delaware Trust's advertising agency revealed that in the twelve months between August 1985 and August 1986 these competitors spent a combined total of $33,600 for fifty-one black and white pages of print advertising about commercial banking. Wilmington Trust's commercial ads appeared most frequently (seventeen times), and WSFS's, least often (eight times). During this same period, Delaware Trust introduced its brand of commercial relationship banking, BusinesSystem Banking, with a four-color magazine ad that ran five times for a total cost of $16,000. Delaware Trust has not advertised or otherwise promoted BusinesSystem Banking to the general commercial marketplace in the past nine months.

Estimates of market share were drawn from the previously referenced Trans Data study. Unfortunately, this study is limited because it includes only businesses with $5 million or more in annual sales. Given that Delaware Trust management is most interested in lending to businesses with annual sales of $1 million or more, the Trans Data study omits a significant chunk of target firms, namely those with annual sales between $1 and $5 million. In the study, firms were asked to name their primary or lead bank. The data revealed the following market share of customers based on major bank relationship.

Bank of Delaware	25.6%
Wilmington Trust	21.5%
Mellon	13.8%
Delaware Trust	13.3%
All others	25.8%
	100.0%

The category "all others" consists mainly of very large Delaware firms whose primary bank is located outside Delaware, for example, the DuPont Company. These firms are not prospects for Delaware Trust or any of our competitors.

Firms were also asked the extent to which various banks were becoming more or less important to them. These were the results, stated in terms of net importance.

Wilmington Trust	+34.6%
Delaware Trust	+15.3%
Mellon	+ 8.8%
Bank of Delaware	- 10.2%

The results show that Wilmington Trust appears to be the best at solidifying existing customer relationships. WSFS is not a significant competitor in the commercial marketplace at present.

Resources and Strengths of Delaware Trust Company

Delaware Trust Company was founded in 1899. Bank management places particular emphasis on good service, as described by Chairman William C. Lickle in a letter to shareholders.

> Quality service is a long-standing tradition at Delaware Trust; it's frankly what sets us apart from our sometimes monolithic competitors. To us quality service means prompt, accurate and courteous service. It is service that is consistent from one employee to another and from one department to another. Quality service is something we work hard at, both with time and money.[6]

This emphasis on service encourages employee creativity and has led to unique solutions over the years.

The bank's emphasis on quality services has not gone unnoticed. The public perceives a positive difference in Delaware Trust's level of service, compared with that of competitors. Based on the results of a 1985 segmentation study, sampling 791 Delaware households, "quality service" was rated the second-most-important bank attribute, and Delaware Trust scored strongly in the minds of respondents.

Delaware Trust operates twenty-two full-service banking offices and four limited-service sites in Delaware. These banking centers are heavily concentrated in the northern third of the state, with nineteen full-service and three limited-service locations in New Castle County.

Delaware Trust's loan-to-deposit ratio has been stable at approximately 68% in the past two years. It is a management goal to raise the loan-to-deposit ratio by employing more deposit dollars as loans.

The Commercial Banking Division

Structurally, the Commercial Banking Division is comprised of five departments that report to a division director. Two sales teams are devoted to servicing existing commercial customers and to developing new commercial relationships. The Real Estate Department manages relationships with builders and developers and works specifically with this market niche on project funding needs. The Branch Loan Support Department functions as a bridge between commercial banking and the banking centers. Branch Loan Support is also the training ground for the Sales Departments. The Commercial Marketing Department plans and implements programs to aid business development and is the liaison to corporate marketing.

Although they fall outside the structure of the Commercial Banking Division, banking centers are an important point-of-contact with commercial customers. The manager of each banking center has responsibility for selling and approving commercial loans within specified dollar limits. These limits are established by the commercial banking director. When the amount of a loan request is above the manager's limit, he or she works with the Branch Loan Support Department on the request.

Commercial Checking Accounts and Loans

As of September 1986, Delaware Trust had a yearly average of 6,800 commercial demand deposit accounts, representing 5,500 customer relationships. This base of core accounts remains relatively stable month to month. Over the past five years, however, the number of accounts has declined steadily by about 2.5% per year, while average account balances have increased disproportionately. Over this same five-year period, Delaware Trust made two major changes that affected commercial demand deposit accounts and that provides some insight into the five-year trends. First, the bank introduced "cash management services" as enhancements to the basic commercial checking product. Secondly, the bank increased "business analysis" pricing, requiring customers to pay more for demand deposit-related activity and optional services.

Commercial loan balances have doubled since 1982. Two forces appear to have aided this growth in commercial loans: changes inside the bank (new divisional management, a new organization structure that is more conducive to a sales culture, more account officers, and sales training) and the healthy economic climate of a state that supports and encourages business growth.

Commercial Customer Mix at Delaware Trust

Delaware Trust's commercial customer base was analyzed alone and in comparison with the general market. Overall, more customers (2,115) fit into the services segment than any other segment, followed closely by customers in the retail trade segment (1,610). Market penetration is greatest in the manufacturing segment (74%), followed by F.I.R.E. (55%), and services (48%). Construction and wholesale trade appear to be underrepresented in Delaware Trust's customer base, when compared with other segments.

Delaware Trust has more commercial customers with annual sales under $5 million than over $5 million. Most of these small businesses were begun by entrepreneurs, and many have been owned and managed by members of the same family for more than one generation.

Twenty percent (20%) of all Delaware Trust commercial checking customers also have commercial loans with Delaware Trust. Of those customers with both a checking account and a loan, more fit into the services segment

(40%) than any other, followed by the retail trade (19.5%) and wholesale trade (11%) segments.

The greatest percentage by industry of Delaware Trust customers with both a checking account and a loan fall in the wholesale trade segment (81.8%), followed by the agricultural (50%) and manufacturing (34.6%) segments.

Present commercial customers represent the biggest sales opportunity to the bank and its account officers. Based on past lending history and the present state economy, Delaware Trust identified the three most profitable industry segments for lending. They are construction, manufacturing, and wholesale trade. We also found that companies with annual sales of $1 million or more were historically more profitable as customers than smaller customers.

Within the construction industry, the bank has sold loans to only 4.9% of its large, borrowing customers. In fact, roughly 81.5% of all large firms in this segment bank elsewhere.

Penetration of large manufacturing firms is good, with roughly 73% of them having a demand deposit account with Delaware Trust and 45% of those also having a loan with Delaware Trust. There is uncaptured customer opportunity of 40% and uncaptured noncustomer opportunity of 26.7% of total large firms in the segment.

Within the wholesale trade segment Delaware Trust has captured only 14% of large firms, but has sold both demand deposit accounts and loans to all of those firms. Uncaptured noncustomer opportunity is 86% of all large, borrowing firms.

Marketing Philosophy
As stated earlier, Delaware Trust emphasizes "quality service." This tradition is the foundation of the bank's marketing philosophy. New products are developed based on the needs of the marketplace and a reasonable return on investment. Divisional managers understand the marketing concept and look for ways to apply it. Well-planned marketing projects receive the funding needed, and marketing staff members work in an atmosphere that is both challenging and supportive.

Structure of the Corporate Marketing Division
The corporate marketing division is comprised of three departments: Advertising, Marketing Research, and Product Management, each with its own manager. Divisional staff includes four senior product managers, a research analyst, a marketing assistant, an advertising assistant, and an executive secretary.

The Birth of BusinesSystem Banking

In a 1985 article for *The Journal of Commercial Bank Lending,* authors Lane Kramer and Dennis McCuistion noted the following small business market need:

> There is a demand for bankers to act as financial consultants. Many small businesses are run by their founders who may be experts in marketing, engineering, or production but who lack the critical skills in finance and management for the firms to grow and survive.[7]

More than a year ago, Delaware Trust had identified this same need among small businesses in our own market. We saw that many small business owners lacked the education and both the internal and external resources needed to make important business decisions. Although they might have a lawyer or an accountant, small business owners cannot rely on these advisors to help with long-range business planning. Malcolm Bund, president of the management consulting firm Malcolm Bund & Associates, addressed the dilemma of the small businessperson and the advisory role of lawyers and accountants in a 1981 speech to the Chesapeake Chapter of Robert Morris Associates.

> The small business owner. . . is not surrounded by experienced employees. He may have a partner with whom he can discuss strategic issues. And he may have a lawyer or an accountant who can be helpful. However, the legal and accounting advice available to the small firm is typically limited to the specific disciplines or narrow experience. In other words, an accountant can tell the entrepreneur what has happened but rarely can tell him why it happened and what the implications for the future could be. The lawyer can discuss the legal implications of what has happened but is not necessarily qualified to advise about future business conditions. This is where, in my opinion, the lender and the consultant can be helpful.[8]

Delaware Trust commercial banking management believes that a commercial banker with the proper background and training can satisfy the small business owner's need for both a lender and a management consultant in the person of the "consultative" account officer. Furthermore, the bank planned to use this approach to develop new business through a program named "BusinesSystem Banking." BusinesSystem Banking is defined as a process of comprehensive business planning emphasizing disciplined growth, transacted between the business decision maker and the Delaware Trust account officer, using financial services that are customized to fit the needs and goals of the business customer, the dynamics of the industry, and the state of the economy.

A print ad introduced the program in January 1986. Unfortunately, after a promising start the program disintegrated. Several other planned marketing tactics that would have supported the program were never developed. Problems with turnover among account officers stretched the remaining staff and temporarily changed the general business development direction from an aggressive search for new business to a defensive position of cross-selling to existing customers and maintaining service levels.

Another reason for the collapse of the BusinesSystem Banking program was a lack of proper coordination and marketing support. Thus, in spite of an advertisement which proclaimed ". . . we just got more aggressive," BusinesSystem Banking all but dropped out of sight in the marketplace.

OBJECTIVES
Delaware Trust plans to more aggressively promote and implement BusinesSystem Banking once again—this time with a more comprehensive marketing plan.

Broad Qualitative Objectives
1. Use the concept of BusinesSystem Banking to differentiate Delaware Trust's commercial bankers from the competition by the end of 1987.

2. Target the program to the three most-profitable commercial industry segments.

Broad Quantitative Objectives
Develop a program, using BusinesSystem Banking as the cornerstone to:

1. Increase commercial loan balances 30% by the end of 1987.

2. Increase noninterest revenue 20% by the end of 1987.

3. Increase the number of commercial deposit accounts 10% by the end of 1987.

Marketing Objectives
Research Objectives

1. Conduct market research in the first quarter of 1987 and again in the first quarter of 1988, segmenting responses by industry, with the following objectives:

   - Measure general commercial market awareness of the name "BusinesSystem Banking" and the respondents' ability to link the brand name to Delaware Trust.

- Determine the makeup of the general commercial market in Delaware by industry segments. Compare results with previous research results (from 1984), and analyze changes.

- Determine the extent to which the bank's customer base is similar or dissimilar in industry makeup to the general market.

2. Analyze secondary research available to the bank in order to monitor commercial market trends and to identify changes in buyer needs.

Advertising and Sales Promotion Objectives

1. Build general market awareness of the name "BusinesSystem Banking" to the 20% level by the end of 1987.

2. Create in the marketplace a positive, differentiated impression of Delaware Trust's commercial account officers by the end of 1987.

3. Generate interest among members of the Delaware commercial marketplace, between January and June 1987, in order to support business development.

4. Target and deliver a message to buyers in the three most-profitable industry segments between January and April to generate sales inquiries.

5. Create messages consistent in tone with those delivered in person-to-person sales calls.

Public Relations Objectives

1. Support advertising and sales promotion objectives by building greater awareness of BusinesSystem Banking among specified target audiences. Coordinate timing with advertising and sales promotion programs.

2. Promote the expertise of Delaware Trust's commercial account officers. Coordinate timing with advertising and sales promotion programs.

3. Build awareness of Delaware Trust's commitment to Delaware businesses. Coordinate timing with advertising and sales promotion programs.

Training Objectives

1. Design product knowledge training for entry-level account officers by February 1987. Training will teach participants about the basics of commercial lending products, commercial deposit products,

and cash management products to enable them to match a Delaware Trust product with a perceived buyer need. Implement training for the first group of account officers by March 1987.

2. By March 1987, design supplemental product knowledge training for advanced account officers to add to their basic knowledge of products and to inform them of product changes.

Business Development Objectives

1. Contact 500 buyers by the end of 1987.

2. Make sales visits to at least 30% of these buyers.

3. Increase commercial loan balances by $77 million, to $335 million by the end of 1987.

4. Increase the number of demand deposit accounts by 680, to 7,480 accounts by the end of 1987.

STRATEGIES AND TACTICS
Research

Research will be targeted to the commercial marketplace in Delaware and will seek to identify the number of firms in each industry segment, the number of firms within various annual sales levels, banks used, satisfaction level of firm with present lead bank, length of time with lead bank, unmet financial services needs, quality of service provided by banks used, number and frequency of solicitations from competitors, and the effectiveness of Delaware Trust advertising. A budget of $20,000 has been allocated for a study in the spring of 1987.

The product manager will be responsible for the following:

- Formulating a list of questions, by February, which the research results are expected to answer.

- Managing internal communications relevant to the project.

- Obtaining internal approvals for all phases of the project by March.

The research manager will be responsible for the following:

- Selecting a random, representative sample of Delaware firms by March.

- Recommending the survey technique to be used.

- Formulating the questionnaire and fielding the survey by April.

- Compiling and analyzing the results by April.

- Forecasting industry growth rates by April.

- Writing a summary of the project, with implications and recommendations by May.

- Presenting the findings to management by June.

Advertising and Sales Promotion
Advertising will deliver the message that through BusinesSystem Banking, small business owners and their Delaware Trust account officers can plan the best long-term growth strategy for the company. Print advertising will be placed in both newspapers and magazines, and will run in all general market and business publications in Delaware between January and June 1987. Newspaper ads will run once a week in daily publications and once a month in community newspapers and business tabloids. Ads will run three out of six months in Delaware's monthly state magazine and in the Delaware subscriptions of four national magazines. A budget of $46,000 has been allocated for advertising production and media purchasing.

The product manager will be responsible for the following:

- Supplying direction and information to the advertising manager for advertising development by the bank's advertising agency by October. (This step has been completed.)

- Obtaining management approval for all phases as needed.

- Coordinating the advertising schedule with other aspects of the program to gain the maximum synergism by October. (This step has been completed.)

- Coordinating communications within corporate marketing and across divisional lines as needed.

The advertising manager will be responsible for the following:

- Liaison with the bank's advertising agency.

- Managing creative development, to be delivered in December.

- Managing media plan development, to be delivered in October and finalized in November. (This step has been completed)

- Supervising the scheduling of media insertions as specified in the media plan, January through June.

- Approving agency billings as budgeted.

Direct mail will be used to leverage the sales staff of fifteen commercial account officers by segmenting and prequalifying prospects. The list, the mailing, and the sales staffs must work closely together for this tactic to be of maximum benefit. To begin, the product manager purchased a targeted list of Delaware firms, with annual sales between $1 million and $50 million, in the construction, manufacturing, and wholesale trade industries. The commercial marketing manager screened the list to remove present credit customers who have already been introduced to BusinesSystem Banking and firms which, for a variety of reasons, do not represent desirable prospects. This process resulted in a list of 300 highly qualified prospects and 200 well-qualified prospects.

In the meantime, the advertising manager worked with the bank's agency to create a direct mail program suitable to the delivery of the BusinesSystem Banking message. Preliminary creative was presented and approved in mid-November. The program is comprised of a three-step mailing followed by personal contact by a Delaware Trust account officer. Each mailing consists of a gift, bearing the bank's logo, a pamphlet whose text ties the gift to a benefit of BusinesSystem Banking, and the business card of the assigned account officer. A prospect will receive three unique packages about three weeks apart. The last mailing will contain a letter from the account officer, who will then telephone the prospect within two weeks after the mailing date. Although progress has been made in this project, the Spring 1987 phase will not be finished until March or April when mailings to the first 300 prospects are completed. Another 200 prospects have been targeted for mailings in the fall of 1987. A budget of $60,000 has been allocated for the direct mail program.

The product manager will be responsible for the following:

- Designing a tracking system for mailing packages and reporting status to account managers.
- Printing and affixing labels, and coordinating mailing dates with account managers.
- Storing and distributing mailing packages and their contents.
- Evaluating and reporting program results.

The commercial marketing manager will be responsible for the following:

- Assigning prospects to account officers.
- Communicating program goals to account officers.
- Evaluating individual account officers on the results they achieve.

The advertising manager will be responsible for the following:

- Liaison with the agency and approval of billing.

Public Relations

Three public relations tactics will be used in the period January through June to supplement media advertising, direct mail, and personal sales calls. They are a news interview with Delaware Trust's director of commercial banking, conducted by a business reporter from Delaware's major daily newspaper; a feature article about BusinesSystem Banking, placed in business trade publications throughout the state; and a seminar promotion for small businesspeople using experts who will speak on topics of particular interest to the audience. A budget of $10,500 has been allocated to the public relations program.

The product manager and the commercial marketing manager will be responsible for the following:

- Briefing the public affairs assistant on BusinesSystem Banking and its benefits. (This step has been completed.)
- Approving copy for feature article.
- Internal communications for all public relations tactics.
- Selecting speakers and topics by February for a seminar promotion.
- Selecting dates and locations by February for a seminar promotion.
- Developing a guest list by January for a seminar promotion.

The public affairs assistant will be responsible for the following:

- Briefing the commercial division director on press interviews.
- Scheduling and coordinating interview with business reporter.
- Writing the feature article by January, and placing it before June.
- Contacting speakers, arranging transportation, lodging, and meals for a seminar promotion.
- Reserving seminar room.
- Printing and mailing invitations.
- Taking reservations.

Training

Entry level account officers, primarily those in the branch loan support department, will receive basic training about Delaware Trust products. A training consultant will conduct the sessions, which will be customer designed, before the end of March 1987. Also by March, product review training will be available to advanced account officers. The specifics of both training programs will be determined with the training consulting firm. A budget of $25,000 has been allocated for the training programs.

The product manager will be responsible for the following:

- Interviewing and selecting a training consulting firm by January.
- Selecting products for product knowledge training and providing information about them to the training consultant.
- Liaison with the commercial banking department and the training department.
- Final approval of training course materials.
- Evaluation of training consultant's performance.

The training coordinator will be responsible for the following:

- Recommending training firms.
- Liaison with the training firm.
- Planning of training sessions—location, audio-visual materials, refreshments, and delivery of training materials.
- Communication with and scheduling of participants.

The commercial marketing manager will be responsible for the following:

- Selection of participants.
- Evaluation of training programs, determination of future product knowledge training needs.

Business Development

The business development tactics are most critical to the success of this marketing plan. Because of the consultative banker approach that is the backbone of BusinesSystem Banking, all sales are expected to occur in person-to-person meetings between the prospect and the Delaware Trust account officer. The direct mail campaign will end with a telephone call from the account officer to the prospect. Each account officer will be assigned twenty prospects. He is expected to telephone all twenty prospects between March and April and to set appointments with at least 30% of them, or six prospects. Furthermore, he is expected to close one piece of business with 80% of his prospects before the end of 1987. The plan for business development of an additional 200 high-quality prospects will be designed for fall 1987, based on the results of the spring program. New commercial lending relationships are preferred, but commercial deposit business or even personal accounts are acceptable because any relationship will introduce a new customer to BusinesSystem Banking. Everyone involved in the planning of this program believes that BusinesSystem Banking has no equal in Delaware, and thus, once a small businessperson samples our brand of consultative banking, they will want Delaware Trust for their primary bank sooner or later.

Account officers will control the beginning date for the first mailing to each prospect. This measure of control will allow them to organize their schedules around personal sales calls, the fourth and final step of the direct mail program.

Prospects have been carefully selected. We began with a list of Delaware companies with annual sales of $1 million to $50 million in the construction, manufacturing and wholesale trade industry segments. Research, confirmed by experience, pointed us toward firms of this size in these particular industries as the most-likely prospects for commercial lending. The prospect list was further screened against a proprietary memorandum file of all noncustomer firms in Delaware. In this file, account officers note their calling experiences with, and personal knowledge of, a firm and its decision maker. Any prospects who were judged to be firmly entrenched with a competitor bank, or not desirable as customers, were eliminated from our prospect list.

The combined budget for advertising, sales promotion, public relations, and training, totaling $141,500, supports the business development plan. However, the direct mail budget is most specifically directed toward the calling effort. It is estimated that the direct mail program will cost $75 per prospect. We reason that it is more cost-effective to spend $75 introducing a prospect to BusinesSystem Banking and piquing some interest via three memorable mailings than it is to send an account officer on two sales calls— the first, to explain BusinesSystem Banking to a prospect who never heard of it, and the second, to close a piece of business. A recent article in *Bank Marketing* magazine placed the cost of an average sales call at over $200.[9] Using this average cost as an estimate, Delaware Trust will spend $275 for direct mail and a personal sales call, instead of $400 for two personal sales calls—an estimated savings of $125 per prospect.

The program will be evaluated at the end of 1987 against the business development objectives previously stated.

The product manager will be responsible for the following:

- Coordinating direct mailing dates with account officers.
- Reporting business development progress to the corporate marketing division director.

The commercial marketing manager will be responsible for the following:

- Establishing goals for each calling officer.

- Evaluating the performance of calling officers.

- Communicating with calling officers.

- Reporting business development results at monthly sales meetings and elsewhere as needed.

CONCLUSION

Delaware Trust has identified a need among small businesses for comprehensive financial service. By implementing BusinesSystem Banking, Delaware Trust's commercial account officers will act both as a lender and a management consultant to their commercial customers. The personal attention afforded by this program should attract new commercial customers, as well as retain existing customers who might expand their relationship with the bank.

If the strategies and tactics of this marketing plan for BusinesSystem Banking are implemented, the marketing and bankwide objectives should easily be achieved. Delaware Trust has the necessary components to make this system work: a well-thoughtout plan, officers who provide quality service, and a market with potential customers. ◆

[1] *Delaware Data Book* (Delaware, March 1985), p. -a-.

[2] Ibid., p. II-3.

[3] Ibid., p. I-2.

[4] Eleanor D. Craig, "Deregulation of Banking in Delaware," *TopLine* (Spring 1986), pp. 12-13.

[5] *FDIC Call Reports* (June 30, 1986)

[6] William C. Lickle, *Delaware Trust Company 1985 Annual Report*, p. 5.

[7] Lane Kramer and Dennis McCuistion, "The Emerging Role of Commercial Bankers as Financial Consultants," *The Journal of Commercial Bank Lending* (June 1985), p. 2.

[8] Malcolm B. Bund, "The Roles of a Consultant and a Lender in the Emergence of a Growing Business," *The Journal of Commercial Bank Lending* (April 1981), p. 39.

[9] Theresa K. Wrobel, "Telemarketing: Not for Retail Only,"*Bank Marketing* (August 1986), p. 12.

CHAPTER 18

Information Management and Business Banking: Establishing a Corporate Database

James M. Roots
Commercial National Bank
$430 million assets

INTRODUCTION
Too Much Information

As an industry, banking has done a good job of collecting information about its customers. The amount of demographic and psychographic data that banks routinely collect in the course of a day's business is staggering, and yet it is only recently that much thought has been given to the marketing implications of this information. The problem has been the sheer volume of information and how to manipulate it.

A good example of this is in the area of business development at Commercial National Bank. Our business officers have a tremendous amount of information available to them: business credit files, on-line access to account information at our data center, and reports from other departments in the bank. Yet putting all these different pieces together into a picture that leads to new business and increased sales is a monumental, if not impossible, task for the individual account officer. Each officer may have a wealth of information about a given customer, but in many instances this information is fragmentary, unconnected, and physically disjointed. In some cases it is difficult to immediately discern something so simple as which bank products a particular customer is currently using. It is also quite difficult for an officer to look at his or her accounts as a whole and to determine areas of strength and opportunity in sales development. The way in which information about our business customers is currently organized is not conducive to cross-selling or officer-call-program management. Thus, information management has become an issue for our business officers.

Borrowing a Solution

It is, thus, clear that effective information management is one of the keys to a successful business development program at our bank. To satisfy this need, we decided to borrow a solution that has already proven successful in many retail industries: database marketing.[1]

The phrase *database marketing* defies a unique definition, and even attempts to explain what it entails or what it provides for its practitioners vary greatly from institution to institution. There are, however, two fundamental aspects of database marketing that are readily apparent: (1) recognition of the concept that customers have individual needs that can best be satisfied on an individual basis, and (2) a reliance on computer technology to handle large volumes of customer data.

While market segmentation is certainly not a new concept, the degree to which promotional activity and selling efforts can now be focused is largely a result of advances in computer technology. It is now feasible for a business to target the specific needs of an individual customer in a cost-effective manner, from both a monetary and temporal standpoint. Indeed, the marketplace of the future, described by Alvin Toffler, in which "every person is a vocal minority of one" [2] is here. And while the marriage of marketing and computers is not new, the days of conflict between marketing on the one hand and data centers and mainframe processing on the other are fast disappearing. The developments in desktop computing power and memory storage have made it possible for marketing departments to have dedicated CIFs, thereby improving their ability to use customer data in a timely and efficient manner.

So far, however, most of the developments and applications of database marketing have taken place in retail environments. This has been true of the banking industry as well. For example, a cursory glance through a recent *Bank Marketing* issue reveals no fewer than three large advertisements for retail-oriented marketing systems,[3] and there are at least a dozen other firms not represented that also provide this service. It has only been within the past year or so that vendors have begun to turn their attention to the corporate side.

Towards a Corporate Database Marketing System

When we first began to explore the possibility of a database marketing system for our business development program, most of the business-to-business databases available from outside vendors at that time were more management tools to track calling and sales performance than true marketing systems. While such tracking abilities were important to us, there were other aspects of our business marketing strategy that we felt could also benefit from a PC-based database. The objectives we identified for our database marketing system were largely derived from those presented by Richard J. Fagan in a 1986 article on officer calling programs.[4] Any system under serious consideration by our bank needed the ability to:

1. Store and retrieve useful information to support the management of our officer-call program. We needed a system with the ability to track officer calls on both existing and prospective customers. The system also needed to provide us with the ability to specifically set calling targets based on such parameters as size of business, location, services used, type of business, or any other criterion for which we have information.

2. Provide our officers with the information to effectively manage the relationships for which they are responsible. In describing bank marketing strategies, Ira Nathanson believes that "what's important is simply this—existing customers are your best source for new business. And the more you know about your customers, the better able you are to satisfy their needs. Period."[5] Providing our account officers with quick access to basic account information was one of the first needs we identified for our bank. Under our old arrangements, an officer might have to access two different computer systems and a number of credit files physically located on another floor of the bank in order to obtain information about one customer.

3. Accumulate information about our customers, market segments, and products, that was useful for analysis, planning, and forecasting purposes. Historically, Commercial National Bank has not had a strong research orientation. A major goal for our business development program in 1988 is to begin to systematically analyze our market position and to use this information to capitalize on our strengths.

A final criterion for our system was the ease with which it could be integrated into our existing programs and marketing objectives for 1988 and beyond. With these objectives and concerns firmly in mind, we began our search for the system most suited to our business development needs.

Outside Purchase versus In-House Development

Our search efforts were immediately confronted with a major decision. Was the system to be purchased from an outside vendor or was it to be developed in-house? Both options offered numerous advantages and disadvantages.

From the very beginning, it had been our intention to purchase our database marketing system from an outside firm specializing in such products. We certainly did not feel any need to reinvent the wheel, nor did we feel that we had the expertise to organize, assemble, and implement such a system entirely on our own. Our bank is still very much in the process of learning how to effectively use personal computers, and any required applications or programming have been exclusively provided by outside sources. We were initially convinced that an outside firm would be able to provide us with a proven, reliable system. From a cost standpoint, we were also convinced that a purchased system would prove less expensive than the staff time needed to develop a system on our own, both in terms of actual people hours and time taken from other vital marketing projects.

What was soon apparent, however, was that even purchased systems would be expensive in terms of staff time because of the following difficulties in implementation, largely a result of our bank's lack of a cohesive information system:

- Since much of our business information is currently contained in "hard" copy (i.e., credit files), there is no way to electronically capture this information for use in our database. As a result, nearly all data entry for our system must be done manually.

- Because customer data is scattered throughout various locations and departments in our bank, the collection and organization of this information requires a large amount of staff research.

- Even where account information is readily accessible and capable of electronic capture, as is the case of data in our CIF, such information is still not organized in an effective manner for relationship management purposes. Our CIF is organized around individual account information, not customers. In other words, looking up a customer in our CIF may or may not give an accurate picture of the total account relationships with that customer. A good example of this is the case of our public funds accounts. Each public body may maintain several different accounts with us, but these accounts are not linked together in our CIF. Thus, an account officer may not know the total deposits a public body is keeping with us. Organizing our CIF data would thus be another area requiring a significant amount of staff time.

A final difficulty we faced with outside systems, and one which ultimately tipped the scales toward in-house development, was the integration of a database marketing system with our existing business development program. Our problem was finding a system that met our specific needs. Some systems we examined were merely calling program tracking systems, which didn't address our need for improved information management. Some systems were designed to function as part of a computer network, with each officer having his own PC workstation. Given the current computer capabilities of our bank and the overall level of computer literacy of our business officers, the hardware costs and training expense that would be necessary to use such systems would be prohibitive. Some systems didn't provide enough information, some provided too much, while still others didn't provide the kind of information we desired.[6] In short, we were having trouble matching a system with the objectives we had established. And yet in-house development did not seem a viable alternative because of the costs that we perceived. With some reluctance, we indefinitely shelved our plans for a business database marketing system.

Two events, in the second quarter of 1987, reopened the issue. The first was attendance of J. MacDuffie Brunson's computer class at the School of Bank Marketing. One of the computer applications that Brunson demonstrated was a very simple business-to-business database that he had constructed using an inexpensive piece of software called Reflex. The ease with which this program could be used and manipulated for a variety of purposes began to change our thinking about developing a database for Commercial National Bank.

The second event of importance was our bank's purchase of a database marketing system for the retail division.[7] The new retail system gave us plenty of food for thought about what steps were necessary in developing a business database. To begin with, the new system, though designed and used for retail marketing, was still a database marketing system, and as such provided hands on experience in PC-based databases. Of equal importance, the retail system, while operating primarily with its own copyrighted programs, also required a working knowledge of Ashton-Tate's dBase III+, a fairly common and easily used database software package.[8] Eventually, we felt fairly confident in our ability to write most of the applications necessary for a business database. In-house development did not appear to be as much of an obstacle.

Another item that became less of an obstacle was the cost of internal development. The actual "hard" dollar costs were very reasonable. dBase III+ lists for under $600, and the only hardware required—an IBM PC with a hard disk—was already available. In terms of staff expense, all the data collection, analysis and processing were going to take up a large amount of time and effort, but this would have been true with a purchased system as well. Given our growing expertise with dBase III+, the actual time spent and the opportunity cost to develop the new system would not be as high as had originally been thought. This was primarily because we were already mastering dBase III+ for our retail system and were convinced that the actual programming required to develop our corporate database would not be difficult at all.

With close cooperation from our bank's business development representative, we began work on our business database in August 1987. By October, the basic elements of our Corporate Information Database (C.I.D.) were completed and had been presented to senior management, who in turn approved the system for implementation in 1988.

There are two tremendous benefits we have received from developing our own system internally. The first is the flexibility it has given us in changing, adapting and adjusting the system to our evolving needs. The second is that we are virtually assured that the system will integrate with our existing business development objectives. This is partially a result of writing the program ourselves, and partly because the system's development included the preparation of a marketing plan for its use, which is the concern of the remainder of this paper.

SITUATION ANALYSIS
Commercial National Bank is located in Peoria, Illinois, and is the lead bank of Midwest Financial Group, a multibank holding company based in downstate Illinois. The bank's current charter dates back to January 14, 1885, while the earliest predecessor of Commercial, the Mechanics National Bank, was founded March 11, 1865. Thus, Commercial has many long-standing ties to the Peoria area.

Market Geography
The primary market area for Commercial National Bank is the Metropolitan Statistical Area (MSA) comprised of Peoria, Tazewell, and Woodford counties. The city of Peoria functions as a major port on the Illinois River, which is part of the inland waterway network connecting the St. Lawrence Seaway with the Gulf of Mexico. The Illinois River separates Peoria county from Tazewell and Woodford counties, although four major bridges foster good intercounty relations. Peoria is approximately equidistant from Chicago and St. Louis, Missouri, and represents the largest populated area in downstate Illinois.

As far as transportation is concerned, Peoria is well-served for a city of its size. Nine major railroads, twelve airlines, sixty-six motor freight lines, forty-four terminal operations, and eight bus lines visit the Peoria area. The Illinois River is also a major artery, with barge traffic passing through the Peoria Lock and Dam exceeding 36 million tons annually.[9]

Peoria is located in a rich agricultural area. The Peoria MSA accounts for more than $290 million in farm production each year.[10] Peoria is also known as a manufacturing city, primarily because the international headquarters for Caterpillar, Inc., is located here. Education is also an important part of

Peoria's economy.   Peoria is home to Illinois Central College, Bradley University, and the University of Illinois College of Medicine. The presence of St. Francis and Methodist medical centers has also made Peoria prominent in medical research and education.

In recent years, operating losses sustained by Peoria's major employer, Caterpillar, Inc., the closing of several other large firms, and unfavorable conditions in general have greatly affected Peoria's economy. However, the past year has seen an economic resurgence in the community, and major expansion and development projects are planned or are already underway. Many laid-off Caterpillar employees are being recalled, and hopes are high for the year to come.

Market Demography

The Peoria MSA has a population of 365,864 persons in 130,927 households.[11]   The Tri-County Regional Planning office is projecting a 3.7% increase in the population of the Peoria area by 1990, and a 9.2% increase by the year 2000, bringing the population up to 400,000 persons.

More important statistics for the purposes of business development are the occupations and industries of the area. Operators, fabricators, and laborers represent 20.3% of the employed persons over sixteen years of age. Managerial and professional specialty occupations, coupled with technical, sales and administrative support occupations represent over 50% of the jobs in this area, thereby lending some support to the claim that Peoria is becoming less of a manufacturing town. This contention is also supported by an examination of the industries represented by these occupations. While manufacturing represents 31.3% of the occupations, services is a close second at 24.9%.[12] This represents a significant shift in our economy, since less than ten years ago one in every five jobs in Peoria was with Caterpillar alone, and other manufacturing firms assured that Peoria was very dependent on manufacturing jobs.

It seems safe to conclude that the growth in service-related jobs will continue, as Peoria's economy continues to mirror national changes toward a more service-oriented economy. These changes are directly visible, as our second- and third-largest employers are now the area's two major hospitals. As a long-range strategy, we should examine and evaluate our products and services in light of these changes. The financial needs of service-oriented firms are different from those of manufacturers, and our business development efforts should reflect this.

Despite trends in the market, manufacturers and light industrial firms continue to represent good business development opportunities. Indeed, the *Peoria Area Manufacturers' Directory* lists nearly 150 principal manufacturing firms. Firms on this list should be targeted for 1988. For example, existing customers can be sold additional services, while non-customers can be approached with new products and services unique to our bank. Another area of opportunity comes from the same source. Ironically, the *Peoria Area Manufacturers' Directory* also lists fifty-five principal non-manufacturing firms. Combined, these two lists represent the major companies who do business in Peoria. Every one of them should be a prospect for 1988.

One other point of demographic significance to business development plans is the location/concentration of area firms. One item immediately stands out: Most of the major retail clusters are concentrated in central Peoria, but we have no facilities in that area. To make matters worse, most of the new development and expansion is taking place to the north and west of town. Only our Pioneer facility is in a good position to take advantage of this growth. Another problem is that our Metropolitan (i.e., business banking) Department is headquartered at our downtown main bank location. Some business calls are made by our branch managers, but most business development is handled through our downtown office. Thus, in terms of convenience to our business customers, our delivery system needs improvement. The situation should improve in 1989, however, with the merger of two holding company banks with Commercial.

Competitive Environment
Financial institutions are well represented in the Peoria area. There are twenty-two banks, fourteen savings and loans and thirty-one credit unions, for a total of sixty-seven establishments representing nearly $3 billion in total deposits.[13] Commercial National Bank holds a 26% market share of total bank deposits, and a 12% share of the total market deposits.

With regard to business banking, a strong competitive indicator is the category of commercial and industrial loans. The table on the following page shows the principal Peoria area financial institutions and the dollar volumes of their commercial and industrial loans.

A cursory glance shows that Commercial National Bank and Jefferson Trust and Savings Bank account for more than half of the commercial loan dollars. Other competitors of note are the Community Banks of Greater Peoria, the First National Bank of Peoria, and the Construction Equipment Federal Credit Union (whose commercial loan figures are unavailable at the time of writing).

Jefferson Bank has been and continues to be our chief competitor for corporate business. They maintain an aggressive calling program, and have been particularly successful in the area of public funds acquisition. Indeed, as of June 1987, the total deposits of state and political subdivisions held by

TOTAL COMMERCIAL & INDUSTRIAL LOANS
(2nd Quarter 1987)

Institution	Amount ($000)	Bank % Penetration
Commercial National Bank	$95,557	38.62%
Bartonville Bank	2,666	1.08%
Community Bnk Gtr Peoria	16,155	6.53%
First Bank	5,602	2.26%
First NB of Morton	7,987	3.23%
First NB of Peoria	15,231	6.16%
Jefferson Tr & Svg	36,909	14.92%
Northwest Community Bk	7,468	3.02%
Madison Park Bk	8,893	3.59%
Prospect NB of Peoria	4,187	1.69%
Sheridan Bk	12,886	5.21%
South Side T & SB	17,237	6.97%
University NB of Peoria	7,323	2.96%
Security S & LA, FA	9,321	3.77%
Total Market	247,422	100.00%

Jefferson Bank was $29,252,000, representing a 25.19% market share (as compared to Commercial's $18,148,000, or 15.63% market share). While Jefferson only experienced a .6% growth in their commercial loan portfolio over the past five years, their growth for 1986 to 1987 was 18.06%.

Another area where Jefferson has done well is in product development, particularly in cash management products. Jefferson is our major competition in payroll processing and was the first local institution to introduce a corporate sweep account. How long they will be able to maintain this competitiveness is uncertain, since their customer base is less extensive than ours, and some of the more sophisticated cash management products, such as outgoing automated clearing house transactions or electronic cash management systems, may be difficult for them to cost justify given their size. Nevertheless, Jefferson's business development efforts will greatly affect our own marketing strategies for the future.

Community Banks of Greater Peoria represent another important competitor. They are one of the fastest-growing Peoria area banks, and they too maintain an aggressive calling program aimed at attracting new business loan and deposit customers. Their main office is located in East Peoria (across the Illinois River from Peoria) and is well-positioned to attract new business customers from Tazewell and Woodford counties, regions where we have not been as aggressive. In a very short period of time, Community

Banks have managed to acquire nearly a 12% market share of commercial loan dollars.

First National Bank of Peoria actively promotes the fact that it is the oldest bank in the Peoria area, but this long-standing relationship with the community does not seem to help its business development efforts. To be sure, the First National Bank is second only to Jefferson Bank in public funds with $25,300,000, representing a 21.78% market share, but this market share has been steadily declining. In fact, from 1983 to 1987, First National lost nearly $6 million in public funds. Their commercial loan situation is not much better.

First National is the third largest bank in Peoria in terms of total assets, yet, ranks fifth in terms of commercial loans. A 14.75% market share five years ago placed them at a close third behind Commercial and Jefferson, but 1987 sees them at 6.16%. This is partially attributable to First National's very conservative underwriting standards, but their 1985 annual report stated that the bank is "finding it more difficult to generate quality loans."[14] The past two years have seen First National with very high, loan loss reserves, so perhaps there has been some "shying away" from the commercial loan market. Nor have we seen any new products from First National on the corporate side. First National appears content to let its business banking market share steadily erode, which suggests that First National's customers might be good prospects to approach with new products.

The **Construction Equipment Federal Credit Union** is our toughest retail competitor. They have surpassed us in total asset size during the last year, and they are capturing a larger share of the total deposit market at the same time that our share is declining. From a lending standpoint, the Construction Equipment Federal Credit Union is very aggressive in the retail market. To date, the credit union has not posed much of a threat to our business banking efforts, but this may be changing. Already our business development representative is reporting that a number of our business customers have recently been approached by the credit union. Clearly, the credit union can no longer be ignored in the business banking market.

So far only local competitors have been discussed. A very real concern is competition from outside our traditional market area. With Peoria reasonably close to both Chicago and St. Louis, we are faced with the threat of large banks penetrating our market with a wave of new products and services that we may not be able to offer cost effectively. Of particular concern is the possibility of a large regional bank purchasing one of our local competitors. Another threat already manifesting itself is the loss of some of our larger customers because of our inability to service their growing statewide and nationwide needs as efficiently as a Chicago or St. Louis bank.

Commercial National Bank's Resources

Despite the growing local and outside competition, Commercial National Bank is still in a strong market position. We are the largest bank in downstate Illinois, with resources adequate to meet a variety of business development opportunities in 1988.

With regard to our distribution system, Commercial currently has three facilities. Our main office is located in an eleven-story office building in downtown Peoria. Our Knoxville facility, which opened in 1977, is situated on Knoxville Avenue exactly 3,500 yards from our main office. This facility experiences a large amount of traffic because Knoxville Avenue is a major north-south artery in Peoria. Commercial acquired a third facility in August 1985 with the purchase of Pioneer Bank. This facility is located in Peoria's industrial park to the north of town and is ideally located to exploit the rapid expansion and development taking place in that area. Commercial also owns an ATM network comprised of twenty-eight machines spread throughout Peoria, including a special ATM-business depository located at Proctor Hospital. However, we don't have a strong presence in central Peoria, which is where the majority of the city's retail clusters are located. In early 1989, Commercial's merger with Prospect Bank and University National Bank, two sister banks in the Midwest Financial Group, should provide us with more opportunities in central Peoria. Another area where our presence is less strong is across the river in Tazewell and Woodford counties. We have a number of customers on the east side of the river, but no facilities there. Our holding company recently purchased a bank in Morton, but Community Banks have better access to the businesses of East Peoria than do we.

Our bank currently employs 413 persons, including 82 officers and 331 nonofficers. Our Metropolitan Department, the area of the bank responsible for business banking, has seven officers and a business development representative. Support is provided by a secretary/receptionist and an administrative assistant. Other areas of the bank involved with corporate banking in a more limited capacity are our Bond, Correspondent Banking, and Midwest Card Services (charge card) departments, plus our Estate Trust and Operations divisions. Additionally, our facility managers are responsible for some business calling. Staffing in our Metropolitan Department appears adequate at the current time, but a large increase in accounts and/or loan demand would seriously affect officer productivity. One alternative in that eventuality would be to hire additional support staff to free the officers for customer calling, prospecting, and loan generation, while leaving more of the day-to-day details of their account management to assistants. This solution is currently utilized in the Employee Benefits Department of our Trust Division with great success and is certainly a cheaper alternative than hiring additional business officers.

Our bank does not have any shareholders per se because we are owned by Midwest Financial Group, Inc., a bank holding company. As of February 13, 1987, the number of holding company shareholders was 3,070. Midwest Financial Group, Inc., has total assets in excess of $2 billion and operates in eight different Illinois MSAs outside of the Chicago area. This diversity of market areas is advantageous to Commercial, because many of our business customers operate throughout Illinois, and Commercial's sister banks provide a means to accommodate their needs. Another area where Commercial benefits is the realization of the various economies and efficiencies possible under the aegis of a multibank holding company.

Commercial National Bank has total assets averaging around $430 million. As of June 1987, our total deposits were $358,273,000, representing a 27.5% market share among our principal bank competitors. Our deposit growth has generally kept pace with the market's growth during the last five years, so our market penetration can be described as good, if stagnant. Our business deposits basically reflect the same trend. In 1987, our average business demand deposits were $72,414,000. Public fund demand deposits represented $6,074,000. Business time deposits were another $27,562,000. Our total average business deposits, including those of correspondent banks, were $129,688,000.

However, one area where our market share is drastically declining is public funds. Our market share in 1985 was over 31%. By June 1987, it had dropped to less than 16%.[15] Call Report information and some discrete inquiries turned up where this money had gone: Jefferson Bank and the First National Bank of Peoria. Unless some positive counter-measures are taken, there is no reason to believe that this trend will stop.

The total loan portfolio for Commercial was $291,032,000 in June 1987. Total commercial and industrial loans at the that time were $95,557,000 for a market share of 38.62% among our chief competitors. This penetration has steadily increased, even given the increased loan demand that our area has experienced during the last year. Indeed, the last quater of 1987 saw our loan-to-deposit ratio in excess of 75% on numerous occasions, and senior management has determined that deposit acquisition will be a major goal for 1988.

Bank Products
Commercial's Metropolitan Department makes a wide variety of products and services available to our business customers. Lending is a primary function of the department, and our business officers routinely handle requests for financing inventory and accounts receivable, purchasing machinery or equipment, business acquisitions and general business expansion. Loan packages are generally customized to each situation and

usually consist of one or more of the following: term loans, accounts receivable financing, inventory financing, industrial-revenue-bond financing (when the bank has an appetite for tax-exempt loans), lines of credit, tax warrants and Small Business Administration (SBA) loans. Commercial National Bank is large enough to allow us to work with a substantial legal lending limit, but amounts in excess of that limit can still be accommodated through participation with our sister banks. Lending currently represents the most profitable aspect of our business banking activities.

On the deposit side, we offer a fairly traditional mix of products: regular demand deposit accounts, NOWs, Super-NOWs, corporate passbook savings and insured money market accounts (IMMAs). Our demand deposit accounts can be set up to operate under one of three different systems of service charge analysis, depending on the expected level of account activity. Complete Analysis is a system designed for accounts with a moderate- to high-level of activity, and as its name suggests, nearly every aspect of a customer's account is subject to analysis. Fundamental Analysis provides a more simplified system and was developed for our smaller customers who would otherwise pay extremely high service charges under our Complete Analysis system. Paymaster Checking is a basic system designed for businesses and organizations that deposit fewer than twenty-five checks each month. Customers pay a fixed monthly cost, plus twenty cents per check written. These three methods allow us to better match our services to the size and resources of our customers. All three systems are profitable for the bank, yet the service charges of each are still competitive in our market area.

One area where Commercial is focusing its corporate product development is cash management. We offer a number of traditional services, such as account reconcilement, money management accounts and various investment vehicles. We also offer a retail lock-box service, which currently involves a great deal of manual processing on our part. On the horizon is automated lock-box processing using optical character recognition (OCR) equipment, which should serve to improve our ability to handle some of our high-volume customers. Last year saw the introduction of our sweep account, which allows customers to invest excess funds in their account on a daily basis. Currently under development is our InTouch Cash Manager. InTouch is a personal computer software program and communications network that provides a direct link between our customers and their accounts. The system allows customers to obtain daily balance information, transfer funds, reconcile accounts, generate cash flow analyses, plus a number of other functions, all through their own computers. This product, presently undergoing beta-testing, is generating a high level of interest among our current customers. Another area of interest is automated clearing house (ACH) transactions. We presently offer a funds concentration service that centralizes funds from multiple outlying banks to a concentration account at Commercial, either through the ACH network or by means of depository transfer checks (DTCs). On the drawing board at this time is an outgoing ACH product that would provide customers with the ability to send or receive funds electronically. It is our belief that cash management is the means with which to differentiate our business banking services and remain competitive in our market.

The list of services described so far represents most of our major products, but is by no means exhaustive. Other miscellaneous services include business MasterCard (locally issued by our bank), charge card merchant processing, and payroll processing. No other financial institution in our market presently offers the number and variety of services that we do, but it is also important to remember that quantity does not always win out over quality and that our competitors are capable of stealing our customers with a simpler or inferior product on the basis of superior service or better pricing.

Current Customers

A research project to determine our market penetration among what we consider to be our prime market target was recently conducted.[16] The market target in question was Peoria area firms with annual sales in excess of $5 million. The research began by obtaining a list of such firms in the Peoria area from Dun & Bradstreet and then noting which companies were currently our customers. The results are summarized below:

Annual Sales	# Companies	# Customers	Market Share
$5-10 million	58	21	36%
$10-25 million	34	22	65%
$25-50 million	15	10	67%
$50 million+	14	11	79%

As can be seen, we have a strong market position with companies over $10 million in annual sales. We do less well in the $5-$10 million category. Though no figures are available at this time, we suspect our market share of companies below $5 million is much smaller. Essentially, our market has been companies of moderate size whose financial needs do not necessitate the services of large money center banks.

One factor effectively limits our future market share growth: time. Customer retention requires a significant amount of time. Local, state, and even national competitors are eternally after our best customers. Thus, besides being service-oriented and competitively priced, we must constantly communicate with our customers. This consumes a great deal of officer time. Prospecting is also very time consuming. Our current market share suggests an area of opportunity among smaller businesses, yet the number of businesses in existence increases geometrically as size decreases. Our business officers are not capable of handling a large increase in prospect calls and business development activities without adversely affecting their current productivity. The hiring of additional staff and improved sales management are two possibilities for resolving the time issue.

Business-to-Business Marketing

As a bank, we are aware that customers don't just "walk in the door" anymore. We know that we have to go out and bring them in with the right combination of price, product, and personal service. More importantly, we are aware that we have to ask for someone's business, and the more personal the invitation to do business with us, the more likely the sale. Accordingly, our corporate marketing strategies do not rely much on advertising or mass media techniques. Rather, marketing at Commercial hinges more on personal selling and our officer call program. We use advertising and publicity in support of officer calling, but not as replacements for it. Our officers do best in one-on-one selling situations, and our marketing reflects this. Every customer or prospective customer is a market segment of one, with specific needs that should be addressed.

We do well in sales training, product development, customer retention, and pricing. Several sales training programs are offered each year, and officers are encouraged to attend seminars and clinics. Our interest in cash management services has sparked a wave of new product development in our Metropolitan Department. Our officers do an excellent job of servicing the needs of our existing customers. As far as pricing is concerned, we keep abreast of the competition and try to be competitive, yet profitable to the bank. Senior management does a good job of supporting our business development programs, both in their personal calling and through their commitment to the bank's sales culture.

There are certain areas that need improvement, specifically media usage, marketing research, cross-selling bank services and prospect calling. With respect to our use of media, we have failed to exploit the potential of direct mail and telemarketing for business development. These two media, if properly employed, could substantially augment our officer calling program. Unfortunately, the negative stereotypes sometimes associated with these media (e.g., junk mail and irritating phone calls) have influenced certain officers against direct mail and telemarketing.

Another problem area is marketing research. Research has never been a high priority at Commercial, but this is slowly changing. There is a growing realization that it is usually more cost-effective to research and analyze the market before blindly rushing into new products and services. There is now a desire to objectify what we have been doing intuitively. With our current customers being the best source for new business, we need to more effectively cross-sell our services. Unfortunately, in most instances our officers are not given the necessary information to enable them to sell additional services. As mentioned earlier, we are having problems providing our officers with complete account information. Finally, we need to systematize the process by which we identify, assign, and approach prospective customers. Our current method of prospecting is at best chaotic, and at worse nonexistent.

Budget

The advertising budget for the Metropolitan Department in 1988 is presented below:

Newspaper	$1,000
Direct mail	1,800
Literature	3,000
Specialities	500
Displays/signs	100
Other	800

Newspaper dollars are allocated for ads in our local newspaper's business section to support a campaign featuring our InTouch Cash Manager. Direct mail funds are also targeted for InTouch. Other budget items allow the Metropolitan Department to produce and maintain brochures and giveaways.

Sales training falls under the budgets of the Marketing and Personnel departments, and is not treated here because it has no direct bearing on the plan outlined in this chapter. One budget item of some importance to the plan, however, is the $7,000 allocated by the Metropolitan Department to purchase an IBM computer.

Marketing Organization

The Marketing Department at Commercial presently consists of three people: a vice president/marketing manager, a marketing analyst , and an administrative assistant. Our marketing manager serves as head of the Marketing Department, chairs the bank's Marketing Committee, and sits on the holding company's Marketing Committee. The marketing analyst is primarily responsible for research but also assists with program and product development. Our administrative assistant coordinates promotional activities and provides support to the marketing manager and analyst. For corporate marketing endeavors, the department works closely with the Metropolitan Department's business development representative. The bank's Marketing Committee, which consists of individuals primarily from customer contact areas, also assists with corporate marketing programs.

OBJECTIVES

One of the keys to a successful business development program is information management. While our own credit file system and CIF provide some support to our officers, they don't furnish information in a manner suitable for business development purposes. Thus, this plan is proposed for the bank's Metropolitan Department to improve information management in order to enhance the personal selling efforts of our business officers. The major component of this plan is a PC-based database marketing system called the Corporate Information Database.

Corporate Information Database (CID)

At its most basic level, our corporate information database (CID) is a means of providing our business officers with easy access to account information. CID currently contains the name, mailing address, street location, phone number, business size, business type, and contact person(s) for both present and prospective customers. CID also includes a service/product matrix that indicates the services each business is utilizing. At a more advanced level, CID is a sales tracking system that maintains information on officer calls, presentations, and follow-ups, and generates a variety of sales management reports. CID is also a useful marketing research tool that allows us to organize and analyze our existing customer base to uncover better methods of retaining customers and satisfying their needs. CID is effective in organizing information on prospective customers as well, thereby providing us with the means of systematizing our prospecting efforts.

The overall objective of CID is to improve information management for our business officers. The following specific objectives have been set for CID this year:

1. Integrate CID with our existing officer call program.

2. Implement CID as a computerized account management system.

3. Use CID as a data collection, storage, and analysis tool for marketing research.

Officer Call Program

The Metropolitan Department first introduced an officer call program last year with mixed results. The goal was fairly simple: Each officer was required to make ten sales calls each month (120 total for the year), consisting of eight calls to existing customers and two calls to prospects. The program can be judged a success on two counts. First, there was a 201% increase in the total number of calls made in 1987 versus 1986. Second, there was a 240% jump in the number of prospect calls last year. However, the total number of calls made in 1987 (580) was only 70% of the 840 calls that were set as a goal (120 calls x seven officers). One of the reasons that the goal was not achieved was limited officer time. Discussions with several of the business officers revealed that some felt that ten calls per month was too much, given their other duties. Another reason was the absence of regular feedback. The officers didn't receive regular reports on where they were in relation to their goal. While officer time is an important issue, information, in addition to the opinions of a few officers, is needed to support the assertion that ten calls is an unreasonable goal. Reporting, however, is a critical issue for our call program's future success.

Our current reporting system is not really a system at all, but rather a list compiled by our Word Processing Department of calls reported during the previous month. Information on this list includes the name of the officer, the company, whether the company was a customer or prospect, the date of the call, and a one-sentence description of the discussion. This report is then cursorily discussed at a monthly sales meeting of all bank personnel who function in a calling capacity. While this meeting serves a useful purpose by communicating who is calling on whom, it does not facilitate a focused, effective selling program.

It is apparent from the above discussion that we do not currently furnish our officers with quantified performance feedback. CID was designed to fill this niche. CID can generate a series of reports as often as necessary that contain as little or as much information as desired regarding our bank's sales calls. Officers can quickly determine such facts as how often they have been calling on their best customers, what percentage of their call quota has been completed, what services were presented during their last call to a particular company, how well they have sold a particular service to their accounts, and a host of other sales management tools. Access to this kind of information will allow officers to better plan and coordinate their sales calls. CID can also be used to generate the call listing for the monthly sales meeting, but in a more flexible fashion. Previously, sales calls have been listed, and hence discussed, in alphabetical order. Now reports can be generated by size of business, product, and type of business, thereby allowing the monthly sales meetings to be more focused.

Account Management
CID was created to provide officers and other concerned parties with quick access to basic account information. CID combines data from a variety of sources in the bank and allows users to organize and sort information according to their needs. While CID does not (and will never) contain all the information about a particular customer, the system does include all of the important sales-related data. CID also makes it possible for an officer to better understand the bank's total relationship with a given customer. CIFs tend to be organized on the basis of accounts rather than on relationships. CID is organized in the opposite manner.

Market Research

Effective business development requires adequate planning and forecasting, which can only be provided by objective review and analysis of past results, trends, and correlations. Planning in the absence of information results in unfocused, ineffective programs.

CID lends itself well to market research projects. Since CID essentially maintains basic customer information in a form that is readily accessed, research based on our corporate customers is easy to perform. Market penetrations (by product, location, size of firm, or any other item on which CID has data) are now simple to determine. The better we know our own customers, the easier it is to sell them additional services. CID can be used to help uncover possible trends and correlations that will assist in sales management, market segmentation, and a variety of other tasks. For example, since charge cards are handled by another department of the bank, the business officers had no way of knowing for certain who already had a business MasterCard and who did not. CID can also be used to model the effects of various marketing decisions, whether it be the introduction of a new product or a price change or the reassignment of an officer's accounts.

Profitability

It is very difficult to determine a specific dollar or percentage growth objective for CID, as CID is a means to an end, not an end in itself. CID is a system designed to assist officers in the total selling process, from planning to closing the sale. CID's value is in providing support to existing programs and, therefore, can be assessed only by the successes or failures of those programs.

What is very clear from the competitive situation in Peoria is that increasing our market share is going to require a very aggressive sales effort on the part of our officers. The strong officer call programs of our chief competitors indicate that we will need to maintain a strong presence ourselves to avoid losing market share. Nevertheless, our bank has set some very aggressive business development goals for 1988.

- The Metropolitan Department will maintain its officer call program this year with the same call quotas. CID can assist in this by providing the tracking and program management that will enable us to meet this year's goal.

- Commercial National Bank has decided to make its presence known in the cash management market and plans to actively promote our InTouch cash management system. The goal here is to have twenty-seven InTouch customers by the end of the year. CID will assist with this by providing the organizational structure for a small direct marketing campaign for InTouch.

- The Metropolitan Department has budgeted a $9 million increase in average annual loan outstandings for 1988, which represents a 14.7% increase.

- Business deposits are budgeted for a 5.4% increase. Public funds deposits in particular are slated for a 16.9% increase.

Because of the low advertising/publicity budget for the Metropolitan Department for 1988, the responsibility for business development will rest squarely on the shoulders of our business officers. If CID can make their time more productive by allowing them to better target and coordinate their sales efforts, then CID can be deemed profitable.

Areas of Concern

The largest concern that we currently have with CID is operational in nature. Who is to run CID? What area will be responsible for data collection, entry, and analysis? In short, the question is one of human resources. Designing and developing CID was easy; implementation and use of the system are not so clear-cut. When we first began to write the software for CID, our original intention had been for the account officers themselves to provide the initial information on their accounts. We had also envisioned the officers as being the primary users of the system. But after discussions with the account officers and management, we realized that this would not be the case because of time constraints and the officers' general unfamiliarity with computers. After all, CID was developed to make account officers more productive, not to create more work for them. As a result, all of the programming and data collection and entry are being done by the marketing analyst and the Metropolitan Department's business development representative. Yet they too have other responsibilities in the bank, and the opportunity costs associated with having two professionals tied up with CID are difficult to assess.

This question of opportunity costs brings up a related issue. Only two people are currently trained to use the system. Although dBase III+ is fairly easy to learn from a user's standpoint, acquiring the ability to program and "troubleshoot" the system requires a substantial amount of time. While training is planned for staff personnel in the Metropolitan Department on how to use CID, there are at the present time only limited plans to train what would amount to a manager for the system.

Another concern involves the account officers themselves. While every effort has been made to involve them in the planning and development of CID so that the system satisfies their needs for sales and account management, there is still the question of whether or not they will use it. While we are convinced that all the account officers will find their productivity increased by the improved information management provided by CID, we are concerned about their initial acceptance of the system.

A final concern with the system involves the quality of the data. CID can only be as useful as the information it contains, as pointed out by the computer cliche, "garbage in, garbage out." It is therefore important to establish a means of assuring the quality of the data entered and of allowing the officers to check the validity of their account information.

These concerns are addressed by the specific strategies outlined in the next portion of this chapter.

IMPLEMENTATION
The major components of CID were in place by the end of October 1987. The basic programs, the types of information to be included, and basic report designs had been decided upon prior to CID's presentation to senior management. We were aware, however, that CID would require modification and adjustment to the "field" conditions of the Metropolitan Department. In order to facilitate this adjustment period, we have divided implementation of CID into several distinct phases, each with its own specific tasks and goals: (1) Development; (2) Testing; (3) Training, and (4) Expansion.

Development
While the bulk of developmental work on CID has been completed, there are still a few remaining items that need to be accomplished. To begin with, there is some minor programming to finish prior to implementing the system. In demonstrating CID to various bank officers, it was discovered that dBase III+, while menu-driven and similar to Lotus 1-2-3 in use, was still too complicated for those not familiar with it. It was therefore decided to add a series of simple menus to "walk" users through the more common applications. People using the menus will lose some of the flexibility of dBase III+ and CID, but CID will still be accessible without the menus. Another programming change that will be incorporated is a password system for security reasons, both to protect sensitive information and to prevent accidental tampering with the database. These changes should be completed by February 15th, 1988.

In a real sense, CID's development will never be finished. As the system is used, feedback from management and account officers should be incorporated to continually adapt the system to the bank's changing needs.

Testing
CID has already been used for a number of marketing research and sales management projects. However, the system has never been tested under

actual working conditions by the users for whom it was designed. Therefore, a formal test period for CID in the Metropolitan Department will begin March 1 and last until May 1. During this time, CID will be used on a limited basis by the department.

First, the information included in CID will be of a limited nature. Only information on major and minor demand deposit customers will be incorporated. Major demand deposit customers are those who maintain balances in excess of $100,000, while minor ones are those with balances between $25,000 and $100,000. Given these parameters, the total number of records included in CID will be less than 400, a manageable number for testing purposes.

Second, all data collection, data entry, and report generation will be performed by the Metropolitan Department's business development representative. The idea is to test the system, not the people using it. Thus, account officers can see some of the benefits of the system, make useful suggestions on how to improve it, and hopefully become familiar with how CID can be used, all without being immediately confronted with a strange computer system. Any unforeseen problems with CID should be uncovered at this time,, so that they can be corrected before the system is fully launched. The usefulness of the information currently contained in CID and possible modifications should also be disovered at this point. The system and what it contains were developed in conjunction with the account officers, but only daily use will determine the kinds of information that are useful. Another area that will be closely monitored during testing is report generation. We have designed a number of reports that should provide useful information to account officers and management, but again, only daily use will determine their utility.

Feedback during this period is critical, so a series of three monthly meetings with account officers is planned to specifically discuss CID and its applications. By involving officers in every phase of CID's development and implementation, CID should become a useful tool for business development at our bank. A side effect of continual officer involvement will be their growing familiarity with the system, thereby making the next phase easier.

Training
Training is probably the most important phase of the entire implementation process, since its success or failure will determine the ultimate fate of CID. If the system is too complicated for the Metropolitan Department to use on its own, then it will not be cost-effective. The goal for this phase is to train others to run CID on a daily basis, thereby allowing the business development representative and the Marketing Department to step away from the more mundane aspects of the system.

The first task is to determine the types of training necessary. There are three different levels of familiarity needed for CID's operation. First, there is the user level. Users are those persons who are merely using the system to access information and who do not need to be very knowledgeable of the system's intricacies. Account officers and management would fall under this classification. The level of training required for users of the system is minimal. A three-hour training session will be held in March 1988 to instruct account officers in the basic functions of CID. The session will be a predominantly hands-on workshop to guide users through the menu system developed for CID.

The second level of familiarity with CID is administrative. The functions performed at this level include data collection, data entry, and report generation. While these tasks seem more clerical in nature, they do require a working knowledge of the basic elements of dBase III+ and, therefore, a greater amount of training. People at this level, in addition to the in-house training described above, would attend a formal workshop in the basic application of dBase III+. Our community college provides such a workshop at a cost of $30 per person for six hours of instruction. The receptionist and possibly the administrative assistant in the Metropolitan Department will attend this workshop. No specific date has been set, but the workshop will be conducted sometime in March. Additionally, these two staff people will work closely with the Metropolitan Department's business development representative during the testing period of CID to increase their familiarity of the system.

The final level of familiarity with CID is system management. Persons at this level need basic programming ability in dBase III+, so that they can troubleshoot problems, modify programs, and develop new applications where necessary. Our community college offers a six-hour workshop in advanced applications of dBase III+, also for $30. We propose to send our business development representative to this workshop so that more than one person at the bank is capable of programming the system. This workshop is also tentatively scheduled for late March.

Thus, by the end of March most of the necessary formal training will have been completed. Formal training, however, is no substitute for hands-on experience. People will be encouraged to actually practice on and "tinker" with CID during the testing period.

Expansion
During this phase, CID will be expanded to eventually include all of the Metropolitan Department's customers and prospects. The process will be as follows. After an officer has completed a sales call, he or she will fill out a customer information sheet which details the business and the particular

call. Having the officer complete this information assures the validity of the data being entered into the system. Additional calls to those businesses previously called upon will require only that the officer report changes since the time of the last call, incidentally giving the officer the chance to review the accuracy of data that has been entered.

The information thus provided by the officers will be entered into CID, along with other related information that has been collected about the particular business by the Metropolitan staff. In this way, CID will gradually expand to include every business that has been called upon by our business officers. This method of expansion serves to spread out the amount of work required to complete the database over a period of time, thereby making the task more manageable. This process will begin as soon as testing is completed. If there are no unforeseen difficulties, this will be May 1. This means that one month's worth of sales call data will be contained in the system as of June 1, which allows CID to assume responsibility for the monthly sales call meeting that same month.

A specific application of CID is planned for the last quarter of 1988 as a final check of CID's capabilities. CID will provide the means to conduct and coordinate a direct marketing campaign aimed at promoting our InTouch cash management system. CID will be used to specifically select potential InTouch customers and to generate a direct mailing to them. Newspaper ads in the business section of our local paper will be used to support the mailing. The mailing itself will consist of an InTouch brochure and a cover letter signed by one of our business officers informing the prospect of our intention to set up a demonstration of InTouch. CID will be used to organize a telemarketing follow-up by our business officers and will also provide the means to track sales leads and coordinate further contact with business prospects. Previous efforts of this nature have met with limited success because of a lack of project coordination and management. CID should provide the means to better coordinate this type of campaign.

CONCLUSION

CID was developed from a need for improved information management in Commercial National Bank's business development program. Increasing our business market share in the face of increased competition requires aggressive calling on the part of our business officers, and effective calling requires focus and planning. CID is the tool with which the bank plans to acquire the structure, organization, and disciplined sales management that are the key success factors in business development.[17]

A by-product of CID is a growing realization at the bank of the many applications of the personal computer to the marketing function. Plans are already under way for the development of an automated sales management system based on CID for our Estate & Trust Division, and other departments of the bank are expressing interest in similar systems. The bank has become aware of the computer's ability to organize customer information along sales-oriented lines. As the bank's sales culture evolves, the computer will become even more important to our selling efforts. As one author has put it, "automated systems greatly facilitate the development of customer information."[18] An increased reliance on personal selling can only mean an increased need for information management, a task ideally suited to the computer. ◆

---

[1] Grace Conlon, "Data Driven Marketing," *Marketing Communications* (October, 1987), pp. 36-40.

[2] Ibid., p. 36.

[3] *Bank Marketing* (December, 1987), pp. 1-3, 17, 26.

[4] Richard J. Fagan, "Making Automated Systems Work for Calling Officers: Part One," *Successful Selling and Sales Management* (May 1986), p. 2.

[5] Ira Nathanson, "The Key to New Business is in Your Files," *Bank Marketing* (October 1987), p. 12.

[6] It is not my intention to list all the systems we examined, as this would be somewhat unfair to the vendors. After all, our situation is unique and systems that we rejected as unsuitable may be well suited to other banks.

[7] The system we purchased was from Customer Potential Management Corporation, 2430 N. Main, East Peoria, IL 61611.

[8] dBase III+ is manufactured by Ashton-Tate, 20101 Hamilton Avenue, Torrance, CA 90502-1319.

[9] *Peoria: Illinois' Other Prime Market*, p. 10.

[10] Ibid., p. 2.

[11] Ibid., p. 6.

[12] Ibid., p. 8.

[13] Ibid.

[14] *1985 Annual Report of the First National Bank of Peoria.*

[15] *BancPen Market Penetration Analysis* (Second Quarter, 1987), pp. 65-67.

[16] Joseph C. Kelley, "Corporate Cash Management Proposal" (unpublished manuscript), p. 5.

[17] Richard J. Fagan, "Structured Calling Programs Mean Business," *Successful Selling and Sales Management* (November 1987), p. 2.

[18] Ibid., p. 2.